Praise for
Next Generation Business Strategies for the Base of the Pyramid

"Ted London's and Stuart Hart's insightful book explores with a fresh lens the challenges facing the economies and communities of the BoP, and offers long-term solutions based on joint value-creation rather than "fortune-seeking." Today's businesses must engage with these communities on a deeper level, to ensure equal understanding of the culture's needs, how to educate BoP business owners, and to uncover ways to move forward—with sustainability as a top priority. This book makes an invaluable contribution to that end."

—Fisk Johnson, CEO, S.C. Johnson

"Around the world, IFC's clients are doing business in innovative ways that create market opportunity, provide goods and services, and improve the living standards of people at the Base of the Pyramid. Our clients and all those seeking to do business with the BoP as consumers as well as suppliers will find insights and inspiration in this book. This book is a milestone in the movement to create inclusive business models to target billions of people for the first time."

—Lars H. Thunell, Executive Vice President and CEO, International Finance Corporation

"An excellent book on how to develop new markets with the Base of the Pyramid, and also enhance the private sector's contribution to solving some of the world's most pressing challenges. At CEMEX, we've put more than a decade into our low-income housing Program, Patrimonio Hoy, as part of a larger effort to promote access to housing and basic infrastructure. London and Hart provide crucial insights to both businesses and sustainable development of the 21st century."

—Lorenzo H. Zambrano, Chairman and CEO, CEMEX

"This book demonstrates that the most socially useful business models to serve the base of the pyramid are those which are created for the market they seek to serve, incorporating appropriate green technologies and innovation-oriented strategies in venture development. Such ventures can go on to achieve the higher purpose of BoP businesses: poverty alleviation."

—Ratan Tata, CEO, Tata Industries

"Anyone interested in the challenges and opportunities faced by the low-income people must read this well-researched book. At a time when intellectual discourse on this important topic is urgently needed, London's and Hart's book combines a wealth of experience in the corporate setting with a deep understanding of economics. Needless to say, we are in the midst of multiple global crises threatening the well-being of all. This book is an attempt to give capitalism new strategies for responding to those crises."

—Muhammad Yunus, Head of Grameen

"This book describes powerful, exciting, and inspirational next-generation business models that are sure to not only improve millions of lives in the years ahead, but also could truly transform the world by unleashing the potential of those people who have been overlooked by society. Through examples like these, the private sector will learn how to grow their businesses by engaging with the Base of the Pyramid as customers, suppliers, and entrepreneurs. These ideas, pioneered by C.K. Prahalad and the authors of this book, are some of the most original in international economics and development of the past decade, and at the Inter-American Development Bank, our Opportunities for the Majority initiative is carrying forward these approaches in Latin America and the Caribbean."

—**Luis Alberto Moreno**, President of the Inter-American Development Bank

"More than a decade ago, C.K. Prahalad and others first opened our eyes to the huge opportunities inherent in Base of the Pyramid markets. This book captures the thinking of the last 10 years, and confirms that those opportunities are greater than ever. As such, it is a fitting tribute to Prahalad and his fellow pioneers—and an essential read for anyone wishing to understand and capitalize upon the real potential of BoP marketplaces."

—**Paul Polman**, Chief Executive, Unilever

"This book offers a new roadmap to guide the thoughts of those who navigate between the formal and informal economies. This is a must-read for anyone wanting to innovate in the Base of the Pyramid field. Above all, this book is about the relationship of two co-existing societies and the broader idea that poverty is not just about lack of financial resources and that business is not just about business, but a way to achieve a more inclusive world."

—**Paulo Mindlin**, Director for the Walmart Brazil Institute

"A crucial and most creative re-framing of the BoP debate: The authors look at the world's poor not just as four billion more consumers, but also as a source of talented entrepreneurs—potential business partners ready to enter the formal economy to put their assets to work and lift themselves, and their countries, out of poverty."

—**Hernando de Soto**, Institute for Liberty and Democracy

"The Base of the Pyramid is a big breakthrough idea that risked being captured as the new conventional wisdom. This clever book by scholars and practitioners averts that by taking the deeply original insight to the next stage. A fitting tribute to C.K. Prahalad."

—**Lord Mark Malloch-Brown**, Former Administrator,
United Nations Development Programme

Next Generation Business Strategies for the Base of the Pyramid

Next Generation Business Strategies for the Base of the Pyramid

*New Approaches for
Building Mutual Value*

Ted London
Stuart L. Hart

Vice President, Publisher: Tim Moore
Associate Publisher and Director of Marketing: Amy Neidlinger
Executive Editor: Jeanne Glasser
Editorial Assistant: Pamela Boland
Operations Manager: Gina Kanouse
Senior Marketing Manager: Julie Phifer
Publicity Manager: Laura Czaja
Assistant Marketing Manager: Megan Colvin
Cover Designer: Chuti Prasertsith
Managing Editor: Kristy Hart
Project Editor: Lori Lyons
Copy Editor: Language Logistics
Proofreader: Williams Woods Publishing Services
Indexer: Lisa Stumpf
Senior Compositor: Gloria Schurick
Manufacturing Buyer: Dan Uhrig

© 2011 by Pearson Education, Inc.
Publishing as FT Press
Upper Saddle River, New Jersey 07458

FT Press offers excellent discounts on this book when ordered in quantity for bulk purchases
or special sales. For more information, please contact U.S. Corporate and Government Sales,
1-800-382-3419, corpsales@pearsontechgroup.com. For sales outside the U.S., please contact
International Sales at international@pearson.com.

Company and product names mentioned herein are the trademarks or registered trademarks
of their respective owners.

Printed in the United States of America

First Printing November 2010

ISBN-10: 0-13-704789-4
ISBN-13: 978-0-13-704789-5

Pearson Education LTD.
Pearson Education Australia PTY, Limited.
Pearson Education Singapore, Pte. Ltd.
Pearson Education Asia, Ltd.
Pearson Education Canada, Ltd.
Pearson Educación de Mexico, S.A. de C.V.
Pearson Education—Japan
Pearson Education Malaysia, Pte. Ltd.

Library of Congress Cataloging-in-Publication Data

Next generation business strategies for the base of the pyramid : new approaches for building
mutual value / [edited by] Ted London, Stuart L. Hart.

  p. cm.

  ISBN-13: 978-0-13-704789-5 (hardback : alk. paper)

  ISBN-10: 0-13-704789-4

  1. Social responsibility of business. 2. Strategic planning. 3. Small business—Management.
4. Organizational effectiveness. I. London, Ted, 1963- II. Hart, Stuart L.

  HD60.N49 2010

  658.4'012—dc22

                              2010031429

*To my amazing mother, Elizabeth; part of you is in this book.
And to my wonderful wife, Danielle;
thanks for all your support and encouragement.*
—T.L.

*To my wonderful family, Patricia, Jaren, and Jane,
for enabling and encouraging my pursuit of this work.*
—S.H.

Contents

*Ted London, William Davidson Institute & Ross
School of Business, University of Michigan;
and Stuart Hart, Johnson School of Management,
Cornell University*

The introduction, by co-editors Ted London and Stuart
Hart, conveys the core message of the book: that the next
generation of BoP business strategies won't be about
"finding a fortune at the base of the pyramid," but rather,
about "creating a fortune *with* the base of the pyramid."
The shift from "fortune-finding" to "fortune-creating" has
implications for how BoP ventures are organized, and
how their strategies are conceived and implemented.
Co-editors London and Hart introduce the three core
sections of the book—Roadmaps for Success, Strategic
Opportunities, and Effective Implementation—and
explain how the contents of each can help venture leaders
approach the challenges and opportunities of BoP
markets.

Ted London's chapter addresses how venture leaders can maximize the chances that their business development efforts in BoP markets will succeed. Which business practices should guide your efforts—and which ones should you be sure to avoid—as your venture moves through the stages of designing, piloting, and scaling? How do you craft initial business models, effectively test these approaches, and create sustainable competitive advantage? Using the perspective of "creating a fortune with the base of the pyramid," London provides a set of guiding principles (a "roadmap") that answer these and other critical questions relevant to both existing and start-up BoP ventures.

Co-authors Robert Kennedy and Jacqueline Novogratz explain how social entrepreneurs and "philanthrocapitalists" are changing the BoP landscape by connecting innovative business approaches to "patient capital"—money that is expected to generate returns over a longer period than is typical of (say) venture capital. They identify four types of innovation that are proving critically important to success in operating in BoP markets, and show how a range of enterprises are applying these approaches in the field.

Part Two: Strategic Opportunities

             Stuart Hart, Johnson School of Management,
             Cornell University

Can the BoP teach the "ToP" (the "top of the pyramid")
anything? Author Stuart Hart says "yes." In the old BoP
model, Western entrepreneurs sought to sell goods and
services to the BoP with little regard to environmental
consequences. Today, Hart argues, the next generation of
entrepreneurs are trying to develop distributed, small-
scale, "small-footprint" products and services that are
more appropriate to the BoP context—and may well point
the way toward better models for the ToP, as well.

             Erik Simanis, Center for Sustainable Global
             Enterprise, Johnson School of Management,
             Cornell University

Market creation, argues author Erik Simanis, is fundamentally different from market entry. And although
the BoP is a "basket of compelling needs," it is not yet a
"market" in the traditional sense of that term. As a result,
entrepreneurs in the BoP context have to think in terms
of market creation—and understand how to achieve that
end in a uniquely challenging context. The wise venturer
in the BoP space, Simanis writes, learns how to frame the
value proposition and manage the innovation process
(through seeding, base-building, and growth and consolidation) in ways that align business strategy with BoP
opportunity. Through a sustained case study involving a
soy-protein product, Simanis illustrates how to stay on
track while building markets with the BoP.

Part Three: Effective Implementation

"The devil is in the details," as the old saying goes. In this chapter, Madhu Viswanathan makes the case that BoP markets have to be understood at the ground level— from the bottom up—if a venture is to succeed in those marketplaces. What are the marketplace-relevant characteristics of poverty? In the one-to-one interactional marketplaces of the BoP, the boundaries between "human" and "economic" issues tend to get blurred, long-term relationships tend to trump short-term ones, "rich networks" make up for resource constraints, and consumption and entrepreneurship can be two sides of the same coin. BoP entrepreneurs, therefore, have to concretize, localize, and "socialize" their products and services.

By enabling breakthrough products, issues of design have come to the fore in the industrialized world, which is leaving behind economies of scale for economies of choice. Contrasting the Apple iPhone with the Chotukool refrigerator, author Patrick Whitney explores the provocative question of whether strategic design techniques that have proven themselves at the top of the economic pyramid might also prove useful—in identical or modified forms— when applied to base of the pyramid markets. His answer is "yes"—albeit with some important caveats.

Social enterprises do good works. But unless they achieve a significant scale, they aren't in a position to serve millions of BoP customers, or to help reshape economies. Author Allen Hammond argues for a combination of both bottom-up and top-down enterprise formation to better reach and serve BoP markets, and explains how that productive mix can be accomplished. Additionally, he suggests, BoP entrepreneurs can build business ecosystems (rather than stand-alone ventures) to support scale. Hammond explains how "hybrid" organizations can serve that purpose—and provides insights from a real-world example.

Co-editors Ted London and Stuart Hart look at "the journey ahead"—both in terms of the future of BoP-oriented ventures, and in terms of the research that needs to be done to help advance our understanding of the field, which ultimately will help those BoP-oriented ventures succeed. They present—and begin the debate about—five core assumptions that underpin the BoP domain, which collectively help set the BoP agenda of tomorrow.

Acknowledgments

This book would not have been possible without the support and guidance of many people. While it is not feasible to name them all, we did want to recognize some key contributors.

First, we would like to thank our co-authors in this endeavor. We believe each chapter in this volume offers unique and important insights in its own right. We are delighted that these thought leaders were willing to share their latest ideas in this book. As we went through the editing process, we pushed each of them very hard to enhance and sharpen their ideas. This meant that each chapter (including our own!) faced continued requests for further clarification and more nuanced discussions. At times, we wondered if we were pushing too hard—and yet, our collaborators always accepted this feedback with the utmost grace and professionalism.

Jeff Cruikshank was a key contributor to this book. He worked closely with all the authors and was the glue that linked the chapters together. Jeff helped us find a common voice and worked with us to ensure that all the pieces fit together. Heather Esper, our colleague at the William Davidson Institute, played a key role in organizing the authors' convening and the conference we hosted in 2009, as well as keeping track of the various pieces of this manuscript. She also provided valuable contributions to the intellectual development of the book and is an emerging thought leader in her own right. Prabhu Kandachar was a valued contributor in the early stages of this journey. He participated in the convening of authors and our conference and played an important role in the shaping of the book's overall design.

We are also indebted to the attendees of our 2009 Conference, *Creating a Shared Roadmap: Collaboratively Advancing the Base of the Pyramid Community*. We much appreciate the time and energy those participants invested in coming to this event and sharing their expertise. We have done our best to capture both their feedback and their key insights.

Thanks go to Bob Kennedy and the William Davidson Institute for supporting this project from its inception and providing us with the initial resources to pursue this adventure. We also want to thank the Cornell Center for Sustainable Global Enterprise for co-sponsoring the 2009 BoP Conference and providing additional support to the effort.

We also would like to recognize Jeanne Glasser, our executive editor at FT Press. Jeanne supported us from the very earliest stages when the project was only an emerging idea. Throughout the process, she has continued to offer advice and encouragement.

Finally, we want to recognize and thank our late colleague, C.K. Prahalad, whose tragic passing occurred before the completion of this book. We appreciated C.K.'s active involvement in and support of this project from its very inception.

Ted London and Stuart Hart
July 2010
Ann Arbor, Michigan

About the Authors

Ted London, co-editor, is a Senior Research Fellow at the William Davidson Institute (WDI) and a member of the faculty at the University of Michigan's Ross School of Business. At WDI, he directs the Base of the Pyramid Initiative, a program that champions innovative ways of thinking about more inclusive forms of capitalism. At the Ross School, he lectures on the opportunities and challenges inherent in developing new business models to serve BoP markets. An internationally recognized expert on the intersection of business strategy and poverty alleviation, London focuses his research on designing enterprise strategies and poverty-alleviation approaches for low-income markets, developing capabilities for new market entry, building cross-sector collaborations, and assessing the poverty-reduction outcomes of business ventures. His numerous articles, chapters, reports, and cases emphasize creating new knowledge with actionable implications. His article, "Making Better Investments at the Base of the Pyramid," (*Harvard Business Review*, 2009), for example, offers a pioneering perspective on listening to the voices of the world's poor to enhance mutual value creation. Over the past two decades, London has also directed and advised dozens of leadership teams in the corporate, non-profit, and development sectors on designing and implementing market-based strategies in low-income markets. Prior to his arrival at the University of Michigan, London served on the faculty at the University of North Carolina, where he also received his Ph.D. in strategic management. Before that, he held senior management positions in the private, non-profit, and development sectors in Africa, Asia, and the U.S.

Stuart L. Hart, co-editor, is the Samuel C. Johnson Chair in Sustainable Global Enterprise and Professor of Management at Cornell University's Johnson School of Management. He also serves as Distinguished Fellow at the William Davidson Institute (University of Michigan) and is Founder and President of Enterprise for a Sustainable World. Hart is one of the world's top authorities on the implications of environment and poverty for business strategy. He has published more than 70 papers and authored or edited seven books with over 5,000 Google Scholar citations in all. His article "Beyond Greening: Strategies for a Sustainable World" won the McKinsey Award for Best Article in the *Harvard Business Review* for 1997 and helped launch the movement for corporate sustainability. With C.K. Prahalad, Hart also wrote the path-breaking 2002 article "The Fortune at the Bottom of the Pyramid," which provided the first articulation of how business could profitably serve the needs of the four billion poor in the developing world. His best-selling book, *Capitalism at the Crossroads*, published in 2005, was selected by Cambridge University as one of the top 50 books on sustainability of all time; the third edition of the book was published in 2010.

Allen Hammond is Senior Entrepreneur and a member of the Leadership Group at Ashoka, where he is applying novel solutions to rural healthcare in emerging markets. Toward that same end, he is also serving as co-founder and chairman of a start-up company, Healthpoint Services, which is deploying eHealthPoint clinics in rural India and, soon, in other countries. Prior to joining Ashoka, he was VP for Innovation at the World Resources Institute. Hammond is also a serial social entrepreneur, serving as principal in five prior ventures in publishing and rural Internet access. He is an expert in market-based solutions to poverty, a global leader in base of the pyramid (BoP) business strategies, and a widely published author in the scientific, policy research, international development, and business literature, with 10 books and more than 150 articles to his credit—including, "Serving the Poor, Profitably" (with C.K. Prahalad, *Harvard Business Review*, 2002), and "The Next 4 Billion: Market Size and Business Strategy for the Base of the Pyramid (World Resources Institute and International Finance Corporation, 2007). He holds degrees from Stanford and Harvard universities in engineering and applied mathematics.

Robert Kennedy is the Tom Lantos Professor of Business Administration at Michigan's Ross School of Business and serves as Executive Director of the William Davidson Institute—a leading think tank that focuses on business and policy issues in emerging economies. Kennedy's research explores international business and strategy topics. He is a well-known scholar, speaker, and educator, and has authored more than 125 articles, chapters, notes, case studies, and computer exercises on emerging market issues. Between 2002 and 2010, his teaching materials were used at every one of *BusinessWeek*'s top 25 U.S. business schools. His most recent work is a managerial book on offshoring, *The Services Shift: Seizing the Ultimate Offshore Opportunity* (FT Press, 2009). Prior to becoming an academic, Kennedy worked as a consultant in more than 20 countries and as a venture capital investor in central Europe and South Asia. Drawing on both his academic and business backgrounds, he has worked with more than a dozen Fortune 500 companies and many smaller firms to design and deliver customized executive education programs. He received his M.S.M. from the Sloan School (1988) and his Ph.D. in Business Economics from Harvard (1995).

Jacqueline Novogratz is the founder and CEO of Acumen Fund, a non-profit venture fund that uses "patient capital" to solve the problems of global poverty. Under her leadership, Acumen Fund has invested almost $50 million in more than 40 companies serving millions of low-income customers in the developing world. She is the author of the best-selling memoir *The Blue Sweater: Bridging the Gap Between Rich and Poor in an Interconnected World*, recently released in paperback by Rodale. The book chronicles her personal quest to understand poverty and challenges readers to grant dignity to the poor and to rethink their engagement with the world. She began her career in international banking at Chase Manhattan Bank and founded Duterimbere, a micro-finance institution in Rwanda. Prior to creating Acumen, Novogratz founded and directed The Philanthropy Workshop and The Next Generation Leadership program at the Rockefeller Foundation. She has received Ernst & Young's Entrepreneur of the Year Award (2008), the CASE Leadership in Social Entrepreneurship Award (2009), and AWNY's Changing the Game Award (2009). She was recently named to *Foreign Policy*'s list of Top 100 Global Thinkers and *Daily Beast*'s 25 People of the Decade. Novogratz received her MBA from Stanford.

Erik Simanis is Managing Director of Market Creation Strategies at the Center for Sustainable Global Enterprise at Cornell University's Johnson School of Management. His applied research focuses on advancing innovation and business development strategies for commercializing new product categories. Simanis has led or consulted to new business ventures in India, Africa, Mexico, former Soviet Union, and the U.S., and has held management positions in the wood products and transportation industries. His most recent work has been published in the *Wall Street Journal, MIT Sloan Management Review*, and the journal *Innovations*. Simanis holds a Ph.D. in Management from Cornell, an MBA from the University of North Carolina at Chapel Hill where he received the Norman Block Award for highest academic achievement, and a BA magna cum laude from Wake Forest University.

Madhu Viswanathan is Professor of Business Administration at the University of Illinois, Urbana-Champaign. His research programs concentrate on two areas: measurement and research methodology, and literacy, poverty, and subsistence marketplace behaviors. His published works include *Measurement Error and Research Design* (Sage, 2005) and *Enabling Consumer and Entrepreneurial Literacy in Subsistence Marketplaces* (Springer, 2008, in alliance with UNESCO). He directs the Subsistence Marketplaces Initiative and has created unique synergies between research, teaching, and social initiatives. He has organized conferences in the area of subsistence marketplaces, bringing together researchers and practitioners to advance nascent research in this area. He designs and teaches courses on research methods and on subsistence and sustainability, including a yearlong, interdisciplinary graduate-level program on sustainable product and market development for subsistence marketplaces. He also founded and directs the *Marketplace Literacy Project*, a nonprofit organization, which—after many years of successful operation in India—is currently being scaled, and drawing up plans to expand to other countries and contexts. He has received several awards, including the Bharat Gaurav (India Pride) Award from the India International Friendship Society in Delhi, India in 2010, given to people of Indian origin around the world for outstanding leadership in their fields.

Patrick Whitney is the Dean of the Institute of Design, Illinois Institute of Technology, and is the Steelcase/Robert C. Pew Professor of Design. Whitney has published and lectured throughout the world about ways of making technological innovations more humane, the link between design and business strategy, and methods of designing interactive communications and products. He writes about new frameworks of design that respond to three transformations: linking insights about user experience to business strategy, the shift from mass-production to flexible production, and the shift from national markets to markets that are both global and "markets of one." *BusinessWeek* has profiled Whitney as a "design visionary" for bringing together design and business. *Forbes* named him as one of six members of the "E-Gang" for his work in human-centered design. *Fast Company* identified him as a "master of design" for linking the creation of user value and economic value, and *Global Entrepreneur* named him one of the 25 people worldwide doing the most to bring new ideas to business in China. He is the principal investigator of several research projects at the Institute of Design, including Global Companies in Local Markets, Design for the Base of the Pyramid, and Schools in the Digital Age.

Dedication

Coimbatore Krishnarao (C.K.) Prahalad
1941-2010

C.K. Prahalad was a visionary, colleague, and friend. Over the years, he provided inspiration and guidance to all the co-authors of this book. C.K.'s tragic passing in April 2010 left us stunned and saddened. We will certainly miss him for the person he was, and for the future contributions he surely would have made to our community.

C.K. was an integral part of the development of this book. In fact, when Ted and Stu initially developed the idea of a co-created book and shared this with our colleagues, C.K. was the first to respond: *"Looks like a great idea. Count me in. Let us do something creative."* He then played an instrumental role when the book's authors convened in Ann Arbor, Michigan in May 2009. He not only presented the ideas for his proposed chapter, but he also offered a compelling vision for the book. He encouraged us to envision a book that would *be on the shelf of every manager in the corporate, non-profit, and development sectors who is thinking about BoP ventures.* That vision became a core foundation in the development of this work.

Ultimately, C.K.'s declining health prevented him from completing his chapter. Still, we wanted his voice to be part of this book. What you will read below is an unpublished summary note he wrote in 2006 in response to some pointed criticisms of his pioneering book, *The Fortune at the Bottom of the Pyramid*.[1] We selected this piece—which C.K. had posted on the Web—because we think it offers the essence of what made him such a brilliant and influential thinker. [2] He had an exceptional ability to identify and amplify weak signals. C.K. did not necessarily always aim for scientific precision. Instead, he strove to influence by demonstrating "dimensionality and directionality."

C.K. was uniquely creative. One of his gifts was to enable people, especially entrepreneurs and business people, to reframe how they looked at current reality. For example, his ground-breaking perspectives on strategy—including the notions of "strategic intent" and "competing for the future"—helped to fundamentally reshape how business leaders viewed that domain, and also provided some of the core premises associated with the base of the pyramid business concept. He taught us to look at things, whenever possible, through the "other end of the telescope." He also taught us to always look for the unintended consequences of any action—the "toxic side-effects," as he liked to call them.

C.K. was also brilliant at asking the right questions. Rather than debating whether globalization was good or bad for the poor, for instance, he preferred to focus on a more practical challenge: how globalization could be made to work better for the poor. Leveraging his unique perspective and ability to reframe the questions we ask, scholars and practitioners could launch both new research agendas and implement proactive practical actions. He taught us to respect criticism and contrary opinions; he also taught that it is far more rewarding (and challenging) to search for creative solutions to difficult and seemingly intractable problems.

In the piece that follows, C.K. demonstrates these qualities. He identifies where he and his critics might see certain issues and core assumptions differently, presents his way of thinking, and offers insight into the questions he thinks we should be asking. We have edited this piece ever so slightly. Our goal was to present C.K.'s response in a way that avoided references to any specific individuals. We have also provided updated citations and reference information. We have not changed the content of his text, nor its relatively warm and informal tone. You are in the room with him as he thinks out loud, and his brilliance and generosity shine through.

As C.K. explains at the beginning of this piece, he is responding to three critiques of *The Fortune at the Bottom of the Pyramid*:

- The measurement problem
- The distinction between consumption and income generation in poverty alleviation
- The fallacy of an opportunity at the bottom of the pyramid

We feel that his views on these important questions could not provide a better backdrop for this book, which we sadly but enthusiastically dedicate to his memory.

Ted London	*Jacqueline Novogratz*
Stuart Hart	*Erik Simanis*
Al Hammond	*Madhu Viswanathan*
Robert Kennedy	*Patrick Whitney*

The Big Picture

C.K. Prahalad, University of Michigan

My thesis is simple. Over 80 percent of the people in the world are ignored as a market by the organized sector (including multinational corporations and large domestic companies). This was and is the "underserved and the unserved market." This population does not typically have access to world-class products or services or to regional and global markets for their effort and production. Awareness, access, affordability and availability continue to be the problems. Yes, I look at both consumption and production. The ITC and EID Parry examples are about production. So is the microfinance example. Creation of transparent markets and a market-based ecosystem is also an integral part of the argument. There is a whole chapter on *transaction governance*, or creating transparent conditions for markets to flourish (Chapter 5). So is a *market-based ecosystem*, including SMEs, single entrepreneurs, NGOs and cooperatives, not just MNCs (Chapter 4). I also talk about how to create products and services for the BoP market to be profitable (Chapter 2). Further, most of the case examples are about personal and family productivity: ITC and EID Parry, Cemex, health (Annapurna, Soap, Voxiva). This totality represents the argument on poverty alleviation: I wonder why some chose to focus on one aspect of the argument—consumption. Yet, examples of production and income generation, such as ITC—that are offered by others as an alternative—are in the book. So is the need to create transparent markets. So is the need for new business models and creativity.

The focus of the book is on 5 billion underserved. They are also poor. But it is naïve to believe that 5 billion represent a monolith (are one segment). Every experiment described in the book does not necessarily have to serve all the segments of the 5 billion underserved. No single business model can do that. My goal was to amplify weak signals and experiments that have potential in this general space. Annapurna and the soap examples are about the difficulty of educating the poor on health benefits as well as how arduous it is to work with multilaterals. Do firms fail in their experiments? Yes, they do.

Data Inconsistencies

I realize the problems of defining poverty using income and even expenditure assessments. Is there a wide variation in the way the "underserved" is described? Yes. Less than $2,000 per capita, $2/day per person are used in the argument. Do 4 billion live below $ 2/day? I and others are very aware of the problems of measurement of the underserved and the poor. The World Resources Institute (WRI) conducted a large-scale effort, with the International Finance Corporation (IFC), to reassess the data from various sources and to arrive at the structure of the pyramid, by country. [3] It is likely to be the most current, and they have used household survey data. It came out in 2006. It shows yet a different view. Let me give you a preview. [4] The data are as follows:

More than $21,730 PPP per capita	0.5 billion
$3,260–$21,730 PPP per capita	2.0 billion
Less than $3,260 PPP per capita ($458)	4.0 billion

The WRI/IFC study confirms that 4.0 billion are below $2/day.

Add to this the underground economy and the remittances from overseas. (India received $21 billion-plus in remittances from overseas last year. Mexico received $18 billion.) The complexity of the problem defies precise measurement. (I am glad that as a result of my drawing attention to this "forgotten population," more people have started to devote their attention to understand this space better.) One way to escape this malaise of measurement is to shape this world differently rather than study, in greater depth, its income characteristics. We know that there is a large population out there—be it 4 or 5 billion underserved. (The size of this market does not depend on its income characteristics alone, but how we can create the capacity to consume. More of this later). *Shaping the world requires a point of view, and some evidence to show that this is possible.* The book is about a point of view. I have tried to apply only one set of tests in my work: Does it change the conversation? Does it show the opportunity? Does it lead to some action?

I respect precision. But to define the poverty line as $1.08 or $1.48 is pseudo precision. So is the ability to compute precisely the total number within those income boundaries. In my work I was looking for *dimensionality and directionality*. My goal was never to measure poverty; much less with great precision. There are others who do this well. My goal is to look for an alternative to the tried and tested methods, including government subsidies and public sector schemes, to remedy this situation.

The broad dimensions of the problem and the opportunity to make a difference are about changing the quality of life of 4 to 5 billion people who are underserved and (most of them) below the radar screen of the organized sector. If it is only 3.5 billion, so be it. It is still a large number, and worthy of our attention.

Consumption—Income—Production

I am surprised that some fall into this trap. Consumption can and does increase income.

Can Casas Bahia (and such other examples of consumption) alleviate poverty? I find this a very interesting argument. Let us start with four propositions:

a. The poor live in high-cost micro-economic systems (see Prahalad and Hammond, *Harvard Business Review*, 2002).[5]

b. They do not have access to good quality products and services (be it water, food, furniture, or credit).

c. They are prisoners of local monopolies, including local money-lenders.

d. They have no recourse to law. The local landlords can and do enforce their will on the local population.

Is the ability of someone at the BoP with volatile wages to get access to credit (at 20 percent rather than 300 percent) improving income? Is a family of four having a small refrigerator and eating better food improving the quality of life? Is someone becoming independent (one blind person means two people without wages—one who cannot see and one who needs to take care of that person)? Is releasing at least one person to do work—even at minimum wages—improving the earning potential of the family? Is helping poor people to avoid diarrhea, helping the family to save on needless costs associated with healthcare, much less, needless death? Is this income? Is this improving the quality of life? Is avoiding mental retardation, at an incremental cost, adding to income? The idea of a "poverty penalty" is real. See the report from Brookings Institution.[6] In the USA, poor families pay more for everything—food, autos, finance; reducing the poverty penalty is adding to real income.

Poverty alleviation is, simply, improving the disposable income for the families—by reducing the costs of services, improving its quality, and releasing their time to do work that is productive.

I also find some dismiss somewhat easily the cell phone revolution. Can you believe in 2009 that more than 50 percent of the cell phones will be sold to the poor in emerging markets, including such desperately poor markets as in sub-Saharan Africa (CelTel) or in South Africa (MTN, Vodacom)? Needless to say in India and China. (All cell phone makers are MNCs, and the new ones from China are also becoming MNCs). Of course they had to invent new business models, from Grameen Phone to "prepaid cards." I am continually humbled by the inventiveness of people who want to serve this population.

Lesson: Creating the capacity to consume is different from serving an existing market. Creating the capacity to consume can increase disposable income (no different from income generation). Creating the capacity to consume can build new and profitable markets at the BoP.

There are many ways to do this:

a. Single serve (Is aspirin OK if shampoo is bad)

b. Monthly payments (Is kitchen cabinet OK if TV is bad)

c. Pay per use (is cell phone OK if videogames are bad)

d. New distribution models (is ITC e-Sagar OK if Shakti Ammas are bad)

e. Low prices (is a water filter OK if iodized salt is bad)

There is another way that consumption leads to income generation. For example, Grameen Phone has 250,000 phone ladies—all entrepreneurs. There are over 100,000 telephone booth operators in Africa, and the number is growing. [Telecom operator] Bharti [Airtel] estimates that it will need about 500,000 individual entrepreneurs to sell "prepaid cards and charge cell phones" for cell phone users in India alone.

I know that some think "Fair and Lovely" is a bad idea. [7] This is an ideological stance. I believe in choice. I believe that the "poor" must have choice. Some may believe that the "rich and the elite can decide what is good for the poor, because they cannot decide for themselves." (Fair and Lovely does have moisturizer and sun block.) I know some do not approve of single cigarette sales; how about beedis, which is more affordable and more deadly? [8] Should a consumer have choice between beedis and cigarettes?

We can also argue that this population does not need PCs. Should AMD, Nicholas Negroponte, and Intel stop all their efforts to create an affordable PC? [9] Should we fix the drainage in Dharavi before we give them access to global connectivity? I just want to show how ideology gets so intertwined with our approaches. I am explicit about my preferences. So should others. State your position with respect to "who decides for the poor." I emphasized the consumer side because, as I stated clearly in the book, "We should commence talking about underserved consumers and markets. **The process must start with respect for the Bottom of the Pyramid consumers as individuals**...Consumers and consumer communities will demand and get choice...we must recognize that the conversion of the BoP into a market is essentially a developmental activity...**New and creative approaches are needed to convert poverty into an opportunity for all concerned. That is the challenge.**" [10]

Is There a Real Market?

Time will tell whether BoP is a market or not. I believe that it is. So do a lot of others (maybe foolishly). ICICI just enhanced the role of rural marketing. They believe that the total market for credit in rural India is Rs. 15,000 billion (now mostly done by moneylenders, at 100 percent, maybe). The banks have just scratched the surface with Rs. 40 billion. Even if the organized sector only got to Rs. 10,000 billion and reduced the interest rate from 100 percent to 20 percent, you can calculate the income generated for the poor. Consumption of credit, even to buy a TV, can create income. Obviously, ICICI expects to make a profit. This is one of their two corporate initiatives—global and rural!! ITC thinks it can make money. P&G, HLL, Nestle all think so.

The World Is Moving Forward

I believe that the world has moved on. The Inter-American Development Bank (focused on Latin America) just adopted the Bottom of the Pyramid as their focus. They call it the "opportunity for the majority." [11] Academy of Management calls it "business for the benefit of all." [12] For the last year I have been talking about "democratizing commerce." So the debate is not anymore about how many are really poor; it is about how to bring the benefits of global standards at affordable prices and increase access.

Hope this helps.

Notes

[1] C.K. Prahalad (2005). *The Fortune at the Bottom of the Pyramid: Eradicating Poverty Through Profits.* Upper Saddle River, NJ: Wharton School Publishing.

[2] The material for this foreword was posted by C.K. Prahalad on the NextBillion.net web site on August 31, 2006.

[3] Allen L. Hammond, William J. Kramer, Robert S. Katz, Julia T. Tran, & Courtland Walker (2007). "The Next Four Billion: Market Size and Business Strategy at the Base of the Pyramid." Washington, DC: World Resources Institute and International Finance Corporation.

[4] The numbers in the final report are slightly different from what is noted here. The authors of the report used $3,000 PPP per capita in 2002 U.S. dollars (or $3,260 PPP per capital when adjusted 2005 U.S. dollars) as the threshold for defining the BoP segment, which totaled four billion people.

[5] C. K. Prahalad & Allen L. Hammond (2002). "Serving the world's poor, profitably." *Harvard Business Review*, 80(9): 48-57.

[6] Matt Fellowes (2006). From "Poverty, Opportunity: Putting the Market to Work for Lower Income Families." Washington, DC: The Brookings Institute.

[7] Fair & Lovely is a skin-whitening cream sold by Unilever in more than 30 countries worldwide.

[8] A beedis is a loosely wrapped cigarette popular in South Asia.

[9] AMD, Nicholas Negroponte, and Intel were working together on the One Laptop Per Child (OLPC) initiative. Intel ended its involvement in the partnership in 2008. For more information, see: http://laptop.org/en/index.shtml.

10 *Fortune*, preface, page xiii. Emphasis in the original text.

11 For more information on the Inter-American Development Bank's Opportunity for the Majority, see: http://www.iadb.org/topics/om/home.cfm.

12 For more information on the Academy of Management and this initiative, see: http://www.aomonline.org/ and http://www.bawbglobalforum.org/.

Foreword

Y.C. Deveshwar
Chairman
ITC Limited, India

A few weeks ago, when Stuart Hart and Ted London asked me to write the foreword for this book, I must confess that I was of two minds. I am familiar with their work and have great regard for their talent and intent. But ever since *The Fortune at the Bottom of the Pyramid* was published, there has been a deluge of conferences, debates, and discussion papers on the subject of the base of the pyramid (BoP). It seemed that everything that could be discussed about the subject's theoretical underpinnings as well as about the handful of corporate examples that characterized this approach was already in the public domain. I was therefore hesitant in adding some more print to this effort.

As I read through the manuscript of this book though, I sensed a welcome change in approach. Far from merely examining opportunities to make a fortune "at" the base of the pyramid, Hart and London and their co-authors had collaborated to highlight the need to create fortunes "for" and "with" the base of the pyramid. This fresh approach was significantly aligned with our own efforts at ITC, over a decade and a half, to co-create sustainable and inclusive societies through innovative business models. A "Triple Bottom Line" approach that has enabled ITC to help create sustainable livelihoods for more than 5 million people, a corporation that is carbon positive, water positive, and waste recycling positive, and a top ranking economic value creator in the Indian economy. It is because of this compatibility between ITC's perspective and the broad ideas presented in this book that I am happy to contribute these introductory thoughts, and to support the efforts of Hart, London, and their co-authors in providing thought leadership in an area of immense importance to societies globally.

It has taken more than a century of material wealth creation to realize that the economic model pursued by the world for so many years is terribly inadequate in creating equitable and inclusive societies. In the last 50 years alone, world GDP has multiplied 60 times. Yet, two-thirds of the world lives in poverty, with more than a billion people in acute deprivation and hunger. UNDP reports have estimated that the top 10 percent own 85 percent of household assets, while the bottom 50 percent own just 1 percent of these assets. Other estimates suggest that the top 10 percent account for 65 percent of world's consumption while the bottom 50 percent consume just 2.5 percent. This disparity is indeed a serious threat to the progress of mankind. It is also a source of social unrest across the world, creating a dangerously vulnerable society. Unstable societies make economic progress unsustainable, and we can only ignore this basic economic fact at our considerable peril.

A century of economic progress also took place with significant apathy toward the need to conserve and replenish the earth's precious natural resources and living systems. In the last half-century alone, the world lost one-fourth of its top soil, one-third of forest resources, more than one-third of global bio-diversity, and witnessed the extinction of many species. Continuing degradation of land, forest, and water resources progressively undermines precious life-support systems, leading to the phenomena that we witness today in global warming, and consequent droughts and floods. Today's inhabitants of the planet inherited a 4 billion-year-stock of natural capital. In less than a century, in the name of material progress, this natural capital has been ravaged. As a result, we have an unenviable global ecological footprint that will demand the equivalent of resources of *two* earths to support an anticipated global population of 9 billion by the mid 2030s. We cannot afford this luxury as we have only one planet—to live together, or perish together.

These threats underscore the undeniable fact that "economic development" and "sustainable development" are not necessarily the same thing. Nor is sustainable development only about creating green economies. Progress and development is also about creating sustainable *and* inclusive societies. Economic growth models must therefore sub-serve a larger need to create greater societal value, and not material wealth alone. That, in turn, requires a far larger focus on the creation of sustainable livelihoods. Given the magnitude of this task on a global scale, this is indeed a formidable challenge for economies around the world today.

The 4 billion people who constitute the base of the pyramid are, by definition, among the poorest in the world. An overwhelming majority of this population live in developing or low-income countries. Predominantly living off the land, they are also the most vulnerable to problems arising out of environmental degradation, including climate change. In the best of circumstances, they are served by inefficient and fragile market systems. At worst, they are at the mercy of exploitation by market intermediaries. Either way, they are trapped in a vicious cycle of poverty. An approach that views this disadvantaged population only as a market for low-cost, low-value products and services contributes precious little to improving their lives or their future. It only implies a "race to the bottom" to garner a small share of a deplorably small wallet. A more enduring and meaningful approach lies in co-creating new economic opportunities that empower them and build their capacity to earn meaningful livelihoods—in essence, increasing the size of their wallets, and integrating them into the economic mainstream. It is this creation of a fortune "with" and "for" the base of the pyramid that will ensure a secure and sustainable future for our planet.

The question is: Can business play a meaningful role in catalyzing this process of sustainable and inclusive development? I firmly believe that it can. Private enterprises, through their operations, have a large number of touch-points in society that constitute the front line of engagement with civil society. Their physical presence in communities around their catchments gives them an opportunity to directly engage in synergistic business activities that can create sustainable livelihoods and add to preservation of natural capital.

In the years ahead, moreover, growing civil society awareness and tougher regulations will compel businesses to adopt sustainable business practices that not only deliver unique customer value propositions, but also enable a twin impact: ensuring a positive environmental footprint and creating sustainable livelihoods. It is my deep conviction that both the competitiveness and profitability of firms in the future will increasingly depend on their relative ability to adopt such sustainable business practices. Corporations of the future will have to innovate strategies to deliver high levels of triple bottom line performance. Their capability to do so will not only define the sustainable corporations of tomorrow, but also create the foundations of a more secure society for future generations.

Our experience at ITC convinces us that it is eminently possible to create larger societal value with business innovations that foster an inclusive and sustainable future. At the heart of ITC's innovative strategies lies the creation of unique business models that synergize long-term shareholder value growth with that of enhancing societal capital. These business models are supplemented by community-based CSR projects that enhance the quality of life of people in rural India.

A much-celebrated example is that of ITC's e-Choupal, described in this book as well. Leveraging the power of Internet and digital technology, ITC's e-Choupal has today become an internationally recognized model of rural transformation, benefiting more than 4 million farmers. By providing farmers with a rich repertoire of agri-based interventions, it not only addresses the core needs of farmers in terms of infrastructure, connectivity, price discovery, and market access, but also provides a significant boost to farm productivity through customized best practices in sustainable agriculture. This has helped transform villages into vibrant economic communities by raising incomes and co-creating markets. Similarly, a strategy to source pulp from renewable plantations, in spite of the availability of cheaper imports, has led to the creation of livelihood opportunities for thousands of poor tribals and marginal farmers. An intensive R&D programme in ITC developed high-yielding, disease-resistant clonal saplings which are today grown by farmers—even on wastelands—providing a huge green cover through forests on nearly 110,000 hectares. In the process, it has created 48 million person-days of employment opportunities. These innovative business models have not only enhanced the competitiveness of the businesses, but have simultaneously created immense value for rural communities.

The deep engagement of e-Choupals with rural communities has also enabled ITC to contribute to the creation of sustainable livelihoods by building community assets. ITC's Integrated Watershed Development initiative has helped create freshwater potential covering over 54,000 hectares in water-stressed areas. In addition, the company's integrated animal husbandry services have reached out to more than 400,000 milch animals, creating avenues for non-farm based livelihoods. More than 200,000 children in rural India have received supplementary education, and more than 20,000 women entrepreneurs have been created through approximately a thousand self-help groups. In addition, several partnerships with state governments have also been formed, to deliver quality projects of high social value through intensive public-private-people partnerships.

I firmly believe that innovation in corporate strategies and an abiding vision to serve a larger societal purpose can significantly transform the future and mitigate many of the sustainability threats discussed earlier. New entrepreneurs, as well as progressive companies, have a great opportunity today to contribute meaningfully to building a secure and sustainable future. So far, open innovation models have synergized the efforts of internal resources, supply chain participants, and even customers to co-create new products and services. To my mind, the need of the hour today is to encourage innovation in corporate strategies and business models that will enable companies to co-create, with local communities, opportunities for sustainable livelihoods, as well as enrichment of natural capital. At the same time, society—including customers, investors, and media— need to be made more aware of the tremendous change they can bring about by encouraging a preference for responsible companies. Innovations will be required to devise a rating system that can provide credible information to civil society to enable them to make an informed choice. Such innovations will spur the creation of a market for responsible and sustainable practices. It will also make sustainability a value proposition that companies will embed in their offerings to society. That will go a long way in creating a sustainable economy for future generations and a secure planet that will continue to nurture and nourish the billions of its inhabitants. I do hope that future innovation will awaken the world to such a promising tomorrow.

I want to compliment the distinguished authors of this book, once again, for collaborating to find engaging solutions that can build new hopes for the many in the base of the pyramid. I also join you in paying my tribute to the late C.K. Prahalad, who helped begin the journey. My very best wishes in this endeavor.

Y.C. Deveshwar
September 2010

Introduction

Creating a Fortune with the Base of the Pyramid

by Ted London, William Davidson Institute & Ross School of Business, University of Michigan; and Stuart L. Hart, Johnson School of Management, Cornell University

The introduction, by co-editors Ted London and Stuart Hart, conveys the core message of the book: that the next generation of BoP business strategies won't be about "finding a fortune at the base of the pyramid," but rather, about "creating a fortune with the base of the pyramid." The shift from "fortune-finding" to "fortune-creating" has implications for how BoP ventures are organized, and how their strategies are conceived and implemented. Co-editors London and Hart introduce the three core sections of the book—Roadmaps for Success, Strategic Opportunities, and Effective Implementation—and explain how the contents of each can help venture leaders approach the challenges and opportunities of BoP markets.

The way we *frame* the opportunities and challenges in front of us matters. In fact, it can be one of our most important choices. When we rely on an established framing, our ideas generally evolve in linear, incremental, and increasingly predictable ways. But when we use a new lens on an old problem, we allow creativity back into the process, and this can enable us to make major leaps forward.

Stated slightly differently, when we *reconsider* our fundamental, often taken-for-granted assumptions, we can help stimulate the emergence of new ideas and approaches. This is true in many human endeavors, and the base (bottom) of the pyramid (BoP) domain is no exception. The BoP domain comprises a broad range of business models, developed by or in partnership with the private sector, and specifically designed to target the poorest segments of society as consumers, producers, and entrepreneurs.

And yet much of the current thinking in this domain, as well as much of the action in the field, seems tethered to a set of assumptions whose time may have passed. For many, their perspective of the BoP domain remains wed to the concept of "finding a fortune at the BoP."

This way of thinking certainly was valuable in generating early momentum, but holding onto this view for too long has limited our collective creativity and impact. Fortunately over the past few years, aspects of a new perspective have begun to emerge, which collectively has the potential to transform the BoP opportunity space. We feel the time has come to connect these emerging ideas together in one place. Hence this book, which offers a fundamentally different starting premise for those companies, nonprofits, social entrepreneurs, and development agencies interested in developing ventures to serve the BoP.

Simply put, we contend that successful BoP business development requires a change in framing to *creating a fortune with the BoP*.

Next-Generation BoP Strategies

Since the BoP domain's initial articulation as "The Fortune at the Bottom of the Pyramid" over a decade ago, interest in the BoP as a market segment, business strategy, and poverty alleviation approach has gained considerable momentum.[1] During that time, a growing number of organizations operating in the business and development sectors launched new BoP ventures and initiatives. With many observers predicting—especially in the wake of the global financial crisis—that the developed world will suffer a prolonged period of slow growth well into the foreseeable future, more and more companies and development agencies are exploring the opportunity to develop self-sustaining—and better yet, scalable—business models to serve BoP markets.[2]

Most BoP business activity and associated intellectual energy, however, remains centered on the prospect of selling products to a seemingly massive and previously ignored and underserved market.[3] Practice and research focus on the role of companies and nonprofit organizations in developing new distribution channels to reach low-income markets and new technological solutions to address unmet needs. This first generation of "fortune-finding" approaches could be described as *business to four billion*.

With some notable exceptions, many of these first-generation BoP ventures have yet to achieve substantial scale. A number have failed, others remain local or regional in character, and a few have been converted into philanthropic endeavors because the financial upside remained elusive.[4] Serving the BoP, it now seems clear, involves more than simply providing low-cost products and extended distribution reach to a hitherto untapped market—one that is passively waiting to be discovered by observant entrepreneurs and business leaders.

Over the past few years, a second generation of approaches with a markedly different orientation and value proposition has emerged. Framed more accurately as *business with four billion*, this "fortune-creating" perspective emphasizes co-creating new business models, technology solutions, and value propositions with the BoP. This more nuanced view of BoP venture strategy extends and enhances our thinking about market development, innovation, capability requirements, and cross-sector partnerships. Most recently, this work suggests that efforts to co-create BoP ventures can also provide important avenues for poverty-alleviation and green-technology agendas.[5] Yet this second generation of BoP business strategies still remains "hidden" from many BoP leaders in the for-profit, nonprofit, and development communities who have yet to shed the old framing.

We assembled the set of essays in this book to help accelerate the transformation in the way the BoP is viewed from a "fortune-finding" to a "fortune-creating" mentality.[6] Our goal is to share some of the latest thinking in this still-emerging perspective for the BoP domain. Based on the idea of creating a fortune *with* the BoP, we have made our best effort to provide useful material for existing and emerging leaders committed to developing better BoP ventures, as well as for those in development and policy-makers interested in the potential social value resulting from these enterprises.

A Different Kind of Journey: Co-Creating a Book

With the rise of BoP business, a robust debate has developed about the business opportunity, poverty alleviation benefits, and environmental impacts associated with such activity. There is growing concern, for example, that BoP business will result in nothing more than "selling to the poor"—in other words, that it's the latest form of corporate imperialism. Others fear that BoP business will spur consumerism among the poor, resulting in accelerating environmental destruction. Some even question whether the profit motive is compatible with sustainable development. If the BoP domain is to fulfill its grandest promise—that is, as a business and development strategy grounded in a synergistic relationship between the generation of economic returns and the solution to social and environmental problems—these issues must be taken seriously and addressed head-on.

This book thus reflects our view that the BoP domain has reached a crucial juncture. The time is ripe for critically assessing what we have learned so far, for exploring the opportunities to incorporate new thinking, and for charting a roadmap that can guide future action. With these goals in mind, we decided to bring together a group of BoP "pioneers"—thought and practice leaders who represent a variety of perspectives—to reflect on the state of the field and creatively consider the opportunities and challenges in moving the domain forward. We were delighted when Al Hammond, Bob Kennedy, Jacqueline Novogratz, Erik Simanis, Madhu Viswanathan, and Patrick Whitney agreed to join us and create chapters for this book.[7] C.K. Prahalad also enthusiastically accepted our invitation to participate in this endeavor. While his declining health ended up preventing him from contributing a chapter, he was nevertheless instrumental in the development of this book.[8]

We viewed this book as an opportunity to connect and catalyze the thinking among the authors; our goal was to co-create a book and infuse it with the latest ideas from the BoP domain. We also wanted to avoid a potential flaw found in many books with multiple contributors: a collection of interesting but often disconnected individual contributions. We believe that stimulating a *dialog among the authors and other thought-leaders*, rather than simply commissioning various experts to write specific chapters in isolation, offered the best path to a final product that would both enrich the recommendations for field-based activities and improve the intellectual development of the domain.

How did we pursue this vision? In May 2009, the coeditors and authors of this book convened for a two-day retreat in Ann Arbor, Michigan. In this intimate setting, each author presented their preliminary thinking, followed by critique and discussion. Gradually, the contours of the book began to emerge, with each of the contributions fitting together to form a cohesive whole. The tangible outcome was a shared vision for the book and an agreed-upon path forward for each of the authors. Each author then began to develop a full draft of his or her respective chapter.

Next, in October 2009 the William Davidson Institute at the University of Michigan and Cornell's Center for Sustainable Global Enterprise hosted a conference during which the authors presented their thinking. Limited to 100 invited attendees, the conference was designed to stimulate dialog and provide a venue for frank conversations and honest feedback. We owe a great debt to those conference attendees, whose names are listed in the appendix at the end of this book. They provided us, as authors, invaluable insight into how to refine, enhance, and even reframe our ideas. They also gave us a welcome recharge of our intellectual batteries with their strong support for the value proposition of this book as well as for the concept of reframing the conversation around creating a fortune *with* the BoP. This helped us to the finish line, which is the final product you see here.

Reframing the Discussion and the Questions We Ask

One of our objectives in developing this book was to move away from some of the old and, frankly, unproductive debates in the BoP domain that end up narrowing the scope of interest and constraining the opportunity for creative thinking. These debates have often centered on a "fortune-finding" perspective, focusing on important-sounding but mainly academic questions such as "Precisely how big is the BoP market?" and "Are BoP ventures good or bad for the poor?"

Both questions, of course, can be answered by "It depends," and the interpretations vary based on the assumptions made. Answers to questions like these will remain elusive and, likely, highly context-specific. At least to the authors of this book, pursuing these lines of inquiry seems to offer limited opportunity to make a substantial contribution to this domain, or to enhance its impact.

Accordingly, we believe that much more attention should be focused on critical questions that emerge from a "fortune-creating" viewpoint. These include, "How can we create a market with the BoP?" and "How can we make BoP ventures better for the poor?" Surely, these questions are more relevant and potentially productive, given that numerous BoP ventures already exist, and their numbers will only grow in the future.

Indeed, BoP ventures are here—for better or worse. Let's focus on how to make them better (and figure out what "better" means!). But before diving into these issues in the chapters that follow, let's first establish some boundary conditions for what constitutes the BoP and BoP business.

Defining the Base of the Pyramid

In the first seminal articles published on the BoP, the global population was divided into a pyramid containing three socioeconomic segments, with the bottom segment being labeled the "base of the pyramid" (BoP). This segmentation was developed from per capita income adjusted for purchasing power parity (PPP). PPP is a measure that equates the price of a basket of identically traded goods and services across countries, providing a standardized comparison of real prices. It provides a useful, albeit crude, measure for dividing the world's population into different income levels.

Since then, different BoP authors have articulated different PPP lines, which has generated some confusion. These values range from $1,500 to $3,000 per annum and $1 to $4 per day per capita, which both provides a broad sense of the variation within the BoP socioeconomic segment and generates some troubling inconsistencies. In the most detailed effort to date, the World Resources Institute (WRI) and the International Finance Corporation (IFC) conducted an in-depth study to develop a deeper understanding of the population size and aggregate purchasing power of the BoP.[9] These authors used $3,000 PPP in 2002 U.S. dollars (or $3,260 when adjusted to 2005 U.S. dollars)[10] as the per capita annual income threshold defining the BoP. Using data from household consumption surveys from Africa, Asia, Eastern Europe, Latin America, and the Caribbean, WRI and the IFC estimate the BoP segment as approximately 4 billion people, with total annual household income of $5 trillion PPP (or $1.3 trillion when adjusted for U.S. dollars).

One outcome of using PPP demarcation lines has been increased scrutiny of some of the earliest claims in the BoP literature about the size of the market opportunity.[11] Given that the BoP was initially framed as a business opportunity (for example, the book *The Fortune at the Bottom of the Pyramid*), these efforts at further clarification are not surprising. Unfortunately this line of inquiry, as noted, ultimately guides the conversation into an arena of diminishing returns. Therefore, we submit that PPP lines demarcating the BoP should instead be viewed as sources of empirical and illustrative convenience, rather than as a rigid definition.

Few would support the notion that an increase in an individual's annual income from $2,999 to $3,001 has a material impact on that person's state of poverty or whether or not they are considered part of the BoP socioeconomic demographic. Few would also support the idea that a business venture should stop serving a person if his or her income moves above some predetermined poverty line. Calculating a specific market size is therefore fraught with difficult-to-defend assumptions and questionable attempts at pseudoprecision. Indeed, the most effective BoP strategies can actually build capacity and generate income among the poor, not simply extract wealth in the form of increased consumer spending. Furthermore, as we will discuss in the following chapters, BoP markets may need to be *created*, rather than discovered, which has important implications for how one assesses potential market size.

The BoP is also not a homogeneous "mass market." In the WRI/IFC report, the BoP is segmented into $500 PPP income increments that are shown to have markedly different characteristics across regions, countries, and industry sectors. If nothing else, this seems to confirm the relative fruitlessness of trying to precisely identify the

BoP segment simply by referencing a specific income level (and also underscores the challenge of scaling, which is addressed in subsequent chapters). Again, as in the debate over poverty lines, income is at best an imperfect indicator of a more complex phenomenon.[12] In the poverty-alleviation community, income is viewed as a measure of convenience and is widely recognized as an imperfect one at best. Again, a specific PPP level—while a potentially useful empirical indicator—has clear limitations as a definition for the base of the pyramid.

How else, then, can the BoP be defined? In the BoP literature, this segment is consistently defined by one characteristic: *It is the population of the world that is generally excluded from the current system of global capitalism.*[13] The IFC and the Asian Development Bank uses the term "inclusive business" to describe efforts to develop new ventures that will serve the BoP. Many other organizations also adopted the term inclusive business or something similar. The Inter-American Development Bank created a special program called "Opportunities for the Majority" to support ventures that focus on improving the quality of life of low-income communities that constitute the majority of the population of Latin America and the Caribbean. The United Nations Development Programme calls it "Growing Inclusive Markets." So an alternative definition of the BoP is *the low-income socioeconomic segment that is not well-integrated into the formal economy*. This perspective aligns with the BoP literature on venture capability-building, which addresses the challenge of business development in the absence of a "Westernized" market environment that is characterized by legally recognized boundaries, enforceable contracts, and property rights protection.[14]

This view also links into important work from the development community. Hernando de Soto, for example, describes how the vast majority of the world's population is excluded from the predominantly western global capitalist system.[15] The poor, while possessing substantial amounts of unregistered assets and entrepreneurial talent, operate in an essentially extralegal environment, in which property rights are not officially recorded, and contracts and other agreements lack legally enforceable mechanisms. In many developing countries, in fact, the informal economy—most of it perfectly legal—accounts for a substantial portion of the current economic activity. Due to the cost, complexity, and unfamiliarity of transitioning to the formal economy, most transactions and business activities conducted by the poor are likely to remain in the informal economy, at least for the foreseeable future. This suggests that the base of the pyramid is the socioeconomic segment that *primarily lives and operates their local enterprises in the informal economy and often has annual per capita income of less than $3,000 in PPP.* (Note: This income line comes from the WRI/IFC report, which based PPP data on 2002 U.S. dollars. The Inter-American Development Bank used $3,260 when it adjusted the same PPP per capita to 2005 U.S. dollars, which again shows the limitation of a "fixed" income line that fails to transcend time and context.)

Managers, development professionals, and academics can therefore define the BoP by a combination of income and characteristics. Income levels, however, hide heterogeneity, and characteristics such as informality can vary depending on how they are operationalized. Those seeking absolute precision could argue about this indefinitely and most likely never reach consensus. Respectfully, we and our fellow authors are less interested in this kind of elusive precision. The key point is that the BoP segment has the following characteristics:

- Is heterogeneous across multiple dimensions.
- Includes the portion of the world's population with the least amount of income.
- Contains local enterprises that generally are not well-integrated with the formal capitalist economy.
- Lives primarily in the informal economy.
- Constitutes the majority of humanity.

Defining BoP Business

BoP businesses (or ventures) are revenue-generating enterprises *that specifically target the BoP demographic described as buyers, sellers, and entrepreneurs.* They sell goods to and source products from the BoP. The two orientations can be termed "serving BoP consumer" or "serving BoP producer," and a specific BoP venture can adopt either or both approaches. Ventures serving BoP consumers bring nonlocal products and services to BoP communities and markets. Ventures engaging BoP producers purchase goods from local producers to sell in various nonlocal domestic or international markets.

BoP business ventures typically *straddle the formal and informal economies*. Unlike the "underground" economy at the top of the pyramid, which is driven largely by the desire to avoid paying income taxes or to conduct illegal activities, the informal sector that characterizes most BoP marketplaces exists because of the difficulty and expense of becoming legally registered due to unreasonable costs, high levels of corruption, and archaic rules. The challenge, therefore, is to bring productive assets from the informal and formal economies together in a mutually beneficial manner. BoP ventures thus seek to combine the best of both worlds—the resources and technological capacity of the formal economy and the indigenous knowledge, human face, and local embeddedness of the informal sector.[16]

BoP ventures *span sector and size*, including initiatives by large multinational and domestic companies, local small- and medium-scale enterprises, and businesses developed by nonprofit organizations and social entrepreneurs. These ventures also *often involve partnerships across different sectors*, including collaborations among for-profit companies, nonprofit organizations, and development agencies.[17] Furthermore, BoP ventures *typically cross traditional industry boundaries*. For example, at the top of the pyramid, industries such as "energy," "health care," and "telecommunications" make sense. When it comes to the BoP, however, given the lack of pre-existing infrastructure, ventures must often cross boundaries to be successful. A BoP health care venture, for example, may need to be premised on telemedicine and must therefore include telecommunications as an important part of its strategy. Similarly, a rural telecom venture may need to also be in the distributed energy business, given that digital power is crucial to telecommunications.

Another distinguishing feature of BoP ventures is the goal of *becoming economically self-sustaining*, meaning that at the least they expect to recover their ongoing operating costs. The objectives of most BoP ventures also include *scalability*. Economic self-sufficiency and scalability, it should be noted, do not preclude access to grants or subsidized support. Many businesses in the developed world—including those in the agriculture, energy, science, technology, aerospace, and medical industries—receive varying levels of short- and long-term support from national and local government. As is discussed in subsequent chapters, ventures serving the BoP can achieve economic self-sufficiency and scalability by combining revenues from serving BoP consumers and producers with resources and "smart subsidies" from the development community and government agencies. Conversely, without access to these types of external support, many ventures will struggle to create markets and demonstrate economic viability.

An Overview of the Book

In selecting authors for this book, we purposely chose BoP thought leaders from different backgrounds, perspectives, and experiences. Accordingly, the book is organized into three sections, reflecting the perspectives of the different authors: Part One, "Roadmaps for Success," provides frameworks and roadmaps for assessing and improving BoP ventures' potential for success. The two chapters in this section offer complementary analytical lenses through which to view the development of any BoP business. They also serve to provide the appropriate context for the more focused material that follows.

In Chapter 1, "Building Better Ventures with the Base of the Pyramid: A Roadmap," Ted London presents BoP venture leaders and development practitioners with a framework, based on the perspective of "creating a fortune with the BoP," to guide their enterprise-development efforts. In particular, he provides core principles that leadership teams should apply at each of the three stages of BoP venture development: designing, piloting, and scaling. London advocates that venture development grounded in mutual value creation offers the best prospect for generating economically-viable enterprises that also enhance the quality of life in BoP communities. He further argues that appropriately applying the core principles at each stage of development can mean the difference between success and failure. London closes his chapter by proposing a new perspective on cross-sector collaboration that can more effectively integrate business effort to build viable BoP ventures with development community investments in creating new market opportunities.

In Chapter 2, "Innovation for the BoP: The Patient Capital Approach," Bob Kennedy and Jacqueline Novogratz describe the "markets versus development assistance" debate, making the point that neither of these traditional approaches has worked particularly well in serving the BoP. They then describe what might be termed a "virtuous convergence": the coming together of social entrepreneurs and "philanthrocapitalists" who have invested in pools of patient capital (i.e., capital that explicitly takes the long view in calculating return on investment). The former create new solutions; the latter bet on the best of those solutions, help build organizational capabilities, and provide the funds needed to scale. Drawing on their own extensive experience with both of these groups, they identify four types of innovations that are critical to success in BoP markets and explore the on-the-ground experience of four BoP ventures.

Part Two, "Strategic Opportunities," addresses two of the principal strategic challenges facing the BoP domain in the coming years: the BoP environmental challenge and the BoP market-creation challenge.

Stuart Hart's Chapter 3, "Taking the Green Leap to the Base of the Pyramid," focuses on the conscious effort on the part of BoP ventures to move beyond the early models of "finding a fortune at the BoP"—which involved adapting environmentally unsustainable products and services to sell to BoP consumers—and to move to a model in which "green" solutions derived with the BoP can serve all strata of the economic pyramid. He contrasts "Green Giant" and "Green Sprout" technologies, with the former being centralized, investment- and policy-driven approaches favored in the developed world, and the latter being distributed, small-scale, small-footprint approaches that are necessary in BoP marketplaces. The "green leap," he argues, will emerge from a creative convergence of the green technology and BoP communities. After citing examples of the green leap in action, he proposes a portfolio of actions and initiatives to help accelerate the Green Revolution around the world.

Chapter 4, "Needs, Needs, Everywhere, But Not a BoP Market to Tap," by Erik Simanis, opens with the surprising example of a product that seemed destined for success in the BoP space and yet failed to match expectations. He makes the case that despite the manifest *needs* in that space, there may not be pre-existing *markets*. The

BoP challenge is more accurately seen as one of market creation, rather than market entry. Market creation, in turn, depends on both framing the value proposition and defining the strategic innovation process in ways that make sense in the very particular environment of the BoP. Yes, Simanis argues—creating new BoP consumer markets is complex, expensive, risky, and time-consuming, and yet that may be where the best opportunities lie.

Part Three, "Effective Implementation," focuses on three critical operational challenges for BoP business, with a particular focus on developing a deep understanding of the nuances of market research, product design, and venture scaling in the BoP context.

Madhu Viswanathan opens this section in Chapter 5, "A Micro-Level Approach to Understanding BoP Markets." He intersperses theory with a "bottom-up" perspective presented by BoP consumers, producers, and entrepreneurs in their own voices. He describes and illustrates the thought processes of those who transact daily in BoP marketplaces and draws out the implications of those thought processes for BoP venture managers. He also draws out the critical coping strategies used by those who live in extremely challenging circumstances and again considers the implications for venture development. He makes the case that to a surprising degree, BoP marketplaces are dominated by ongoing relationships, rather than one-time transactions, and concludes the chapter with practical advice for designing and implementing enterprise solutions for the BoP.

Patrick Whitney's chapter, Chapter 6, "Reframing Design for the Base of the Pyramid," comes at the design challenge from a very different yet still complementary perspective. He argues that new design principles being adopted to create breakthrough products at the top of the economic pyramid also can be used to create successful innovations for the BoP. He notes the surprising similarities in the "reframing" design principles of the iPhone and those of the Chotukool refrigerator (designed for use by consumers in India who had never owned—or even dreamed of owning—a device that could keep produce cool and fresh for extended periods). In the case of the refrigerator-producing company, the designers spent enough time "on the ground" to imagine a scenario whereby customers might also become "partners" generating income for themselves by selling refrigerators to family and friends. Whitney argues that the "direct design" model (whereby companies analyze markets and create new offerings) is less relevant to the BoP than "strategic design," which allows for a radical reframing of the design process. But because developed-world companies like Apple are already well-versed in strategic design, businesses designing for the BoP should take heart, follow suit, and adapt accordingly.

The third and final chapter in this section, Chapter 7, "BoP Venture Formation for Scale," by Allen Hammond, tackles the aforementioned issue of getting to scale. This is critical for any BoP venture that hopes to become sustainable, and for any enterprise that hopes to have a meaningful social impact (as most BoP ventures do). But scale has tended to be elusive among both corporate and *de novo* business startups, in part (Hammond suggests) because many bottom-up new ventures simply don't plan adequately for scale. He explores in detail two alternative scaling-up strategies. One focuses on the business structure—and urges BoP ventures to plan to be both global and local (both bottom-up and top-down) at the same time, the better to source capital and technology, while also paying attention to local needs and challenges. The second focuses on activities outside the business structure, and urges BoP entrepreneurs to build a supporting ecosystem for the venture as well as the business activity itself. One particular form of such a supporting ecosystem is a hybrid model—one or more partnerships between the venture and civil society entities—that enable a diverse ecosystem and hence multiple sources of solutions. The chapter also illustrates how such strategies might be put into action with examples from a new BoP venture that Hammond and a number of collaborators have launched.

We close the book with our thoughts and reflections looking forward. Our goal in writing this book is to present the underpinnings of a new perspective for the BoP domain. We are well aware that more work needs to be done, and in our conclusion, we draw attention to important issues that need further consideration. What new problems and challenges have been identified? What areas have not been adequately tackled? What gaps remain?

The BoP domain is at a critical juncture. We hope this book offers insight into the way forward. We believe that the next generation of BoP ventures should emphasize the opportunity to create a fortune with the BoP. The evolution of the domain, clearly, is not finished. We are on a learning journey, and these are exciting times for BoP venture leaders and their partners. We must continue to extend the boundaries of our understanding. We must not stop asking, "Where do we go from here?

Notes

[1] A working paper by C.K. Prahalad and Stuart Hart titled "Raising the Bottom of the Pyramid" was first circulated in 1998. It took four years for it to be published as C.K. Prahalad and Stuart Hart (2002) "The fortune at the bottom of the pyramid," *Strategy+Business*, 26:1–15.

[2] This argument is made very strongly in Jeffrey Immelt, Vijay Govindarajan, and Chris Trimble (2009) "How GE is disrupting itself," *Harvard Business Review*, October: 3–11.

[3] It should be noted that some work has also been done on ventures designed to source from BoP producers. See, for example, Ted London, Ravi Anupindi, and Sateen Sheth (2009) "Creating mutual value: Lessons learned from ventures serving base of the pyramid producers," *Journal of Business Research*, 63(6): 582–594.

[4] Some of the BoP ventures that have scaled include Grameen Phone, Hindustan Lever, and ITC.

[5] See Ted London (2009). "Making better investments at the base of the pyramid," *Harvard Business Review*, 87(5): 106–113 and Stuart Hart (2010). *Capitalism at the Crossroads.* Upper Saddle River, NJ: Wharton School Publishing.

[6] For more on the distinction between "discovery" and "creation," see Sharon A. Alvarez and Jay B. Barney (2008). "Discovery and creation: Alternative theories of entrepreneurial action," *Strategic Entrepreneurship Journal*, 1(1): 11–26 and Saras D. Sarasvathy (2001). "Causation and effectuation: Toward a theoretical shift from economic inevitability to entrepreneurial contingency," *Academy of Management Review*, 26(2): 243–263.

[7] We would also like to thank our colleague Prabhu Kandachar from Delft University of Technology for his active and valued participation during the convening and conference.

[8] C.K. Prahalad passed away on April 16, 2010. C.K. was the first to accept the offer to join us on this endeavor, and his contributions helped shape this book. As such, we have dedicated this book to him.

[9] Allen L. Hammond, William J. Kramer, Robert S. Katz, Julia T. Tran, and Courtland Walker (2007). *The Next Four Billion: Market Size and Business Strategy at the Base of the Pyramid.* Washington, DC: World Resources Institute and International Finance Corporation.

[10] In a similar study with the Inter-American Development Bank, WRI examined the BoP in 20 countries in the Latin America and Caribbean region. This report finds that the BoP population in these countries totals 361 million and that these individuals have an aggregated annual income of $510 billion. See World Resources Institute (2006). *The Market of the Majority: The BOP Opportunity Map of Latin America and the Caribbean*. Washington, DC: Inter-American Development Bank.

[11] For a good example of this critique, see Aneel Karnani (2007). "Misfortune at the bottom of the pyramid," *Greener Management International*, 51: 99–110.

[12] For a detailed discussion of the multi-dimensional nature of poverty, see Amartya Sen (1999). *Development as Freedom*. New York: Anchor Books.

[13] See Stuart Hart (2010) *Capitalism at the Crossroads*. Upper Saddle River, New Jersey: Wharton School Publishing.

[14] See Ted London and Stuart Hart (2004). "Reinventing strategies for emerging markets: Beyond the transnational model," *Journal of International Business Studies*, 35(5): 350–370.

[15] See Hernando de Soto (2000). *The Mystery of Capital: Why Capitalism Triumphs in the West and Fails Everywhere Else*. New York: Basic Books.

[16] Hart, *Capitalism at the Crossroads*.

[17] For more information about the unique challenges of cross-sector collaborations, see Ted London and Dennis Rondinelli (2003). "Partnerships for learning: Managing tensions in nonprofit organizations' alliances with corporations," *Stanford Social Innovation Review*, 1(3): 28–35.

Part
One

Roadmaps for Success

1

Building Better Ventures with the Base of the Pyramid: A Roadmap

by Ted London, William Davidson Institute & Ross School of Business, University of Michigan

Ted London's chapter addresses how venture leaders can maximize the chances that their business development efforts in BoP markets will succeed. Which business practices should guide your efforts—and which ones should you be sure to avoid— as your venture moves through the stages of designing, piloting, and scaling? How do you craft initial business models, effectively test these approaches, and create sustainable competitive advantage? Using the perspective of "creating a fortune with the base of the pyramid," London provides a set of guiding principles (a "roadmap") that answer these and other critical questions relevant to both existing and start-up BoP ventures.

Leaders in the corporate, nonprofit, and development sectors are increasingly seeing the base of the pyramid (BoP)—that is, the four billion people living in low-income markets in the developing world—as a socioeconomic segment that business could serve more effectively. These leaders also believe that BoP venture development offers the prospect of helping to alleviate poverty. Despite the promise of generating both economic and societal returns, however, building successful BoP ventures remains a challenge. Some such ventures have demonstrated economic sustainability and have gone to scale. Others, launched with much fanfare and promise, have failed to develop viable business models or have remained endlessly mired in the pilot phase.[1]

I argue, though, that venture leaders and their development professional partners should not view these mixed results as unexpected or disappointing. Launching successful new ventures is a challenging endeavor in *any* context. Leaders considering developing a BoP venture must further account for the fact that entry into BoP markets is certainly not "business as usual" for most organizations. Indeed, BoP venture leaders must understand how to create business models and operate enterprises in a market environment governed by different rules of the game, energized by different stakeholder expectations, and implemented with unfamiliar customers, suppliers, and partners. As outsiders with limited experience in these markets, the venture team must be willing to reconsider traditional views about expertise in designing, approaches to piloting, and capabilities for scaling. They must understand the key principles required *to create a fortune with the BoP*.

What BoP leaders currently lack is a roadmap that enables them to respond to the unique opportunities and challenges that these enterprises face.[2] The goal of this chapter is to present a set of principles that the BoP leadership team can apply at each of three stages—*designing, piloting*, and *scaling*—to increase the chances of success in the venture-development process. Specifically, these managers must: 1) design based on creating market opportunities and crafting solutions with the BoP; 2) pilot by orchestrating effective experiments and managing failures; and 3) scale through generating co-mingled competitive advantage, as well as leveraging and transferring social embeddedness. The path, however, is not necessarily always linear. Lessons learned from pilots, for example, may require revised designs. Similarly, a venture that scales in one market may return to the design phase as it explores opportunities in new markets. Furthermore, the leadership team must attend to all these principles, as missing even one can generate challenges across all the stages of venture development.

BoP venture leaders also must embrace the perspective that *success at each of these three stages is grounded in demonstrating and enhancing mutual value*. When based on creating a fortune with the BoP, venture development can generate economically viable enterprises that also enhance the quality of life and respect the natural environment in BoP communities. To achieve this, however, the leadership team must commit to continually assessing the value created and exploring opportunities for improvement as the venture moves through the designing, piloting, and scaling stages.

The seven key principles of BoP venture development—our "roadmap," if you will, for creating a fortune with the BoP—are depicted in Figure 1-1 and are described in detail in subsequent pages. As this figure implies, these principles are interrelated and complementary, and each should be thought of as a critical part of a greater whole.

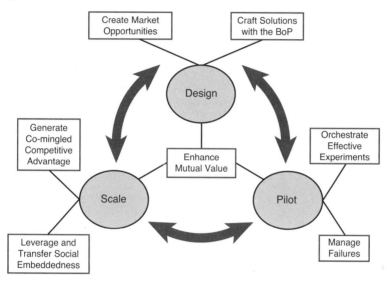

Figure 1-1   BoP venture development: Seven key principles for creating a fortune with the base of the pyramid

Creating Market Opportunities

Let's start by looking at a key challenge in the design phase: that of creating market opportunities. The allure of tapping into the "fortune" in BoP markets has helped catalyze interest in developing business models to serve the poor. But most ventures that attempt to serve BoP markets will not find a fortune just waiting to be discovered. Like the proverbial $10 bill on the sidewalk, if it existed, it would have already been picked up. So instead of focusing on "finding a fortune at the BoP," these ventures must consider the possibility that they will have to take an active role in *creating* the market opportunity.

To succeed, BoP ventures must expand their focus beyond designing products, developing business models, and generating competitive advantage. They must also consider market creation: a process that requires exploring strategies to enhance consumer demand, reduce transactions costs with suppliers, and facilitate the development of public goods. This means the venture leadership must consider a broader portfolio of investment needs, as well as prospects for accessing resources from a diverse set of partners.

At the top of the pyramid, market entry mainly focuses on identifying and exploiting existing market opportunities. For the most part, a venture's strategy assumes that while the market exists, a particular opportunity may remain undiscovered. Once the opportunity is identified by an observant entrepreneur or firm, standard business development approaches apply. In evaluating the size of the opportunity, revenue projections rely on assessing available disposable income and the prospects of convincing customers to change purchasing habits. In estimating supply, projections start from measures of current productivity and the opportunity to persuade existing producers to sell to a new buyer. As a rule, the enterprise leadership team can safely assume that both the consumers and producers are willing and able to actively participate in the market.[3]

In BoP markets, the approach is very different. First, markets don't necessarily exist in any organized form, and market awareness and demand may not yet be sufficiently developed. For example, if potential customers do not understand the link between dirty water and disease, a water purification venture will struggle to generate interest. Even if awareness exists, the poor may not have sufficient disposable income to create adequate demand for the product. While the poor may need little education about the dangers of malaria, they still may lack the resources to afford the mosquito bed net or indoor residual spraying that can reduce transmission.

Ventures seeking to serve BoP producers also can face market-creation issues.[4] BoP producers can be unaware of or unable to take advantage of new channels to sell their goods. Without an investment in information-sharing, for instance, local farmers may not realize that alternative markets exist or understand what they need to do to meet buyer expectations in terms of quality and quantity. Even if farmers are aware of and interested in participating in a new channel, a failure to address local infrastructure constraints may prevent these BoP producers from capitalizing on the perceived opportunity.

In addition to their focus on enterprise development, therefore, BoP ventures must also assess the need for market creation. If a gap is found, the leadership team should explore the potential for partnership with the development sector. Let's look at the example of Kenya-based honey producer Honey Care. Honey Care recognized early on the need for market creation and leveraged a variety of partnerships to overcome these challenges. The company first focused on understanding why beekeeping was not a thriving local business and what the company and its partners could do about this. Honey Care's business model involved creating a guaranteed market for local beekeepers. With financial support from several development-sector collaborators, Honey Care established a "money for honey" program, whereby it committed to buying all the locally produced honey from company-supplied hives at a fixed minimum price. Collecting honey directly from the producers in convenient locations—and also paying on the spot—helped catalyze local acceptance of this venture. As part of their design efforts, the Honey Care leadership team also worked with partners to generate a robust end-market for the final product.

At the same time, the venture also introduced a new product, the Langstroth hive, and helped local farmers learn the necessary technical skills. As this technology was considerably more expensive than existing hives, Honey Care looked to develop partnerships with local nonprofit organizations to provide the financing and training that supported the development of a more consistent, higher-quality supply of honey. Specifically, these partners were asked to provide micro-financing to prospective beekeepers, subsidize training courses, and monitor local honey production. These investments helped ensure that the local beekeepers could provide the quality and quantity of honey needed to meet market expectations.

Crafting Solutions with the BoP

Another key reason why many BoP ventures fail to gain traction in the design phase is that their learning processes are fundamentally flawed. Too often, the leadership team begins with incorrect assumptions about the marketplace and a misplaced sense of expertise. Successfully designing any new venture requires careful consideration of the sources of information its managers use to understand, evaluate, and address new market opportunities. Venture development in BoP markets is particularly challenging in this regard; most important, the venture's leadership team must surface any implicit biases about the poor and the ways in which their organizations can serve them. They must actively engage with the BoP, seek their advice, and incorporate this learning into the design of ventures.[5]

Unfortunately, too many managers and development professionals fail to recognize and calibrate for their existing biases about the BoP. One good test of this is to ask them to articulate the first references that come to mind when they think about the "BoP." Some are surprisingly disrespectful of the members of the BoP community, saying something along the lines of: "The poor are lazy, lack intelligence, or are helpless; if they were not, they would not be poor." Other descriptions focus less on individual shortcomings and more on structural disadvantages. Here you might hear terms such as "uneducated," "limited resources," or "isolated from opportunities." While more charitable, this latter view still fails to recognize the poor as having the capacity to productively participate in the venture-development process as thoughtful colleagues and resourceful experts. People who are characterized as uneducated, limited, or isolated are unlikely to be viewed as strong potential partners in a design process.

Actively crafting solutions with the BoP requires this fundamental shift in thought and deed. BoP venture leaders must ground their dialogue in mutual respect. Of course, many can *claim* they are doing this, and yet their actions often indicate otherwise. Respect requires a deep appreciation of the value the BoP can bring to the problem-solving process, including embracing a perspective that honors their ideas and input.

This means venture leaders must adopt three guiding perspectives as they develop relationships in BoP communities: *be patient, stay longer,* and *come back.* These perspectives provide an on-going reminder of the need for humility and the importance of listening and learning. A venture's management team can't rely predominantly on secondary data or truncated field observations to gain a deep understanding of the opportunities and challenges in BoP markets. If their goal is to craft solutions collaboratively, they can't plan to interact with BoP communities for only a short time. They need to *build relationships* in local communities—relationships grounded in mutual respect and trust.[6] These types of relationships take time to develop. They require a commitment to remain actively engaged in dialogue across an extended time period and over multiple interactions.

Managers for CEMEX's Patrimonio Hoy initiative adopted this three-part orientation. CEMEX, one of the world's largest cement manufacturers, identified a substantial business opportunity in serving the home-building needs of low-income communities in Mexico. But Patrimonio Hoy only gained momentum after its leadership team made what they called a "declaration of ignorance." Even though they were operating in their home country, the team developed enough humility to see that they had limited knowledge of the home-building constraints faced by the low-income segment in Mexico. After some early struggles in designing an effective business model, Patrimonio Hoy's managers decided they needed to spend more time engaging directly with the local community.

Through their declaration of ignorance, they signaled that even after careful analysis of secondary data and extensive discussions with existing partners, their organization did not possess the requisite expertise. By explicitly recognizing that they didn't understand the BoP market, team members could more easily drop their biases and focus on opening up, learning, and sharing. Rather than seeing the BoP as a community that they were going to help, they viewed them as a community that could help them.

The Patrimonio Hoy leadership team embedded itself for several months in the local community to develop mutual trust and forge deep connections. The team initiated and maintained conversations with a wide variety of stakeholders during (and after) this extended immersion. Such an intensive interaction enabled team members to develop a deeper understanding of the barriers that limited the poor's home-building efforts. A key to the depth and quality of this dialogue was role reversal. The venture's leaders did not view the poor as supplicants, pupils, and constituents. Instead, they saw them as colleagues, teachers, and advisors. Truly hearing the voices of the poor requires this level of respect.

Orchestrating Effective Experiments

After a venture leadership team has crafted a preliminary business model based on input from BoP communities—assuming they have also assessed and addressed any need for market creation—they can move to the pilot stage. Here's where "humility" (for lack of a better word) again enters the picture. The piloting stage in BoP venture development requires a willingness to experiment, learn, and innovate based on what is learned. Committing substantial resources before the business model or technology is proven can be a recipe for disaster, especially when serving BoP markets in which much learning needs to occur. As a rule, investments in BoP pilots should start small, with a view toward testing their potential for sustainability and future scalability. It is an *iterative* process; as these experiments unfold, the venture team may find that it needs to return to the design stage to revise its thinking.

To effectively experiment, BoP venture teams must incorporate two components into their piloting efforts. First, the leadership team must ensure that the venture's development is assessed based on the appropriate metrics. The team must do its best to avoid measures that require demonstrating immediate economic returns and resist pressures to make premature claims of social impact. Without longer-term metrics (and associated expectations) in place, internal and external partners may pressure the team to show immediate results, which can short-circuit the key processes of learning and improvement. Like most early-stage experiments, these initial pilots will likely need enhancement. At this phase of the venture-development process, failure may generate more useful knowledge than success. The venture team should develop metrics that support a process of trial-and-error—for example, partnerships developed, experiments launched, lessons learned, and improvements generated.

Effective experimentation also requires testing specific hypotheses about a business venture. This means establishing a pilot with explicit outcomes in mind. A pilot can evaluate specific components of a business model, or it can be designed to test the entire model (although most ventures start with the former before moving to the latter).[7] Testing specific aspects of the venture's model allows for a focused assessment of particular challenges. Subsidizing the cost of a product, for example, can allow for a careful assessment of the possible reach of a distribution channel without having to initially address the capital requirements of local distributors. Once the venture formulates a strategy to maximize awareness and reach, the leadership team can then focus on identifying the working capital needs of the appropriate set of distributors. After this round of experimentation, the venture may have sufficient information to test a full commercial model for sustainability and scalability.

CEMEX's Patrimonio Hoy, for example, started with an approach based primarily on incrementally modifying its top-of-the-pyramid business model. The venture's first pilot, based on conversations with its existing distributor network, involved providing its existing product in smaller and more affordable sizes. This approach generated disappointing results. But CEMEX did not waver in its commitment, in large part because Patrimonio Hoy's metrics were grounded in a long-term learning orientation.

How did this come about? At Patrimonio Hoy's earliest stages, CEMEX's top management had located the initiative in a so-called "corporate greenhouse." Protected from the influence of short-term expectations, the initiative received the resources, time, and space needed to invent a new business model. The venture leaders used this opportunity to experiment with various designs, while also developing metrics that tracked progress but did not curtail innovation. Rather than focusing on the number of bags of cement sold, the team adopted a radically different metric: *success in building homes*. This metric forced the Patrimonio Hoy team to take a much "deeper dive" into understanding local constraints. As a result, the venture developed a robust business model that comprised architectural services, affordable financing, and efforts to reduce the power imbalance with local intermediaries—all issues that had impeded home construction (and cement purchasing) in the past.

Patrimonio Hoy tested various components of its model in different experiments. For instance, the leadership team explored several approaches to addressing local financial constraints. Initially, the venture leveraged an existing group-lending model, called *tandas*. After testing this approach, the team decided to discard it in favor of CEMEX financing. Rather than having ten people in a group, as in the tanda model, Patrimonio Hoy moved to a model that required each customer to join with two other people. In addition to smaller groups, working outside the tanda system allowed the borrowers to avoid pre-existing expectations and competing demands. Experimenting in this fashion allowed the venture team to create a financing system better coordinated with the other emerging pieces of their business model.

Over the course of its first two years, Patrimonio Hoy produced results that would not have satisfied traditional internal business metrics grounded in short-term expectations. Sales were low, and profits were non-existent. Again, to its credit, CEMEX accepted the need for experimentation, learning, and persistence. The company valued the lessons learned and continued to support the venture as it repeatedly went back to the drawing board in its efforts to develop an appropriate business model. CEMEX's commitment to the initiative was rewarded over time: within five years, the initiative had become a $25 million revenue generator with intriguing growth prospects.

Managing Failures

As Patrimonio Hoy's efforts demonstrate, unsuccessful trials can provide substantial insight into improving the business model during the piloting stage. By its nature, good experimentation fosters variable levels of success. Leaders of BoP ventures investing in multiple experiments should have the flexibility to continue funding only those pilots that offer the opportunity for further insights into successful venture development. These leaders should also ensure that the post-mortem analysis focuses on capturing knowledge—as opposed to allocating blame—in order to maximize the value of any failed pilots. Yet even if venture managers have the flexibility to end disappointing pilots and the freedom to capture the lessons of failure, they must remain attentive to unintended outcomes that can sabotage these potential benefits. Two oversights in particular may limit the opportunity to capture the full breadth of knowledge that could be gained from these experiments.

First, rather than seeing piloting as one phase on a longer journey to developing a sustainable and scalable venture, managers may instead decide to prop up failures. The team may be reluctant to admit failure, or it may be too vested in demonstrating success. When this happens, a *learning-oriented pilot* turns into a *philanthropic project*, requiring continued funding and having little chance of becoming self-sustaining. Of course, philanthropic support to maintain a project is not necessarily a "bad" thing. Yet managers must explicitly recognize the transition from pilot to project and understand the associated changes in the value proposition, including the diminished likelihood of generating insights about achieving sustainability and scalability.

The second challenge to successfully managing failures may arise when the pilot is brought to a close. The venture cannot simply abandon its partners when a pilot ends, especially when these efforts have targeted the BoP. The individuals and communities vested in this venture must have the benefit of a soft landing. The venture's leadership team must ensure that any potential negative local impact caused by the pilot's termination are carefully considered and properly mitigated. In this market environment, concluding a pilot earlier than initially planned can create unique challenges. Failure, however, is not a license to abdicate responsibility. Venture managers must prepare for the end of the pilot—including the potential for premature closure—in setting initial expectations, in their implementation activities, and in their decisions about how to conclude the effort. Before pilot launch, the team must clearly articulate their plans to all partners. During implementation, the pilot must not require local partners, communities, or individuals to take substantial risks or make significant investments without also providing a safety net in case of failure.

Ventures ignoring these requirements do so at their own peril. Beyond the fundamental ethical considerations, managers must also recognize the increasingly rich network connecting the players involved in BoP ventures across the globe. The venture team's approach to managing its pilots has substantial implications for its future ability to find willing partners. Word can spread with amazing speed about the behaviors of specific organizations. Even for business ventures that articulate positive poverty-alleviation goals, the global community of potential local partners remains skeptical about motives and is highly sensitive to past abdications of responsibility. Bad management of failures means the leadership team will almost certainly find it difficult to recruit partners for its future activities.

Procter & Gamble's (P&G) approach to piloting its water-purifi-cation product, PUR Purifier of Water, offers insights into managing disappointing outcomes in a way that respects local partnerships. A powdered compound offered in sachets that can decontaminate 10 liters of water, PUR was one of P&G's first products specifically tar-geted to low-income markets in the developing world. The company worked closely with the Centers for Disease Control and Prevention (CDC) in several trials focused on assessing the efficacy of the prod-uct and evaluating usage patterns in local households. In these pilots, the product was provided free of charge.

The outcomes of these trials underscored the potential effective-ness of the product. The results also suggested that establishing regu-lar in-home use required a greater investment in education about the benefits of continuous treatment of water. P&G conducted test mar-kets in Guatemala and the Philippines using this knowledge. The product was sold at its expected retail price, but the company subsi-dized distribution and awareness. The goal was to see if customers would regularly purchase the product at this price. Awareness cam-paigns yielded modest results in terms of product perception, with repurchase rates reaching up to 25 percent in some locations. But P&G was spending a considerable amount to sustain these communi-cation campaigns, resulting in a disappointing return on investment.

Based on what they had learned, P&G launched a new pilot in Pakistan, where a revised model incorporating substantial community-based awareness efforts led to higher repurchase rates. Encouraged by these results, and after securing funding from the U.S. Agency for International Development (USAID), P&G then con-ducted an 18-month trial of the full commercial model in Pakistan. This trial failed to generate sufficient purchase rates to establish a sus-tainable business for P&G, even though it was launched in conjunc-tion with a high-profile campaign on the importance of clean water.

In short, the company's investments in market creation were not yielding a sufficient return. Given this, the company decided to transi-tion the PUR venture into a not-for-profit operation primarily sup-ported by the company's sustainability arm. The new noncommercial effort, called the Children's Safe Drinking Water (CSDW) program, focused on collaborating with partners that already had an existing infrastructure at the community level. The CSDW program now works with 70 partners across 50 countries.

As it developed the PUR venture, P&G considered the implications of ending the trial at each phase of the piloting process. The company worked with its partners to set initial expectations among all stakeholders and ensured that pilots were concluded in an orderly and well-considered manner. The CDC continued to partner with P&G as the company navigated through the initial series of pilots.

The venture team had also prepared a fall-back plan that transitioned the initiative into the not-for-profit domain when the traditional for-profit business failed to materialize as expected in Pakistan. P&G decided to provide PUR at cost for disaster relief and to a network of nonprofit partner organizations. The company saw benefits from these efforts in terms of organizational reputation and as a platform for gaining knowledge about marketing and distributing products to BoP markets. Additionally, P&G's commitment to managing the piloting process has helped establish and maintain partnerships with nonprofit organizations like Population Services International, which continues to help distribute PUR in a number of countries.

Establishing Co-Mingled Competitive Advantage

To achieve scale, BoP ventures (like all ventures with a goal of long-term self-sufficiency) must create and sustain competitive advantage. But because these ventures must straddle the border between the formal and informal economies, they face unique challenges in generating that competitive advantage. Unlike businesses operating solely in the formal economy, BoP venture leaders cannot rely on establishing competitive advantage based on investments made within and secured by the firm's protective boundaries or by a country's legal system. Businesses operating in the informal economy must accept the possibility of copyright infringement, the presence of counterfeiters, a limited ability to enforce contractual terms, and the prospect of product adulteration.[8]

At the same time, unlike businesses operating solely in the informal economy, BoP ventures cannot rely on a strategy that primarily depends on extracting value already present in these markets, such as accessing locally-available expertise or utilizing pre-existing infrastructure. These assets may be limited, and—as goods commonly available in the marketplace—are also available to other competing firms. Common availability levels the playing field, and nearly all local businesses that operate in the informal economy remain small.[9]

To scale a venture that straddles the formal and informal economies, the leadership team must embrace a perspective geared toward *identifying, leveraging,* and *enhancing platforms* that already exist in the BoP marketplace. These platforms could include network infrastructure, such as existing distribution systems and local self-help groups; social infrastructure, such as relationship capital and informal leadership; and physical infrastructure, such as underutilized business assets and existing resources previously used for nonbusiness purposes.[10]

To gain access to these platforms, BoP ventures must recognize and respond to two issues. First, these platforms are often developed and managed by nonprofit or community-based organizations that place a premium on development goals. BoP ventures must therefore understand and commit to creating the kinds of value that these partners pursue. Unlike partnerships with other businesses, social returns—not profits—predominate. A collaboration with a development-oriented organization is likely to remain viable only as long as that partner is comfortable with the type, amount, and allocation of the value created.

Second, these platforms may well require additional investment if they are to support business development. By investing in the platform, the venture enhances the partner's ability to achieve its social mission, while also strengthening its own business model. These investments, however, are made outside the venture's boundaries and are unlikely to be protected by any sort of contractual mechanisms. Once made, they probably can't be recovered. Obviously, this type of investment generates some sunk costs and associated risk for the venture. At the same time, it can help demonstrate the commitment necessary for cross-sector collaborations to flourish.

To sum up: achieving co-mingled competitive advantage necessitates gaining some level of exclusivity to platform-type assets controlled by development-oriented organizations and also typically requires making nonrecoverable investments outside the venture's boundaries. This co-mingled competitive advantage is only sustained when parties with different orientations toward economic and social returns 1) see value in maintaining the relationship and 2) see disadvantages in changing partners, even if neither party is contractually bound to the partnership.

Unilever's Shakti initiative has scaled in large part due to its ability to build and sustain co-mingled competitive advantage. Unilever, one of the world's largest fast-moving consumer goods companies, launched Shakti in 2000 as part of its Millennium Plan, which focused on identifying new sources of growth in India. Shakti relies on a network of entrepreneurs, primarily women, to distribute its retail goods to remote communities and villages outside Unilever's traditional distribution network. Shakti recruits many of these entrepreneurs through collaborations with nonprofit organizations and self-help groups (SHGs). To scale its business model, Shakti developed partnerships with over 350 organizations, one of which is CARE.

CARE, a global humanitarian organization, has worked in India since 1949. CARE's initiatives in India include facilitating the development of local SHGs. These SHGs are designed to empower women in poor communities. CARE and its local partners provide training, organizing skills, and connections to new opportunities to the SHG members. By establishing a partnership with CARE, Shakti positioned itself to potentially gain access to a platform of over 70,000 SHGs across four Indian states.

The partnership between Unilever and CARE is grounded in co-mingled competitive advantage. Both organizations are free to withdraw from the partnership but see benefits in continuing it. Shakti invests in the platform by offering training to the women; generating awareness about health, child care, and social justice issues; and providing access to potentially profitable enterprise opportunities. In return, CARE allows Unilever to leverage its relationships with local partners and BoP communities. Although focused on different success metrics, both parties see value in maintaining their partnership. As Shakti scales, Unilever expects economic returns to support their investment, and CARE anticipates an increase in socially beneficial outcomes.

Leveraging and Transferring Social Embeddedness

As illustrated by Unilever's Shakti initiative, BoP ventures can scale a well-developed business model across familiar contexts by generating co-mingled competitive advantage with an expanding set of partner relationships. This approach to growth can be called *scale up*. Ventures, however, may also want to *scale deep* (that is, serve the same customers in an existing geography but offer new products and services) or *scale wide* (offer similar products or services but target new customers in unfamiliar contexts requiring a different value proposition). When a venture scales deep or wide into a new market environment, it has to "start over," in the sense of designing and piloting new business models. After these new models are in place, they can then be scaled up using the techniques of co-mingled competitive advantage just described.

Let's look more closely at this idea of "starting over." Obviously, few organizations have the resources or patience to approach each new opportunity as a blank slate, with no prospects for economies of scope or scale. The leadership team must therefore ensure that it can transfer the venture's hard-won skills and knowledge about BoP market entry to new contexts. In particular, as a venture scales deep or wide, it must move more rapidly through the phases of the venture-development process—design, pilot, and scale up—by efficiently and effectively accessing and interpreting local knowledge about a different set of local needs and a new market environment.

The leadership team must therefore ensure that the venture develops what can be called *social embeddedness*—that is, the capability to gain a deep sense of the social context and a detailed knowledge of the intrinsic economic rationale of the local economy.[11] As it builds its social embeddedness, the venture can more smoothly design and pilot new business models, as well as enhance its ability to establish co-mingled competitive advantage that enables scale-up of these new models.

Developing social embeddedness requires skillful execution along two dimensions. One involves how a venture *gains access to* critical market-specific information, and the other focuses on how the leadership team *interprets* that information. Gaining access to important and relevant information requires the ability to develop deep, mutually beneficial connections with a diversity of local stakeholders. These connections can yield market intelligence, links into established networks, and insights into how things really work in these environments. Establishing and maintaining relationships with a diverse set of partners is a valuable skill, and the venture leadership team must ensure this capacity is recognized, nurtured, and transferred.

The venture team must also use an appropriate perspective in order to effectively interpret the information collected. Developing social embeddedness requires venture leaders to look beyond the relatively obvious limitations of the local economy and an associated impulse to fix "what is wrong." The team must instead frame its analysis around identifying opportunities to leverage and enhance "what is right." With this orientation, the leadership team can then most constructively engage the existing resources in BoP markets in designing, piloting, and scaling. The venture can improve its ability, for example, to craft solutions with the BoP, develop appropriate pilots, and generate co-mingled competitive advantage. When successfully developed, social embeddedness enables the leadership team to both efficiently assemble critical knowledge about BoP markets and effectively use this information while moving through the venture development process.

ITC, one of India's largest companies, operates in a variety of top-of-the-pyramid markets, including tobacco, paperboard, retail, and hospitality. ITC's International Business Division launched eChoupal to improve access to locally produced agricultural products. In its initial market-entry efforts, the venture began developing its social embeddedness capability. After scaling up, the leadership team then used this capability to both scale deep and scale wide.

First focusing on soybeans, eChoupal ("choupal" is the Hindi word for meeting place) followed the venture development stages discussed earlier. The leadership team spent considerable time gaining a deep understanding of the opportunities and constraints faced by these local farmers. They also considered the need to create a new market channel. The team then piloted various models based on deploying personal computers at the local village level, intended to provide information on the price of soybean transactions occurring in distant auction markets. In addition to creating price transparency,

ITC used the computer kiosks to announce its guaranteed forward price for next-day procurement of the commodity.

After a systematic process of iterating between design and a series of pilots, ITC felt it had developed a scalable business model. The company then invested in providing computers and training to carefully selected farmers to create a network of eChoupal kiosks. These specially trained farmers (called sanchalaks, the Hindi word for coordinators or directors) valued the prestige and recognition associated with serving as the official intermediaries between the farmers and ITC. ITC benefited from gaining trusted partners in these communities. The company was able to lower its purchasing costs by reducing the buying power and the associated margins of the existing intermediaries. In providing a guaranteed price, lower transaction costs, and prices that were aligned with produce quality, ITC generated greater returns and—significantly—shared some of this surplus with the local farmers. The eChoupal venture then relied on establishing and maintaining co-mingled competitive advantage to scale up a model in which the key stakeholders—including the company, the local farmers, and the sanchalaks—were all satisfied with the returns they received.

Success for ITC, however, required further scaling, and the company looked to both scale wide and scale deep. First, scaling wide, ITC explored the opportunity to procure other commodity products, such as wheat and coffee, grown in other regions of the country. To do so, the company transferred its burgeoning capability in social embeddedness to these new markets in order to identify and address the constraints faced by these BoP farmers. The leadership team quickly established strong local relationships, and demonstrated its skill at interpreting the information generated. This enabled the venture to rapidly design, pilot, and scale up its business model for these different crops.

ITC then investigated additional opportunities to scale deep—that is, to address additional needs of BoP farmers they currently served. Recognizing that the productivity of the local farmers suffered due to low-quality inputs, ITC used its procurement platform not only to source products from BoP producers, but also to provide a channel that local farmers could use to purchase high quality seeds, fertilizers, and pesticides. After this new business model went through the design and pilot stages and then reached scale, ITC and farmer success became further intertwined. The farmers purchased better inputs from ITC and produced better yields, while ITC received a more consistent and stable source of supply and provided greater returns to the farmers.

The venture then further leveraged its social embeddedness to gain an even deeper understanding of how to enhance the quality and reliability of the produce from local farmers in its existing markets. ITC, for example, made available the advice of agriculture scientists through their eChoupal kiosk network—enhancing the information farmers could find at this central location—and started extensive agricultural productivity improvement training. The venture leadership team also provided soil-testing services at nominal cost, so farmers could apply the most appropriate fertilizers. In addition to developing stronger relationships with BoP farmers, the soil-testing service had the additional benefit of yielding a data warehouse of the soil properties of local agricultural lands, which proved valuable for ITC's ongoing engagements with fertilizer and pesticide companies. In each new endeavor—whether the venture scaled deep by providing new products and services to existing customers or scaled wide by meeting producer and consumer needs in new market environments—leveraging and transferring social embeddedness proved critical to the ultimate success of these efforts.

Enhancing Mutual Value

Perhaps most important, a leadership team going through the BoP venture development process must remember that success in each stage is grounded in the proposition of *mutual value creation*. Of course, this is wisdom that is as old as business itself: The better the venture meets the needs of their customers, suppliers, and partners, the greater the likelihood of long-term viability. BoP ventures are no different. They will thrive only if their economic success is tied to creating value for BoP communities. Without a deep understanding of how their efforts meet—or fail to meet—local needs and changing expectations, customers may not return, suppliers may explore alternatives, and partners may become disenchanted.

Assessing and enhancing mutual value creation, however, remains problematic for many BoP ventures. While most of these ventures have metrics to evaluate their economic performance, many fail to invest in a systematic approach to continually improve their poverty-alleviation impacts—a surprising lapse, given the importance of maintaining an ongoing dialogue with those they seek to serve. Venture leaders instead tend to rely heavily on selected anecdotes, output-oriented measures, and ungrounded assumptions—in other words, information that is insufficient to convey the voices of their BoP customers and suppliers. These leaders also often pay scant attention to environmental implications. As ventures scale to serve hundreds of thousands or millions of consumers or producers, the environmental issues magnify. At the risk of stating the obvious, the world simply can't sustain BoP models of production and consumption that mirror those of the top of the pyramid.[12]

A leadership team that fails to develop a holistic understanding of potential value creation (and value destruction) will face challenges at each stage of the venture development process. In the *design* stage, venture leaders must develop a deep appreciation of how their business model might create value for the BoP and their partners. Successful piloting requires an ability to test these hypotheses about value creation and to identify opportunities to improve. To scale, the venture must continually demonstrate to its partners that it is indeed creating the value that they desire.

One way to quickly assess the depth of a venture's understanding of mutual value creation is to see if its impact assessment analysis reveals any negative outcomes. The law of unintended consequences suggests that it is nearly impossible to predict and respond in advance to *all* possible outcomes. So it is rare for *any* intervention, in any field, to have no unintended consequences or negative outcomes. Yet many of the assessments of BoP ventures that I've reviewed describe only positive impact. How can this be?

I submit that the problem is *a failure to probe deeply enough*, which in turn seems to stem from two root causes. One is the kinds of incentives that can infuse a venture with a development orientation, and thereby shape its view of "success." The development community has their own stakeholders to satisfy: To justify their investments in specific poverty-alleviation efforts, they are motivated to identify and highlight success stories. The development community also often provides funding in stages. Ventures that can demonstrate success—as opposed to exploring opportunities for improvement—are more likely to secure follow-on funding. As a result, optimistic estimations by the management team based on field observations, combined with heart-warming stories about changes in the lives of specific individuals, often suffice as measures of success.

The second root cause is hubris and an associated over-confidence in the local value creation potential of the business model. Providing a new service or offering a better product to the BoP (as this thinking goes) will *surely* generate positive results. After all, for people who have nothing, any improvement is good. In this case, even ventures that *do* decide to more deeply evaluate their performance can run into trouble, as the data they collect is frequently insufficient to generate a holistic picture.

For those that adopt this mindset, the key to assessing venture success lies in optimizing operational performance. The leadership team, therefore, primarily collects data on venture outputs, especially ones that they can observe, control, and manage in the short-term: clients served, products delivered, jobs created, revenues generated, training programs held, and so on. Under this logic, the venture need not overly worry about investing resources to hear the voices of the BoP. It wouldn't make sense—the argument continues—from a cost-benefit perspective to collect more data; the return on hearing from those we seek to serve is too low to justify the investment.

While potentially useful, these output-oriented metrics fail to give a complete picture of the type of value created or destroyed (increasing revenues by locating and training female entrepreneurs can, for example, generate more revenues, empower women, *and* lead to increased tension in the women's households as well as negatively impact other local businesses) or its allocation (the venture may be making a profit, perhaps, but the type and amount of value that actually reaches the BoP stakeholders can remain unclear). In this scenario, metrics demonstrating "success" can blind a venture's leaders to opportunities for enhancement. And, as stressed earlier, any business that fails to develop and maintain a holistic sense of its impact and an orientation centered on assessing and enhancing can expect to struggle as it moves through the venture development process.

VisionSpring has adopted an approach designed to obtain a full picture of its impact assessment. In partnership with this author and his colleagues, the VisionSpring leadership team has implemented a tool—the BoP Impact Assessment Framework—that assesses local impact on buyers, sellers, and the community across three dimensions of well-being and also spells out a process for continuous improvement.[13] The venture's business model relies on equipping local entrepreneurs with the skills and product portfolio needed to provide low-cost, high-quality reading glasses to the BoP. Left untreated, the individuals whose livelihoods depend on near vision—such as tailors, bookkeepers, and mechanics—face diminished economic productivity and quality of life.

VisionSpring's management team used the BoP Impact Assessment Framework to understand who within the BoP was impacted by their venture and how they were affected. The assessment helped address some challenges, including the fact that some of the venture's most successful female entrepreneurs were dropping out. Deeper probing of the situation revealed that the success of these women created tension in local family structures typically dominated by the husband. Understanding this dynamic allowed the leadership team to develop strategies to gain the support of the husband at a much earlier stage, thereby helping to retain some of the venture's most successful entrepreneurs (and some of the venture's most valuable assets).

Collaborative Interdependence: A More Perfect Union

The core premise of this chapter is that venture development, based on *creating a fortune with the BoP*, will best flourish when leadership teams adopt seven principles to help guide them through the design, pilot, and scaling stages. As discussed in the preceding pages, these principles include creating market opportunities, crafting solutions with the BoP, orchestrating effective experiments, managing failures, generating co-mingled competitive advantage, leveraging and transferring social embeddedness, and enhancing mutual value. (See Table 1-1 for a summary of these core principles and associated key components.) Effectively applying these principles can mean the difference between venture success and failure. And as indicated earlier, paying insufficient attention to any one of these principles—especially early in the process—can have substantial negative consequences in later stages of the venture-development effort.

TABLE 1-1   Key Components for Each BoP Venture-Development Principle

Stage	Core Principles	Key Components
Design	Create market opportunities	• Assess market-creation investment needs • Explore potential partnerships with development sector
	Craft solutions with the BoP	• Dialogue grounded in mutual respect • Adopt appropriate mindset: Be patient, stay longer, come back
Pilot	Orchestrate effective experiments	• Utilize metrics that support a process of trial-and-error • Explicitly identify and test specific hypotheses
	Manage failures	• Avoid turning learning-oriented pilots into philanthropic projects • Ensure soft landing for BoP when pilot ends
Scale	Generate co-mingled competitive advantage: *scale up*	• Gain access to and invest in existing platforms • Ensure partners' value creation goals are achieved
	Leverage and transfer social embeddedness: *scale deep and wide*	• Generate access to rich and diverse sources of information • Frame analysis based on identifying and enhancing "what is right"
All Stages	Enhance mutual value	• Remain open to local value creation opportunities • Invest in listening to the voices of the BoP

In closing, I offer one additional recommendation. Viewing the BoP as an underserved or unserved market opportunity offers the potential to connect profits and poverty alleviation. Yet for BoP ventures to truly achieve their economic and social promise, business managers and donor community professionals must break away from their traditional paradigm of working independently. In the developing world, businesses and donors have generally operated in relative isolation from each other. Businesses use market transactions to meet the needs of those with sufficient disposable income, and the donor community provides aid to serve those without such resources. Maintaining this arm's-length mentality, however, limits the economic and social potential of BoP ventures.

Business and donor-community leaders must instead embrace an orientation based on collaborative interdependence. Only by breaking free of the mindset of independent responsibilities can business enterprises and the donor community truly unlock the potential in these BoP markets and forge the new business models needed to create the value demanded by all stakeholders.

At the design stage, both sectors should carefully evaluate opportunities to co-invest in ventures that align business-oriented activities with donor community goals. In the piloting and scaling stages, the partners should openly explore ways to keep the venture on track in terms of generating value commensurate with their investment objectives. Throughout, a commitment to a transparent process of mutual value creation—including agreeing on a holistic set of impact assessment metrics geared toward learning and improving—is crucial to establishing and maintaining collaborative interdependence.

Collaborative interdependence, however, remains difficult to initiate. Business leaders often hold the view that grants and other types of development support will make BoP ventures unsustainable or overly constrained to achieve non-economic goals. My research suggests that the opposite is true: This early-stage support can be crucial in making ventures economically viable. For example, donor-community investments can enhance demand through awareness campaigns or voucher programs. Donors can also lower the cost of reaching local suppliers by supporting infrastructure development or by offering BoP producers technical assistance and business training. Finally, donors—or the organizations they fund—can invest in a venture directly by providing access to low-cost "patient capital" and other resources.[14] Without garnering support and investment from the donor community, many ventures might not make it through the design or pilot stages, as top management may perceive that the anticipated return is too low or too risky.

The donor community must also recognize their biases about these types of partnerships. While public-sector assistance to facilitate business development is well established in the developed world, this thinking has yet to take hold in BoP markets. Resistance to the idea of business ventures making money from serving the poor (in the developing world) remains a powerful ideological framing. Yet business development can help alleviate poverty, and the development sector will be remiss if it does not proactively consider if and when their resources can best facilitate these efforts.

For all of these reasons and more, business leaders and donor-community professionals must be willing to engage one another in a deep dialogue aimed at bridging the current divide between the sectors. Becoming more interdependent and co-investing in venture development may well enable both parties to better achieve their respective goals. Decisions on whether to partner should stem from pragmatism, rather than ideology.

The seven core principles discussed in this chapter provide a roadmap for creating a fortune with the BoP. These venture-building efforts are further enhanced if they are closely integrated with donor-community investments that support business activities. BoP venture development, energized by collaborative interdependence, offers the prospect for generating new opportunities for businesses and providing development practitioners with a new approach to poverty alleviation. Exploring the promise of these ventures, therefore, ought to command the attention of both sectors.

Notes

[1] I would like to thank the following individuals for their comments on earlier drafts of this chapter: S. Sivakumar and Parvathi Melon (ITC); Israel Moreno and Henning Alts (CEMEX); Vijay Sharma and Prasad Pradhan (Hindustan Unilever); Farouk Jiwa (Honey Care); Greg Allgood (Procter & Gamble); and Jordan Kassalow (VisionSpring). I also much appreciate the insightful feedback from Stuart Hart (Cornell University) as I developed this chapter, as well as the helpful comments from the attendees at the "Building a Shared Roadmap: Collaboratively Advancing the Base of the Pyramid Community" conference in 2009.

[2] See the introduction in this book for a more detailed discussion of the differences between an orientation based on "finding a fortune at the BoP" and one based on "creating a fortune with the BoP."

[3] See Erik Simanis's chapter in this book for an exploration of approaches that managers can use to engage the community in a process of mutual ownership that can facilitate market creation.

[4] See Ted London, Ravi Anupindi, and Sateen Sheth. 2010. "Creating mutual value: Lessons learned from ventures serving base of the pyramid producers," *Journal of Business Research*, 63 (6) 582–594, for more information on the constraints that BoP producers face and the strategies that ventures can use to overcome them.

[5] See Madhu Viswanathan's and Patrick Whitney's chapters in this book for more details on how venture leaders can integrate the voices of the BoP into the design process.

[6] See Erik Simanis's and Stuart Hart's chapters in this book for further discussions of the role and importance of trust in building relationships with BoP communities.

[7] See Ted London. 2010. "Business model development for base-of-the-pyramid market entry," In Leslie A. Toombs (Ed.), *Proceedings of the Seventieth Annual Meeting of the Academy of Management*, for more on applying an innovation-oriented approach to BoP business model development.

[8] See Hernando de Soto. 2000. *The Mystery of Capital: Why Capitalism Triumphs in the West and Fails Everywhere Else*, Basic Books: New York, for more on the characteristics of the business environment in the informal economy.

[9] See Abhijit Banerjee and Esther Dufflo. 2007. "The economic lives of the poor," *Journal of Economic Perspectives*, 21(1): 141–167, for more detailed information about entrepreneurship among the poor.

[10] See Allen Hammond's chapter in this book for more information on how BoP ventures can build ecosystems and develop hybrid organizations to facilitate scaling.

[11] See Ted London and Stuart Hart. 2004. "Reinventing strategies for emerging markets: Beyond the transnational model, *Journal of International Business Studies*," 35(5): 350-370, for an empirical assessment of the need for social embeddedness to complement existing capabilities when multinational corporations enter BoP markets.

[12] See Stuart Hart's chapter in this book for more about the environmental issues associated with BoP venture development and the leapfrog innovation needed to respond to these challenges.

[13] See Ted London. 2009. "Making better investments at the base of the pyramid," *Harvard Business Review*, 85(5): 106–113, for a full description of this framework.

[14] See Jacqueline Novogratz's and Bob Kennedy's chapter in this book for more details on sources of patient capital, and how BoP ventures are accessing and using this type of financing.

2

Innovation for the BoP: The Patient-Capital Perspective

by Robert Kennedy, University of Michigan and WDI, and
Jacqueline Novogratz, founder and CEO, Acumen Fund*

*Co-authors Robert Kennedy and Jacqueline Novogratz explain how social
entrepreneurs and "philanthrocapitalists" are changing the BoP landscape
by connecting innovative business approaches to "patient capital"—i.e.,
money that is expected to generate returns over a longer period than is typical of (say) venture capital. They identify four types of innovation that are
proving critically important to success in operating in BoP markets, and
show how a range of enterprises are applying these approaches in the field.*

*The past decade has witnessed a revolution in thinking about how to
address the persistent issue of poverty. Thoughtful observers in government, business, and nonprofits are moving beyond the old "markets versus
development assistance" debate and are now converging on a new
approach to addressing poverty.*

What is driving this convergence? Simply put, neither traditional
markets nor traditional development assistance has worked well.
Globalization has lifted millions out of poverty in countries like Mexico, Brazil, China, and India. But those benefits have largely bypassed
those living in base of the pyramid (BoP) marketplaces. As noted
elsewhere in this volume, more than two billion people still subsist on
less than $2 per day, and the gap between rich and poor is growing—
a disparity that in the long run is not sustainable.[1]

---

* The authors acknowledge and thank Rob Katz for his support in researching and
writing this article.

45

But traditional approaches to development assistance have not worked either. Over the past 60 years, more than $1.5 trillion has been disbursed as aid-based grants and donations to developing countries, with little improvement in poverty measures.[2] William Easterly, Dambisa Moyo, Robert Calderisi, and others have argued that traditional top-down development programs, while well intentioned, inevitably fall short of their goals because they neglect individual incentives, create opportunistic behavior, and fail to tap into the innovative potential of citizens in recipient countries.[3]

While this history is discouraging, new approaches that combine the best of the markets with the best of traditional aid are showing much more promise. Two complementary developments are transforming how we think about development. First, a new group of so-called "philanthrocapitalists" has taken an interest in global poverty.[4] Organizations such as the Gates Foundation, Omidyar Network, Google.org, and Virgin Unite are devoting new resources to social investment. Unlike traditional development organizations, however, they are insisting on the adoption of business tools and techniques in their programs: using private capital organizational forms to get incentives right, pushing for efficient and effective use of resources, insisting on rigorous measurement, and so on. The goal is to identify and scale organizations that can have a large impact.[5] One important outcome is the emergence of a new "patient capital" sector—a set of intermediaries with private capital structures who direct their energy toward creating social returns. Examples include Acumen Fund (with which one of the authors is affiliated), New Ventures, E+Co, Root Capital, and TechnoServe.

A second development is the rise of "social entrepreneurs"—individuals who create innovative organizations to address social needs. Like classic entrepreneurs, social entrepreneurs look for unmet needs, organize resources in new ways, and bring their solutions to the marketplace.

When they work together, social entrepreneurs and patient capitalists can have a transformative effect on BoP markets—in sectors as diverse as housing, water, sanitation, agriculture, and health care. The social entrepreneurs innovate and create new solutions. The patient capitalists identify the best ideas, help build organizational capabilities, and provide the capital to scale.

This chapter draws on our experience with patient capital organizations to explore what it takes to run a business that serves the BoP community. The answer is much more complex than simply importing successful business ideas from the top of the pyramid (ToP). BoP markets differ from ToP markets in important ways and thus require unique solutions. The factors that make BoP markets unique are discussed in more depth elsewhere,[6] but five key factors are briefly highlighted here:

- There are many *unaddressed needs* at the BoP. These range from services where the government often does not meet its mandate (clean water, sanitation, and so on) to needs that are neglected because people are perceived as being too poor to buy (health care, housing).

- BoP markets are beset by *poor infrastructure* (roads, water, power) and inadequate distribution networks. As a result, firms cannot count on the basics—connectivity, roads, water, power—when they are setting up a factory, warehouse, bank branch, or sales office. Poor infrastructure also means that the low-income customer generally has poor access to education and information—which makes marketing and service delivery different from a company's approach to ToP customers.

- *Corruption* is common, sapping economic value from the system and adversely affecting those who follow the rules.

- *Low purchasing power* makes it difficult for new products and services to enter the market. A 2007 study indicates that there are more than 4 billion people living in conditions where they are subject to a "poverty penalty," whereby the poor pay significantly more for products and services than their middle-income counterparts (in some cases, up to 40 times more).[7]

- *A lack of equity capital.* Traditional capital providers typically bypass BoP entrepreneurs, including those who are trying to solve tough problems in healthcare, water, sanitation, and alternative energy because they are perceived as highly risky.

Taken together, these factors make BoP markets very different than ToP markets. We see this in the types of products and services

offered, how ventures are run, and in the ways in which organizations innovate to design and deliver products and services to their
customers.

This chapter is organized into four parts. The first provides a brief
introduction to the patient capital sector. The second introduces and
explains four types of business model innovations that are critical to
succeeding in BoP markets. The third explores the experience of four
successful BoP ventures. The conclusion serves as a summary and—
we hope—a call to arms.

The Emerging Patient Capital Sector

The patient capital sector is relatively new, but it is growing rapidly and having an important impact. BoP firms often require nontraditional financing. In many of the situations described in this chapter,
firms require some type of patient capital. Why? Because the innovations and advances undertaken by BoP firms usually take time to
pilot, develop, and grow. Patient capital is not a grant; it is an investment intended to return its principal plus interest, which may be at or
below the risk-adjusted market rate. It does not seek to maximize
financial returns to investors; rather, it seeks to maximize social
impact and to catalyze the creation of markets to combat poverty. On
the spectrum of capital available to both nonprofits and for-profits,
patient capital sits somewhere between traditional venture capital
and traditional philanthropy and also between development aid and
foreign direct investment.

Patient capital organizations differ from traditional capital
providers in at least four ways. These are:

- *A longer time horizon.* Patient capital is often appropriate
  for BoP firms because there are few opportunities for quick
  exit. Whereas a traditional venture capitalist might hope to exit
  a company after three or four years, a patient capital investor
  may need to be willing to tie up money for ten years or longer.

  This is also a sharp contrast to the short time horizon of many traditional development aid programs. A renewed focus on accountability among bi- and multi-laterals has led to the proliferation of

three-year funding cycles for many development projects, including project ramp-up, wind-down, and evaluation. This only leaves somewhere between 18 and 24 months for the "real work" to be done. Our experience is that firms operating at the BoP find it difficult to prove their concepts within such a short time frame.

- *A willingness to forego maximum financial returns in exchange for social or environmental impact.* Different organizations approach this trade-off very differently. Some start with expected market rates of return, and—if an investment has high social or environmental impact—indicate their willingness to forego some return (for example, 15 percent as opposed to 20 percent). Other firms take the opposite approach, seeking to maximize social returns with some lower bound on acceptable returns. These organizations strive for break-even on a commercial basis, with the primary goal being maximum social impact.

- *A greater tolerance for risk than traditional investors.* The source of patient capital may be philanthropy, investment capital, or some combination of the two. Many patient capital investors raise their money from foundations or socially oriented individuals who have no expectation that their capital will be returned. This allows for greater experimentation with the knowledge that many investments may not succeed but will still lead to learning that benefits the entire sector. When investments do succeed, the money is returned to the fund and thus becomes available for future investments. For many social investors, the opportunity cost of *not* investing is perceived to be high. Their aim is social change, which leads to a tilt toward experimentation and action, as opposed to conservation of capital.

- *Capital is typically bundled with intensive support for social entrepreneurs as they grow their enterprises.* This assistance may take many forms, including formal training programs; informal mentoring of executives; assistance with writing business plans or obtaining financing; technical advice on manufacturing, sourcing, and distribution; and sponsorship for conferences and exchange programs. Patient capital investors often spend more time and effort nurturing and growing their investee organizations than they do providing financial capital.

We should emphasize, though, that patient capital is not "easy capital." It invests because it believes in a company's ability to become self-sustaining and to serve low-income markets at scale. It expects accountability and requires repayment on an agreed-upon schedule. Critically, repayment is part of a social contract that helps avoid the tension that can arise when poor entrepreneurs are expected to repay well-off investors. When they repay the patient capitalist, the social entrepreneur is enabling the patient capital investor to support other social entrepreneurs serving the poor.

To provide a better sense of the kinds of organizations that populate the patient capital sector, we briefly profile five of them here:

- *Acumen Fund* was founded in 2001 to help build a world in which all individuals have access to quality, affordable critical goods and services. This nonprofit venture capital fund for the poor has invested in 46 organizations with $40+ million in approved investments, which range from $200,000 to $2 million in both debt and equity vehicles. Acumen Fund now has offices in Hyderabad, Karachi, Nairobi, and New York. Its investments have helped create more than 20,000 jobs and delivered services to tens of millions of customers.

- *E+Co* is a clean-energy investor focused on developing countries. The firm finds promising entrepreneurs and helps them start or grow companies that provide energy services to low-income customers. E+Co makes debt and equity investments, ranging from $25,000 to $1 million. The firm not only invests capital, but also provides tools and business know-how to help make clean energy businesses successful.

  Since it was established in 1994, E+Co has invested $32.4 million in more than 200 small enterprises, giving 5.6 million people access to energy and generating an overall return of 8.4 percent.[8]

- *New Ventures*, a program of the Washington, D.C.-based World Resources Institute, was an early pioneer in the patient capital sector. New Ventures promotes sustainable growth in emerging markets by supporting and accelerating the transfer of capital to businesses that deliver social and environmental benefits in the base of the economic pyramid markets.[9]

  New Ventures supports small- and medium-sized enterprises seeking capital in the range of $100,000 to $5 million and located in such fast-growth sectors as ecotourism, renewable energy, clean technologies, and water management. New Ventures works with its firms to open new markets, grow sales, and become leaders in their sectors. Since its inception in 1999, it has helped entrepreneurs attract more than $175 million in investment.

- **Root Capital** invests in small, grassroots agricultural businesses such as coffee farmer cooperatives and artisan associations. Root Capital targets businesses that are caught in the "missing middle"—too small and risky for mainstream banks but too large for microfinance organizations.

    Since 1999, Root Capital has provided more than $140 million in credit to 254 grassroots enterprises in 30 countries in Latin America and Africa. The organization boasts a 99 percent repayment rate from its borrowers and a 100 percent repayment rate to its investors.[10]

- **TechnoServe**, founded in 1968, focuses on developing entrepreneurs, building businesses and industries, and improving the business environment. It identifies and capitalizes on good business opportunities that help transform the lives of the rural poor by generating jobs and creating markets for their products and services.

    TechnoServe works to develop the skills and resources that entrepreneurs need to launch or expand businesses. It does so by sponsoring business plan competitions and entrepreneur training, while also working to foster a culture of entrepreneurship. After a company has launched, TechnoServe often remains engaged to assist with developing business plans, linking to markets and sources of capital, improving management skills, producing higher-quality products and services, and operating more efficiently.

    Every year, TechnoServe assists thousands of small businesses, generating ripple effects in terms of employment, sales, and income generation in low-income countries.[11]

As these five organizations illustrate, patient capital is helping to create and support an economic ecosystem that allows BoP ventures to thrive. The sector is nurturing businesses that provide maternal health care, village-level clean water solutions, low-cost green lighting solutions, and sanitation. Patient capital investors and the social entrepreneurs they support are moving beyond an artificial separation between aid and the market and are jointly creating a new path to prosperity.

Business Model Innovations

We now turn to exploring the types of innovations that are frequently observed in successful BoP ventures. But first, a bit of context may be useful. Both authors have extensive experience with BoP ventures. Novogratz is the founder and CEO of Acumen Fund, which has invested in more than 40 BoP ventures. Kennedy has worked with dozens of BoP ventures in advisory roles, documenting their experiences in case studies, and as director of the William Davidson Institute (WDI).

The framework presented here draws on several years working together on Acumen Fund projects and many long discussions about how to nurture and grow BoP ventures—in Acumen Fund's portfolio and elsewhere. To be clear, the framework is not the outcome of structured hypothesis testing or of extensive data gathering and analysis.

But as discussed in the introduction, BoP markets differ in important ways from ToP markets. Most ventures that succeed in the BoP environment operate very differently than ToP ventures in the products and services they offer and in their business processes.

Our experience indicates that four innovations are key. Most successful BoP ventures have adopted at least one of these innovations. Many have adopted more than one. Not all are present in every case, but this is the tool kit from which social entrepreneurs often draw. Briefly stated, these are:

- Introducing radical cost reductions in some value activity
- Building a BoP-centric management team, which consists of constantly rebalancing the social impulse (that is, the will to serve the poor) with the more traditional business skills needed to build a successful business
- Implementing human-centric design thinking to products and services

• Establishing trust with the BoP in order to create and grow markets

We briefly discuss each innovation and then use examples from BoP ventures affiliated with Acumen Fund to demonstrate how these concepts are operationalized in practice.

Introducing Radical Cost Reductions

To operate sustainably in the BoP marketplace, organizations must be able to cover their costs. A common misconception is that because BoP customers have low incomes, companies must sacrifice quality to make products and services affordable. For some consumer products businesses, this may be the case (for example, Nirma Detergent in India).[12] But many BoP organizations have managed to lower costs without sacrificing quality.

Aravind Eye Hospital is one example. Based in Madurai, India, Aravind screens more than 3 million people annually for eye problems and performs more than 250,000 cataract surgeries. In developed countries, a cataract surgery costs $2,500 to $3,000. Aravind has lowered this cost by a factor of around 50 (to between $50 and $75 per surgery) through a radical restructuring of the hospital's workflow.

There are three key elements to Aravind's radical cost reduction:

• ***Massive scale.***   A leading eye hospital in the U.S. might perform 3,000 to 5,000 surgeries per year. Aravind performs more than 50 times this volume, allowing it to optimize workflows.

• ***A focus on paraskilling.***[13]   Aravind employs hundreds of low-cost orderlies and junior nurses who perform routine monitoring and patient care services. This frees up doctors and nurses to focus on the activities that truly require their expertise.

• ***A relentless focus on optimizing scarce resources.***   A surgeon at Aravind performs 3,000 to 5,000 surgeries per year, compared with 200 to 300 for a typical U.S.-based surgeon. Paraskilling and other workflow innovations allow surgeons to complete a cataract operation in three to five minutes and to start on the next patient less than one minute later. Because surgeons are, by far, the most expensive resource in the hospital, workflow innovations that improve their productivity have a dramatic effect on costs.

While Aravind is a low-cost provider, its quality measures are equal to or exceed those of U.S. hospitals. Because of this high quality—and also because of the rare opportunity to gain a great deal of experience in a short time—surgical residents from around the world offer their services in exchange for training in the Aravind system. Cost reduction innovations like these allow Aravind to price its services so that even the poor can afford high quality eye care.

Building a BoP-Centric Management Team

Finding the right talent at the right time is critical to the success of BoP ventures. Top management teams need two distinct skill sets: *the will and imagination* to create solutions for BoP markets and the *skill* to manage a significant business. The challenge is to balance these needs effectively as the venture matures.

Successful BoP ventures go through distinct stages. During launch and startup, it is vital to have a dedicated social entrepreneur who recognizes a need, has an insight, and throws herself into creating a solution that creates value for her customers. At this stage, the staff is typically small and cohesive; operations, finance, and HR issues are straightforward and can be handled effectively on an ad hoc basis.

If and when the concept is proven and the BoP venture scales (often very rapidly), the organization becomes much more complex and frequently grows beyond the capabilities of the founder. The staff grows in size, and it becomes difficult to create a shared mission. This makes onboarding and HR policies more important. Scale brings new operational challenges (such as multiple locations or product lines) and a heightened need for financial and operational controls. While *will* and *imagination* remain important, *business skills* in specific functional areas now become the critical factor. Of course, this is the classic entrepreneurship challenge, but it is magnified in the BoP setting because the characteristics of the early stage social entrepreneur are so unique.

So why is innovation needed to build a BoP-centric management team? Because traditional approaches rarely work. At the senior management levels, it is difficult to find highly skilled individuals who have a good sense of low-income consumers while also knowing how to build a complex business. High achievers have an enormous range of professional choices available to them. This is especially challenging in rural areas, where it is tough to convince high achievers to live. Asking them to work for relatively low salary, in a rural area, in a risky venture is a major hurdle. For many organizations, it wipes out the pool of candidates.

At the middle-management level, high growth companies serving the BoP often face the challenge of hiring leaders who will take initiative rather than just follow directions. Many companies (LifeSpring Hospitals, WaterHealth International, D.light Design, and so on) are pursuing decentralized distribution models. These models rely on solid managers who know when and how to make strategic decisions, improve processes, and bring new ideas to top management when appropriate. Developing a team of managers that shares a common culture, set of values, and approach to operations, while bringing a keen sense of judgment to the work, is critical and challenging.

In short, organizational success creates new management needs. Those interested in social entrepreneurship rarely have the functional skills necessary to run large, complex organizations. And skilled functional executives are rarely available for the salaries and circumstances that BoP ventures can offer. It is not unusual for the inspirational founder of an organization to find herself a poor fit as it becomes a successful BoP venture. Balancing these needs—will and skill—is a key challenge.

Successful BoP ventures often pursue alternative methods of recruiting key executives. Two innovations have proven useful for matching functional specialists with the needs of growing BoP ventures:

- ***Connecting with experienced managers from the private sector.*** More and more such executives are joining the social enterprise sector as a second or third career. These executives are financially secure and looking to make a difference. Programs that place them with BoP ventures for up to a year provide quick shots of functional expertise, along with mentoring for the social entrepreneurs. One example is Acumen Fund's Senior Fellows Program, which sends experienced managers on assignments with investees such as Drishtee (India), Jassar

Farms (Pakistan), First Micro Insurance Agency (Pakistan), and Insta Products (Kenya).

- **Connecting with idealistic young professionals.** More and more young professionals are taking a break after their bachelors' or graduate degree programs for a service year. Acumen Fund, Kiva, and Drishtee all run "Fellows" programs that place young professionals in BoP ventures. Programs such as Engineers for Social Impact and MBAs without Borders connect volunteers with BoP ventures in many geographies and sectors.

Patient capital investors play a key role in making these programs work. Few BoP ventures have an accurate perception of their management gaps or the management bandwidth to select an appropriate fellow. But patient capitalists can identify the gaps, screen candidates for multiple organizations, and work with founders to bring in outsiders and entrust them with key activities.

Implementing Human-Centric Design Thinking

A central challenge facing BoP organizations is to offer products or services that meet at least three conditions:

- **They are valued** by BoP consumers. Some services are simply private sector alternatives to items that governments provide in ToP markets (that is, electricity, clean water, sanitation). Others address needs that are specific to the BoP (such as asynchronous Internet access and mobile telephone banking services).
- **They are affordable** for BoP consumers.
- **They can be delivered efficiently enough** so that the organization can cover costs at the BoP price. Ideally, both fixed and variable costs can be covered. But in some cases, "smart subsidies" may be needed to cover start-up, fixed, or even some portion of operating costs.

For all three of these reasons, design is a key element of many successful BoP ventures.[14] This usually involves immersion in the local context to understand consumers' needs and usage patterns to achieve "human-centric design" for BoP consumers.[15] Something that is learned early in many organizations is that product, service, and system designs that work in ToP markets often do not translate to BoP markets. In many cases, products and services from the ToP are not suitable given the culture and context of the BoP or are too expensive for BoP customers to afford.

Human-centric design begins with attempt to understand the wants and needs of customers—and well beyond what a typical market researcher might find useful. The point is to better understand the way people think, feel, and live at the BoP before, during, and after designing products or services.[16]

An example of human-centric design is WaterHealth International's (WHI) experience with home water delivery. WHI is discussed in more detail in a later section, but one insight is worth noting here. WHI builds and operates village-based water purification systems. The standard model is to operate a WaterHealth Centre in a central location, where villagers can come to purchase water and transport it home. In an early effort to generate incremental revenues, WHI experimented with a home delivery service. The thinking was that WHI could charge rich households a premium for delivery (approximately two times the price of the water) and use these fees to subsidize water for the poor.

The service was an immediate success, but somewhat surprisingly, day laborers were the customer group most likely to use the service. It turns out that rich households had servants and perceived no incremental cost to sending them to transport water. But the day laborers put a high value on their time. They needed water in their homes and couldn't spare the time to pick it up—but they were willing to pay for a service that was vital to them. Immersing itself deeply into the local community and listening carefully to its customers allowed WHI to develop an important but counterintuitive understanding of its target customers.

Establishing Trust with the BoP to Grow New Markets

Trust can be a scarce commodity in BoP markets. In the commercial sector, the deck often seems stacked against the BoP. Farmers may be compelled to deal with monopolistic intermediaries that are the only suppliers of agricultural inputs or buyers for the harvest.

Villagers hear the promises made by politicians—a new road, a new school, a new clinic—around election time and then see many of those promises broken. Mistrust extends, as well, to the well-intentioned development organizations and charities whose funding or organizational priorities prevent them from "being patient, staying longer, and coming back" (to quote our editor and co-author Ted London).

So it should not be surprising that many BoP customers are extremely skeptical of many of the solutions offered to them. After all, they have seen it all before. Combine this with the fact that for understandable reasons, the poor tend to be more risk-averse than other market segments, and you have a recipe for customer inertia and even resistance.

Consider the case of Ms. Gupta, a samosa vendor who works outside the D.light headquarters in Noida, India.[17] (D.light is an international consumer products company that targets consumers with no reliable electricity source, to which we will return later in this chapter.[18]) In May 2009, D.light's product development team gave Ms. Gupta a solar-powered lamp as part of a one-month market test. At the end of the month, Ms. Gupta would have the option to purchase her lamp or give it back to D.light.

She immediately replaced her hot, dirty, expensive, and unsafe kerosene lamp with the new Nova S150 lamp and reported fantastic results.[19] The Nova gave off a better quality light, so Ms. Gupta hung it from the corner of her cart to get a better view of what she was doing, resulting in fewer charred samosas. The smokeless light attracted customers who wanted to eat their samosas in the absence of a noxious kerosene cloud. At the end of the working day, she used it as the cart's headlamp on the way home—something not possible with the kerosene lamp.

At the end of that first month, with more customers, more volume, and less waste, Ms. Gupta discovered that she had *doubled* her income. The D.light team showed her glowing projections—the light would pay for itself in kerosene expenditure savings, not to mention all the non-monetary benefits—in less than five months. All signs seemed positive, and the D.light team asked if she wanted to buy the lamp. She declined politely, implying that she might buy one sometime in the future.

An irrational decision? Not from Ms. Gupta's perspective. Consider two aspects of the decision-making process: trust and the "bluff." First, D.light was a start-up company, then in India for less than two years. It was not yet a trusted brand. Even though the lamp worked well for one month, there was no track record to suggest that it would continue to perform well.

Compounding the problem for D.light was the track record of traditional development aid. Western aid organizations were and are well-known for giving things away for free. Ms. Gupta figured that if she hesitated, perhaps the company would just *give* it to her.

Ms. Gupta's decision-making process is not atypical. Closing any sale is difficult, but in a low-income market, it can be far more so.

Innovations in Action

We now delve into the experiences of four BoP ventures to see how these organizations applied these approaches to innovation in a real-world setting. The organizations are:

- *LifeSpring Hospitals*, a maternity hospital chain delivering low-cost, high quality services to low-income people in India.
- *Ecotact*, a firm that builds and operates pay-per-use toilets and shower facilities in urban centers throughout Kenya.
- *WaterHealth International*, the low-cost provider of clean water solutions to the poor that was introduced earlier.
- *D.light Design*, the lighting and consumer-products manufacturer also introduced earlier.

Each of these organizations relies on several of the innovations described in the previous section (as summarized in Table 2-1). For each organization, we introduce the problem being addressed, describe the organization's key business model innovations, report results to date, and use the organization's experience to highlight one of the four innovations. We also briefly note other secondary innovations adopted by each organization. (The reader may want to refer back to Table 2-1 periodically to help keep the larger conceptual framework in mind.)

TABLE 2-1   Innovations in Four Organizations

	LifeSpring	Ecotact	WHI	D.light
Radically reducing costs	XX			
Building BoP-centric management	x	XX		
Using human-centric design		x	x	XX
Developing trust			XX	x

LifeSpring Hospitals

In developed countries, the lifetime risk of maternal death is 1 in 8,000; in developing countries, the ratio is 1 in 76. Worldwide, more than 500,000 women die each year due to complications during pregnancy and childbirth.[20] According to the World Health Organization, nearly 25 percent of these deaths occur in India.[21]

One problem is that only 43 percent of Indian women are cared for by a skilled attendant during childbirth.[22] True, Indian government policy focuses on the public provision of healthcare services, but the public system performs very poorly. The maternal mortality rate is more than nine times that of China and thirty times that of the United States. Maternal and child mortality also affect whole populations and countries: USAID estimates that $15.5 billion a year in productivity is lost when mothers and newborns die.

In some ways, Anant Kumar was the least likely person to get involved with maternal care. As an executive with Hindustan Latex Limited (HLL)—India's largest condom manufacturer—his job was to prevent pregnancies, not facilitate them. But in his role as the head of Social Franchising at Hindustan Latex Family Planning Promotion Trust (HLFPPT), Anant saw firsthand the conditions at public hospitals and the unwillingness of the private sector to move downmarket.

He launched the first LifeSpring Hospital in December 2005 as a pilot within HLFPPT. This was not his initial foray into the development space; he had previously served as program manager of the Andhra Pradesh Social Marketing Programme as well as a regional manager for HLL. These dual positions gave him the skill to run a business and the will to serve the poor. With a post-graduate diploma in rural management (equivalent to an MBA) from the Institute of

Rural Management and a post-graduate diploma in health care and hospital management from Symbiosis Institute, he was in many ways the ideal entrepreneur to run a BoP enterprise.

Today, LifeSpring Hospitals is a network of hospitals operated as a joint venture between Acumen Fund, HLL (a private company), and HLFPPT (a quasi-governmental agency). The goal of the partnership is to provide low-income customers access to affordable maternal and child healthcare services in urban areas through a chain of small hospitals (20 to 30 beds).

LifeSpring's business model starts with respect. All prices are clearly written on the wall. Doctors are fairly compensated and on salary, which means that there are fewer "surprises," like emergency (and unnecessary) Caesarian sections. Providing information in advance about how much the services will cost and helping clients plan for their deliveries have proven to be two of LifeSpring's strongest selling points.

Radically Reducing Costs

LifeSpring has radically reduced costs across its business lines. Its narrow specialization and high customer volume are the foundation of its business model, allowing it to maintain high quality without incurring expenses that would prevent it from serving a BoP clientele. LifeSpring's hospitals focus on normal deliveries, Caesarian sections, and hysterectomies; more complicated procedures (and their associated high costs) are referred to affiliate hospitals. The cost of a delivery at LifeSpring ($32) is about one-sixth the cost of a delivery at local private hospitals (approximately $200).

Each hospital is laid out in exactly the same way, with the same clinical and administrative procedures. Think of it as the McDonald's of hospitals—that is, franchised facilities in which everything is standardized. As the Monitor Inclusive Markets team reports, "LifeSpring hospitals are strictly no-frills operations: no canteens, outsourced pharmacy and laboratory services, rented rather than purchased properties, and old hospital buildings rather than new ones. Most beds are in general wards, with basic furnishing and no air conditioning."[23]

LifeSpring doctors earn fixed salaries rather than the per-procedure consulting fees of their peers in private clinics. Each site employs an administrative specialist who is responsible for all paperwork, thus enabling physicians to focus on clinical care. The doctors are LifeSpring's most expensive variable cost—so they employ up to 12 nurses per doctor to support them and increase productivity.

The hospital is organized so that it increases the use rates of other key assets—ranging from diagnostic machines to the obstetricians themselves. LifeSpring's high throughput business model leads to strong productivity that drives profitability.

Focusing on inpatient gynecology and obstetrics leads to standardization and lower costs. The hospital has defined more than 90 standard procedures, from standardized surgery kits to clinical protocols. LifeSpring uses a narrow range of drugs and equipment for large numbers of repeat procedures, making it possible to purchase standard equipment and generic medicines at volume discounts. Standardization also enables the hospital to use Auxiliary Nurse Midwifery nurses in some roles where, typically, more expensive General Nurse Midwifery nurses would be used.

There are important lessons for the public sector in LifeSpring's model. It typically costs the Indian government 5,000 rupees ($110)—or more than three times the price LifeSpring charges—for a normal delivery. As the model has been developed, LifeSpring has emerged as a powerful example of private innovation driving public change.

By mid-2009, LifeSpring had treated more than 65,000 patients in nine hospitals, conducting 3,500 safe deliveries.

Other Innovations: Building a BoP-Centric Management Team

LifeSpring aims to double its current size, to 18 hospitals by 2012, so human capital strategy is central to its growth plan. The company has added hundreds of employees in the past two years and plans to double its staff in the next two.

To reinforce the importance of a customer-centered culture at LifeSpring, new employees go through an innovative onboarding program. Each new worker spends a day shadowing a LifeSpring outreach worker. The worker spends time with existing and potential customers—mothers and mothers-to-be—in low-income areas. This helps middle-class staff see life through the eyes of low-income customers and experience first-hand LifeSpring's social mission.

New workers also visit a government-run hospital. Seeing the "competition" firsthand is a powerful experience for the new employee. The third aspect of the onboarding is an overnight stay at a LifeSpring Hospital. The onboarding program focuses on culture and the ways in which LifeSpring differs from the norm, and the firm is able to get its workforce engaged and up to speed quickly.

Ecotact

More than 2.6 billion people—or almost 40 percent of the world's population—lack access to basic sanitation.[24] The situation is worst in sub-Saharan Africa, where 63 percent of the population lacks this access.[25]

Kenya's capital of Nairobi is home to some of the world's largest and most densely populated informal settlements. The World Bank has labeled the city's public toilets as unhygienic and barely functional. (It has been more than 30 years since the government last invested in public sanitation facilities in the capital.) The lack of functioning toilets and showers in Kenya exposes BoP communities to health risks and affronts their dignity. Many slum residents dispose of excrement at night in plastic bags, which are commonly thrown from residences into the street, leading to the colloquial name "flying toilets."

David Kuria is an entrepreneur who is deeply familiar with these challenges. An architect by training, he has worked for years to create solutions for the urban poor, including experimenting with different water and sanitation models. Among other initiatives, Kuria built toilet facilities in slum areas where local residents could pay a small fee to use a safe and clean toilet and could also take showers if they paid slightly more.

In the early days, Kuria was the epitome of the startup social entrepreneur: securing land concessions, writing grant applications, supervising construction, hiring and supervising workers in the facilities, and acting as the general manager.

His early models were grant-funded, but Kuria found that the demand was so great that fee income would cover operating costs and generate a surplus. He came to realize that if he could use operating surpluses to secure private financing for the capital cost of his systems, he would be able to scale more quickly than if he continued to rely on grants for each new system.

Acumen Fund found this idea compelling from both the social and financial perspectives. Acumen worked with Kuria for more than a year to create a business plan for his company—christened "Ecotact"—and invested $757,000 to finance 30 facilities. The toilet facilities themselves are branded as IkoToilets. "Iko" means "there is" in Kiswahili. As such, the name tells customers that "there is a toilet" here. The toilets' slogan is "thinking beyond a toilet," an effort by the company to remove stigma from sanitation and make it an aspirational purchase for its customers.

Incorporated in 2006, Ecotact today builds and operates public pay-per-use toilets and shower facilities in urban centers throughout Kenya. The company uses a Build-Operate-Transfer model, where municipalities grant the use of public land—in most cases, for a period of five years. The company then constructs and operates a sanitation facility. After five years, Ecotact transfers ownership of the operation to the municipality, sometimes negotiating the rights to operate the facility for additional years.

At each facility, there are a total of 24 toilets and 8 showers—half for men and half for women. Each facility employs two or three uniformed workers, responsible for managing, cleaning, and maintaining the operation. Customers are charged 5 KShs (about seven cents) to use a toilet and 20 KShs (about 29 cents) to take a shower. Additional revenue is earned from renting space to vendors (such as shoeshine services and newspaper stands) and by selling advertising space.

In early 2010, Ecotact operated 22 facilities serving more than 15,000 customers daily, with the total usage for 2009 exceeding 4.3 million visits. Facilities operate in the central business districts of Nairobi, Naivasha, Machakos, Nanyuki, Othaya, Eldoret, and Embu, as well as two of the capital's slum areas.

The firm plans to add 30 additional facilities by 2012. To extend its reach even more, Ecotact has also begun to explore a franchise model for new facilities; Ecotact would charge a franchise fee based on location and volume of customers. To help make services more affordable to users in informal settlements, Ecotact is now offering a family membership plan, whereby a family pays 100 KShs ($1.30 USD) a month for the use of a facility.

Building a BoP-Centric Management Team

Ecotact's success to date is due in large part to Kuria's passion for and ability to execute on his ambitious vision. But that is not nearly enough to ensure success. Growth—from only a handful of facilities in 2007 to 22 in 2010 and an anticipated 50+ in 2012—has created huge organizational challenges. It is impossible for any one person, no matter how passionate or committed—to drive a social enterprise to scale.

Kuria is working with Acumen Fund to transform his organization from a founder-run startup to a professionally managed growth company. Together, they are working to build the company along four distinct issue areas, each of which will require a manager-level presence to ensure continued growth and success. These four issue areas are:

- Preconstruction operations: permits, construction management
- Post-construction operations: staff training, cash collection, toilet staff supervision
- Communications and advertising
- Finance and cash management

In short, Ecotact has become orders of magnitude more complex than it was only two years ago. A committed entrepreneur can conceivably manage the first round of facility construction and operation. But an organization with dozens of facilities, hundreds of employees, and numerous complex contracts with government agencies won't survive long by will alone. Kuria is working with Acumen Fund to recruit an experienced, professional team that shares Kuria's vision, passion, and *will*, while bringing additional talent and experience (in finance, HR, marketing, and operations)—the business *skills*—that are necessary for growth.

Acumen Fund has supported this transition by providing Ecotact with Acumen Fund Fellows, external consultants, and extensive management support. It is a time of growth and promise, but also of uncertainty for Ecotact. The challenge with a business focused on BoP markets—like Ecotact—is to recruit top talent without diluting the founder's vision of serving low-income customers.

Other Innovations: Human-Centric Design

Design is also key to Ecotact's vision and success. As noted, Kuria is a trained architect. Solid engineering and visual appeal—tools of a good architect—are built into the company's facilities. For example:

- Ecotact's facilities (called "IkoToilet malls") are architecturally distinctive, incorporating odd angles into the building design. These angles are not merely a flourish—they enhance ventilation and facilitate maintenance—but they also set IkoToilets apart from surrounding buildings.

- Ecotact's uniformed attendants greet customers and sell services, while also continuously cleaning the facility. This signals professionalism, enhances the customer experience, and increases their willingness to pay.

- The interior of an IkoToilet mall is painted in unique colors, and popular music is piped into the bathrooms and showers. Customers remark of the "beauty" of the IkoToilet—not the reaction one might expect to such a facility.

WaterHealth International

Worldwide, some 1.2 billion people don't have access to safe drinking water; of this population, roughly 480 million live in India.[26] At any point in time, half of the world's hospital beds are likely to be occupied by patients suffering from waterborne diseases. Aside from the human suffering involved, there is also a tremendous impact on people's productivity. In India alone, water-borne diseases cost the nation an annual $600 million in lost production and medical treatment.[27]

Individuals in rural communities often spend hours a day collecting and transporting water from contaminated sources. Their counterparts in urban slums have little or no access to municipal water and as a result, pay a premium of up to 37 times to buy sanitary water from tanker trucks.[28]

In this situation, we once again see the inability of two traditional models to solve the problem. The government, on the one hand, has invested in infrastructure, but not in maintenance, so the wells may provide water that is unsafe to drink. Commercial vendors of water products, meanwhile, don't see the rural poor as a market and don't invest in building water businesses that serve them.

As a Ghanaian, Tralance Addy had a personal connection to this aspect of rural poverty: His family came from a small and impoverished village in the country. He had an opportunity to get an education in the U.S. and eventually took a job with Johnson & Johnson, where he worked for more than 25 years. Clean drinking water was always his passion, however; he wanted to switch gears to build an innovative business with major social impact. In 2001, Tralance acquired a company, WaterHealth International (WHI), that used a pioneering ultraviolet filtration system to quickly and easily clean water, at a cost of just five cents per ton of water.

Today, WHI attempts to serve the market that both the government and incumbent private sector players do not. WHI manufactures and markets community water systems (CWSs) that use a proprietary UV-based water treatment system. The company sells these cost-effective water filtration systems, called WaterHealth Centres, to organizations serving both rural and urban communities in India, the Philippines, Ghana, and Mexico. The majority of WHI's systems are now installed in India.

A WaterHealth Centre can provide a community of 7,000 people with up to 20 liters of safe, affordable drinking water per person per day. WHI sells 20 liters of water for just INR 3 rupees (about six U.S. cents), enough to meet the daily water needs of most families. The company currently reaches more than 400,000 individuals in India alone and has served as a model for an emerging water sector focused on rural villages.

Developing Trust

During its initial ramp-up, WHI focused on producing and delivering CWSs to villages. This led to the development of the UV Waterworks treatment system and the WaterHealth Centers. But as the centers began to come on-line, WHI noticed there were unexpected issues along several dimensions. These included education about clean water issues, social conventions around access to clean water, and the "last mile" problem of transportation and storage.

WHI partnered with the Naandi Foundation, a trusted local non-governmental organization (NGO). This allowed WHI to focus on building, operating, and maintaining the WaterHealth Centres, while Naandi conducted customer awareness and education campaigns focused on the health benefits of drinking clean water. WHI and Naandi co-branded the plants and shared revenues from the WaterHealth Centres. The partnership led to increased sales for WHI and allowed Naandi to deepen its impact in the communities where it works.

A lack of consumer awareness about the links between contaminated water and waterborne diseases continues to be a major challenge. A WHI study showed that many living at the BoP believe that as long as water looks clean, it is drinkable. In addition, many people hold longstanding cultural beliefs that are hard to change, such as a family's history of drinking from a certain well, the taste and health benefits from drinking tap water, and the idea that dead bodies thrown into ponds will later produce purified water.

WHI realized that it could not rely on traditional forms of communication and marketing (such as posters, flyers, and handouts). These forms were not trusted by locals, and were generally ignored. WHI therefore launched a series of village information sessions, which continue today. They attract customers by mounting street fairs with clowns and other entertainment. When a large enough audience has gathered, WHI employees project microscopic images of both contaminated and clean water onto large screens, showing the differences between the two. WHI workers then answer questions from the crowd and demonstrate WHI's filtration systems. These sessions have helped to communicate WHI's value proposition and increased trust among villagers. At the sites where these information sessions were conducted, WHI has seen a four- to seven-fold increase in revenue and enjoys more repeat customers.

Team members are working with local entrepreneurs to design marketing programs and business ecosystems around WaterHealth

Centres that will improve acceptance, sales, and WHI's bottom line. Recently, this came to a head as the company rebranded its entire product line under the name "Dr. Water" to emphasize the health benefits of drinking clean water.

Other Innovations: Human-Centric Design

On the last-mile issue, WHI has taken a different approach. The organization worked with IDEO and Acumen on the "Ripple Effect" project, which tackled water transportation and storage. The team identified several challenges:

- While WaterHealth Centres were providing clean water at the central gathering point, much of this water was transported back to the home and stored in unsanitary containers.
- Villagers had both expected and surprising expectations regarding price. Many asked: *Why pay for something that we can get for free?* After all, water from the Centre looks and tastes like that collected from the local well or pond. The immersion process, however, also revealed that these same consumers are willing to pay for a variety of other features—including water temperature, flavor, clarity, packaging, and transportation.

WHI pondered these challenges and moved to position their product as a value-added set of products and services. For example, product designers worked with villagers to design and prototype new water transport and storage containers. These narrow-mouth containers prevent users from dipping their hands into the water, a common practice. The containers are also ergonomically designed to allow children and women to easily transport a day's supply of water in one trip.

By building trust through partnerships and using human-centered design principles throughout their business, WHI has positioned itself for growth just as the CWS market in India is taking off. By 2009, the company had nearly 300 Dr. Water WaterHealth Centres up and running and was preparing to push into the market for government tenders that would fund the construction of hundreds more.

D.light Design

More than 1.5 billion people in the world lack access to electricity. These households spend approximately $38 billion on fuel-based lighting, including kerosene lanterns and candles. In India, some 580 million people lack access to safe, reliable electricity—most of them in rural areas, where even those connected to the grid get only eight hours of power per day or less. Stated differently, 44 percent of Indian households have no access to electricity. In rural areas, that percentage rises to more than half.[29]

The government of India has been working to address this problem. In 2005, for example, it launched a rural electrification scheme to electrify more than a million villages by 2010. As of 2009, however, it was less than halfway to this ambitious goal, mainly because the necessary infrastructure was not in place.[30]

Kerosene, the most prevalent type of fuel-based lighting in rural India, is a health hazard, emitting significant particulate pollutants of the type that cause 36 percent of all lung infections in India. It produces low-quality, inefficient lighting, often requiring the need for multiple lanterns to read or work, which in turn increases the risk of fire in the home. Kerosene is expensive; in some low-income households, more than 10 percent of income is spent on fuel-based lighting.[31] Finally, the use of kerosene alone accounts for approximately 100 million tons of carbon emissions per year. Finding clean, safe, affordable substitutes thus promises enormous social impact.

Sam Goldman, D.light's founder, knows the disadvantages of kerosene all too well. As a young Peace Corps volunteer in Benin, he depended on kerosene lamps for reading and cooking light. Eventually, he persuaded a friend in the United States to ship him a light emitting diode (LED) headlamp, commonly used by backpackers, so that his eyes and respiratory system could get a break. In addition, Sam's neighbor in Benin nearly died from burns inflicted by a tipped-over kerosene lamp—a tragedy that left a lasting impression on Sam.

These experiences led Sam and his partner Ned Tozun to cofound D.light Design, a for-profit company whose mission is to "[e]nable households without reliable electricity to attain the same quality of life as those with electricity. [This] begins by replacing every kerosene lantern with clean, safe, and bright light."[32]

Taking advantage of advances in LED technology, the founders developed a solar-powered LED light that provides an alternative to kerosene lanterns and candles. LED units can provide a quality of light comparable to a fluorescent strip but are significantly cheaper, more durable, safer, and longer lasting.

D.light's product offering began with the Nova, an all-purpose portable LED lamp that provides up to 40 hours of light on a full charge. Thanks to effective innovation in its design and marketing strategies, D.light has expanded its product line, offering a Nova model that also charges mobile phones, as well as the ultra low-cost Kiran—a $10 solar-powered LED lantern that has been widely praised.[33]

By 2009, D.light was selling more than 50,000 LED units annually and recorded revenues of $1 million. Early surveys show significant increases in income among purchasers as well as gains in health and general well-being. Since its founding, D.light also claims to have helped offset more than 30,000 tons of carbon emissions. The company is aggressively expanding sales operations in India and is also working to scale operations in East Africa.

Using Human-Centric Design

The company requires that all managers based in its Noida headquarters (including the CEO) spend a few days each year living in rural areas. Additionally, all new staffers have to spend at least one night in a rural, kerosene-lit village during their first month of employment.

D.light has a staff of eight full-time designers at headquarters, and the members of this team spend additional time immersed in village life—an immersion that moves the designers beyond mere technical specifications to really understanding needs, habits, and usage. Having staff consistently spending time in rural villages gives the company a short and straightforward feedback loop: Marketing/sales staff can directly communicate customer reaction to product designers. This has allowed the company to continuously innovate its core product—the Nova. The original Nova design was simple: An ultra-efficient LED was enclosed in an unbreakable plastic casing with a connection to a single-watt solar panel. The product was well received. After the Nova went to market, D.light's immersion research helped uncover a series of insights that allowed for continual improvement. These included:

- A need to hang the light from hooks and poles to better light an entire room. D.light responded by adding an ergonomically designed strap to the top of the light.
- A desire for multiple light settings.
- A need to respond to different ways in which the lamps were used—outdoors, for reading, for general lighting.
- A desire for after-sale service (rather than just a warranty).
- A desire for dual charging options (solar and A/C). After realizing that customers wanted both functions on a single device, D.light added an A/C-charge feature to the Nova and phased out its A/C-charge model, the Vega.

The latest version of the Nova—the S200—incorporates a mobile phone charger outlet: a design innovation that has been a major selling point since its introduction in early 2009. The model can provide up to 32 hours of light and recharge a standard mobile phone in 2 hours. The S200 also improves durability with a sturdier encasement.

The "Kiran," D.Light's newest product offering, goes a logical step further. The Nova was charged by plugging the lantern into a small solar panel, separate from the unit. While this is standard practice for solar products around the world, customer feedback indicated that the separate panel was damaged or lost easily. In response, the Kiran incorporates the solar panel directly into the lamp. The Kiran also features a metal handle—replacing the strap on the Nova—that gives the user up to 10 ways to hang or position the light. Finally, the Kiran gives off 360-degree light, whereas a Nova focused light only in one direction.

Other Innovations: Developing Trust

D.light is attempting to create a new product category and position a new brand in a rural market—an extremely challenging endeavor. This requires the company to persuade customers to change behaviors and buying habits that have been in place for generations. For some potential customers, the economics can be confusing. While LED lamps have much lower operating costs, they require larger up-front outlays—anywhere from $10 to $25 per lamp. A kerosene lamp involves a lower capital expenditure but much higher lifetime operating costs.

From a lifetime cost perspective, buying a D.light should be an easy decision for most low-income households. The D.light Nova S150 retails for INR 1500 ($32)—equal to the annual operating cost of a wick lamp. The D.light lamp's 50,000 hour life would last for more than 30 years if used four hours per day—yielding an annual operating cost of less than a dollar. When contrasted with a hurricane or mantle lamp, the economics are not just compelling—they are staggering (see Table 2-2). The ultra low-cost Kiran model, introduced in late 2009, makes the economics even more compelling.

TABLE 2-2   The Economics of Kerosene and LED Lighting

	Kerosene Wick Lamp	Kerosene Hurricane Lamp	Kerosene Mantle Lamp	Solar LED Products
Hours/Day	4	4	4	4
Lamp wick or bulb life (hours)	200	400	1000	50,000
Replacement wicks/Lanterns per year	7.3	3.7	1.5	0.03
Replacement costs	$1.61	$3.70	$2.25	$32.00
Annual fuel (liters)	15	44	109	0
Fuel costs annual	$29.48	$86.47	$214.20	$0.00
CO_2 emissions (kg/year)	38.7	113.52	281.22	0.0
Total Operating Costs ($ / year)	$31.08	$90.17	$216.45	$0.94

But selling a product is not as simple as educating a consumer about the unit economics. We've already told the story of Ms. Gupta, the samosa vendor and reluctant consumer who works outside the D.light headquarters in Noida, India. When a light is put into someone's hands with a one-on-one demonstration, the consumer purchases it more than half the time. But this type of distribution is extremely expensive. Meanwhile, dealers often demand high markups, which can put the lamp out of reach for many BoP customers.

Conclusions

At first glance, our four examples—ranging from hospitals, to lighting, to clean water and toilet and shower facilities—have little in common. And indeed, each of these companies is unique: invented in a specific locale to meet a specific need for specific BoP consumers.

And yet, when you look across the thriving BoP landscape, you can see an emerging set of approaches to innovation (and innovative approaches to funding) that can be employed across a range of BoP-oriented businesses. These four innovations are critical building blocks for many BoP organizations. Not all organizations will use all four, but they collectively make up a useful toolkit from which social entrepreneurs can draw.

It is an exciting prospect. In fact, there has never been a more exciting moment in history for accelerating the delivery of goods and services to underserved markets. We are seeing social entrepreneurs who are increasingly approaching low-income communities as *customers* and even *partners*, rather than merely objects of charity.[34] We are seeing examples where patient capital is enabling entrepreneurs to take risks they might not otherwise take to serve the BoP.

The emerging sector is necessarily messy, as many players struggle to figure out what works and—just as important—what doesn't. Our collective challenge is to build on this trend. We need to share lessons and ensure the ongoing extension of the global economy so that it includes, ultimately, *everyone*.

As William Gibson, prophet of the digital future, famously said, "The future is already here—it's just not evenly distributed."[35]

Notes

[1] World Development Indicators, 2008.

[2] $1.5 trillion as measured in current US dollars. Calculated from the World Development Indicators database (http://data.worldbank.org/indicator/DT.ODA.ALLD.CD) of the World Bank, accessed 11 June 2010. The measured indicator is net official development assistance and official aid, for all countries with data, from 1960 to 2008.

[3] Easterly was a long-serving economist at the World Bank and is now a Professor at NYU's Stern School of Business. See for example, *The Elusive Quest for Growth: Economists' Adventures and Misadventures in the Tropics*, 2001, MIT Press; or *The White Man's Burden: Why the West's Efforts to Aid the Rest Have Done So Much Ill and So Little Good*, 2006, Penguin Press. See also D. Moyo, 2009, *Dead Aid: Why Aid Is Not Working and How There Is a Better Way for Africa*, Farrar, Straus and Giroux; and R. Calderisi, 2007, *The Trouble with Africa: Why Foreign Aid Isn't Working*, Palgrave Macmillan.

[4] Bishop, Matthew and Michael Green, 2009, *Philanthrocapitalism: How Giving Can Save the World*, Bloomsbury Press.

[5] See Al Hammond's chapter in this book for a further exploration of scale.

[6] See Erik Simanis' chapter in this book for more details on the unique aspects of the BoP context.

[7] Hammond, Allen, William Kramer, Robert Katz, Julia Tran and Courtland Walker. *The Next 4 Billion: Market Size and Business Strategy at the Base of the Pyramid*. World Resources Institute and International Finance Corporation, 2007. See also Prahalad, C.K. (2004) *The Fortune at the Bottom of the Pyramid*, p. 11.

[8] Source: E+Co web site: http://www.eandco.net/impact (Accessed November 12, 2009).

[9] Source: New Ventures web site: http://www.new-ventures.org (Accessed November 12, 2009).

[10] Source: Root Capital web site: http://www.rootcapital.org (Accessed November 12, 2009).

[11] Source: TechnoServe web site: http://www.technoserve.org (Accessed November 12, 2009).

[12] Nirma is a leading, low-priced laundry detergent in India. The firm has radically lowered production costs by avoiding most nice-to-have features—such as fragrance, whitening, etc. Nirma is somewhat harsh on the skin and rough on clothes. But it is much better than no detergent at all, and has achieved a leading market position with its "low-cost, low-feature" positioning.

[13] Karamchandani, Ashish, Michael Kubzansky and Paul Frandano. *Emerging Markets, Emerging Models: Market-Based Solutions to the Challenges of Global Poverty*. Monitor Inclusive Markets, March 2009. See page 55 for a detailed discussion of paraskilling.

[14] See Patrick Whitney's chapter in this book for more on designing for BoP marketplaces.

[15] http://www.ideo.com/work/item/human-centered-design-toolkit/.

[16] See Madhu Viswanathan's chapter in this book for more on a micro-level approach to understanding BoP marketplaces.

[17] A samosa is a popular fried Indian snack food, something like a dumpling.

[18] http://dlightdesign.com/about_who_we_are.php

[19] For the full story, see: http://www.socialedge.org/blogs/let-there-d-light/archive/2009/05/04/samosa-150.

[20] http://www.childinfo.org/maternal_mortality.html.

[21] http://www.childinfo.org/maternal_mortality_countrydata.php.

[22] Maternal Mortality in India, Center for Reproductive Rights, via http://acumen-fund.socialtext.net/data/workspaces/acuwiki/attachments/maternal_mortality_in_india_center_for_reproductive_rights_2009_report:20090225160931-4-28516/original/maternal_mortality_in_india_2009.pdf (internal site).

[23] Karamchandani, Ashish, Michael Kubzansky and Paul Frandano. *Emerging Markets, Emerging Models: Market-Based Solutions to the Challenges of Global Poverty*. Monitor Inclusive Markets, March 2009. Pages 48-49.

[24] World Health Organization and United Nations Children's Fund Joint Monitoring Programme on Water Supply and Sanitation.

[25] Progress on Drinking Water and Sanitation: special focus on sanitation. UNICEF, New York, and WHO, Geneva, 2008.

[26] Source: Human Development Report, 2006 http://hdr.undp.org/en/media/HDR06-complete.pdf.

[27] Source: Child Survivor Fact Sheet, UNICEF. http://www.unicef.org/media/media_21423.html.

[28] Prahalad, C.K. (2004) *The Fortune at the Bottom of the Pyramid*, p. 11.

[29] Modi, Vijay. "Improving electricity services in rural India." Working Paper Series, The Earth Institute at Columbia University. Dec 2005.

[30] "Rural Electrification Scheme to Miss Target" The Press Trust of India, June 1 2009.

[31] Household Consumer Expenditure in India, 2006-2007. National Sample Survey Organisation, Ministry of Statistics and Programme Implementation, Government of India. October 2008.

[32] http://www.dlightdesign.com/about_who_we_are.php.

[33] http://www.dlightdesign.com/about_who_we_are.php.

[34] See Ted London's chapter in this book for more on crafting solutions with the BoP.

[35] http://en.wikipedia.org/wiki/William_Gibson.

Part Two

Strategic Opportunities

3

Taking the Green Leap to the Base of the Pyramid

by Stuart L. Hart[1], Johnson School of Management, Cornell University

Can the BoP teach the "ToP" (the "top of the pyramid") anything? Author Stuart Hart says "yes." In the old BoP model, Western entrepreneurs sought to sell goods and services to the BoP with little regard to environmental consequences. Today, Hart argues, the next generation of entrepreneurs are trying to develop distributed, small-scale, "small-footprint" products and services that are more appropriate to the BoP context—and may well point the way toward better models for the ToP, as well.

We have indeed come a long way since 1998 when, together with C.K. Prahalad, I first proposed that companies focus attention on serving the needs of the 4 billion poor at the base of the pyramid (BoP).[2] Indeed, over the past decade, it has become apparent that the BoP offers both enormous opportunities and challenges for enterprises operating only at the top of the economic pyramid.

Once companies recognized the opportunity, many set their sights on achieving the price points needed to "penetrate" the BoP with stripped-down versions of their existing products. To achieve this, they adopted wholesale changes in their business models, turning to local sourcing and production, extended distribution, single-serve "sachet" packaging, microfinance, NGO partnerships, and a variety of other innovations. With early success stories like that of Hindustan Lever providing inspiration and practical guidance, scores of companies, NGOs, and multilaterals launched new BoP business initiatives aimed at serving the poor profitably.

79

This is indeed an exciting and positive trend. As with any emergent phenomenon, however, innovation tends to create new problems while it is solving old ones. The BoP is no exception. As commercial momentum in the BoP has grown, new problems have now become apparent. In the quest to ramp up sales and profits rapidly, for example, many companies have chosen to simply adapt environmentally unsustainable products and services to sell to the poor and aspiring middle-classes.

But left unchecked, this path leads inevitably to environmental oblivion. The average American consumes 17 times more than his or her Mexican counterpart, and hundreds of times more than the average Ethiopian.[3] Per capita consumption rates in China are still about 11 times below those of the U.S. If the whole developing world were to suddenly catch up, world consumption rates would increase *eleven-fold*.[4] By some estimates, humankind already uses more than 40 percent of the planet's net primary productivity—that is, the total amount of the sun's energy fixed by green plants.[5] If, as projected, the human population increases from the current 6.7 billion to between 8 and 9 billion over the next 30 years, and if growth in consumption rates continues at its present pace, we could literally destroy the natural systems—soils, watersheds, fisheries, forests, and climate—that underpin all economic activity and indeed, human existence. The planet simply can't sustain 8 to 9 billion people consuming like Americans.

Serving the BoP sustainably therefore requires "leapfrog" green innovation: the incubation today of the environmentally sustainable technologies and industries of tomorrow. Indeed, new technologies—including renewable energy, distributed generation, biomaterials, point-of-use water purification, wireless information technologies, sustainable agriculture, and nanotechnology—could hold the keys to addressing environmental challenges from the top to the base of the economic pyramid. Yet, because green technologies are frequently "disruptive" in character (that is, they threaten incumbents that serve existing markets), the BoP may be the most appropriate socioeconomic segment upon which to focus initial commercialization attention. Learning to close the environmental loop in the base of the income pyramid is thus one of the key strategic challenges—and opportunities—facing companies pursuing the BoP in the coming decade.[6]

I call this approach the *Green Leap*—a strategy for commercializing green technologies through BoP business experiments aimed at leapfrogging today's unsustainable practices, with each having the potential to grow and become one of the twenty-first century's "next-generation" businesses. If such a strategy were widely embraced, the developing economies of the world could become the breeding grounds for tomorrow's sustainable industries and companies, with the benefits—both economic and environmental—ultimately "trickling up" to the wealthy at the top of the pyramid.

The Green Leap is a strategy that can tap into the entrepreneurial spirit in all of us: It can empower and motivate change agents in global corporations and NGOs, social entrepreneurs, residents in underserved communities, investors, and public servants alike. It is a strategy that can potentially unite the world—east and west, north and south, rich and poor—in a common cause, fostering peace and shared prosperity. Perhaps most important, it is a strategy that starts small and grows from the bottom up, beginning with the world's poor and underserved: the base of the pyramid.

Beyond the Green Giant

Before proceeding further with the development of the Green Leap concept, we should first distinguish between two fundamentally different types of green technologies: large-scale, centralized applications and small-scale, distributed solutions (see Figure 3-1). The first variety, which I call *Green Giant*, typically requires policy change, public investment, and a centralized deployment strategy to implement. Because of their scale and scope, Green Giant technologies are more readily developed by large, incumbent firms with much to gain through government subsidy or procurement. Think big wind, centralized water treatment, and massive solar farms.

Two Shades of Green Technology

Green Giant	Green Sprout
Centralized	Distributed
Large-Scale	Small-Scale
Remote	On-Site
Capital Intensive	Labor Intensive
Centrally Planned	Self-Organizing
Standardized	Localized
Trickle Down	Bottom-Up
Big Footprint	Small Footprint

•Solar Farms •Big Wind •Nuclear •Clean Coal •Water Plants	•Distributed Generation •Biofuels •Microturbines •Small Head Hydro •Point-of-Use Water

"Bigger is Better"   "Smaller can be Beautiful"

Figure 3-1   Two shades of green technology

The "go big" approach can be politically advantageous because it gives the appearance of tackling big problems with bold and sweeping solutions. The problem, of course, is that there is little margin for error: Betting on a few big solutions on a technological frontier almost always produces nasty—and expensive—surprises. Remember nuclear power in the 1960s and 70s? The vision of electricity that would be too cheap to meter short-circuited with Three Mile Island, Chernobyl, and other nuclear mishaps. In the end, the law of unintended consequences almost always prevails. Even today, with the rebirth of nuclear power in a carbon-constrained world, the industry exists only because of massive government subsidies and supports—to limit corporate liability, finance construction, and assume responsibility for growing stockpiles of nuclear waste. Today, hundreds of billions of dollars once again are being bet on next-generation nuclear power plants; history suggests that it will take only one major disaster to bring it all tumbling down.

In sharp contrast, the second variety, which I call *Green Sprout*, is small in scale, distributed in character, and almost always disruptive to incumbent firms and institutions. It is almost impossible to overemphasize this point. Because existing players in the utility, energy, transport, food, and material sectors have so much invested in yesterday's technology, it is enormously difficult for the entrepreneurs developing decentralized solar, small wind, fuel cells, biomaterials, point-of-use water treatment, and other distributed solutions to gain traction in established markets. The power of incumbency produces formidable barriers to innovation—witness, in another realm, the backlash against the Obama administration's efforts to reform health care and address climate change. Indeed, Clay Christensen's work on disruptive innovation strongly suggests that the early incubation market for such technologies is found outside of the mainstream in underserved or ignored spaces.[7]

This is why the base of the pyramid becomes so attractive as an early incubation space for emerging Green Sprout technologies: The poor are typically poorly served and must pay exorbitant prices for goods and services that are inferior or inappropriate.[8] That's the bad news, but it's also the good news. Rural villages and shantytowns typically do not have pre-existing physical infrastructures, and there are few large incumbents with significant positions to lose. Even the declining industrial cities in the developed world offer the opportunity to "start again," with thousands of acres of vacant and abandoned "brownfield" sites in Midwestern urban centers (for example) and an underutilized population that is hungry for new opportunities.

The Great Convergence

Unfortunately, the vast majority of Green Sprout technology ventures pursue strategies focused on the "top of the pyramid," where, as noted, they encounter significant resistance due to their disruptive nature. In addition, entrepreneurs in this space focus inordinate amounts of attention on R&D, evidently in the belief that their resulting green technologies will somehow automatically be transformed into commercially viable products and services. Comparatively little attention is paid to creative commercialization strategies (such as focusing on the underserved), which raises the concern that large numbers of these ventures may be destined to fail in the coming years.

Commercial experiments for serving the BoP, in contrast, have often relegated environmental sustainability to the back seat—or ignored it altogether. Yes, dozens of global corporations and hundreds of smaller social enterprises around the world have initiated or deepened commercial commitments to serve the 4 billion poor who to date have been largely bypassed by economic globalization. Yet as we have seen, many have chosen to simply adapt existing (unsustainable) products and services to sell in the BoP "mass market"—with potentially devastating environmental consequences.

Thus, Green Technology and BoP ventures have developed largely independent from one another. Each has evolved with its own particular dominant logic and core assumptions. In some respects, each represents a separate "community" with its own set of beliefs, priorities, and culture. Indeed, C.P. Snow—in his 1959 classic *The Two Cultures and the Scientific Revolution*—observed that the breakdown in communication between the sciences and the humanities was a major hindrance to solving the world's problems.[9] The existence of these two cultures, he suggested, resulted in policy solutions that failed to combine the wisdom inherent in each.

The schism between the advocates of Green Technology on the one hand and the Base of the Pyramid on the other is a modern-day manifestation of Snow's "two cultures" problem. At the risk of oversimplification, Green Technologists tend to see the road to sustainability as paved by new, "sustainable" technologies that dramatically reduce or eliminate the human footprint on the planet. Their focus is on technology and the early penetration of high-end "green" markets at the top of the pyramid, with the promise of eventual "trickle down." For example, most efforts to commercialize fuel cells to date have focused on pie-in-the-sky visions of fuel cell cars for the wealthy at the top of the pyramid. Comparatively little attention has been paid to the potential of fuel cells to provide stationary power in off-grid applications in poor, rural communities, where biofuels can be efficiently produced to provide the hydrogen needed to run them.

BoP advocates, in contrast, tend to focus on new, more inclusive business models for reaching and serving the poor. Confronting poverty and the humanitarian crisis is the primary societal focus, and there is often little attention paid to the environmental implications of such strategies. Witness the proliferation of spent single-serve, sachet packages that now litter the countryside throughout much of the developing world. Diesel generators have also been the technology of choice for distributed generation, rather than Green Sprout technologies like small-scale solar, wind, or fuel cells.

A key element of the Green Leap is, therefore, the merging of these two strategies in a *Great Convergence* (see Figure 3-2). Given the urgency of the need and the scale of the opportunity described here, Cornell University recently launched the Global Forum on Sustainable Enterprise, focusing on the Great Convergence.[10] The goal of the Global Forum is to accelerate the shift toward the Green Leap, with a particular focus on entrepreneurial strategies for the growth and scaling of Green Sprout ventures at the base of the pyramid. The inaugural Global Forum was held in New York City, June 1–3, 2009. More than 100 of the world's leading intrapreneurs, entrepreneurs, and financiers on the forefront of the Green Leap participated. Task groups focused on strategies for accelerating the commercialization of distributed generation of energy, point-of-use water treatment, biofuels, biomaterials, renewable energy, sustainable agriculture, and point-of-service health technologies.

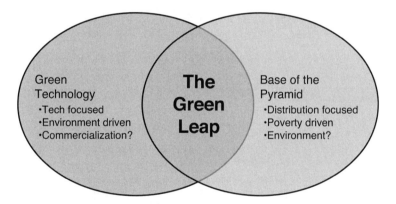

Figure 3-2   The Great Convergence

The Green Leap thus holds the potential to adapt and commercialize the most advanced green technologies from the rich world in the underserved spaces in the base of the pyramid. Once established, such disruptive technologies and business models could then "trickle up" to the established markets at the top of the pyramid—but only after they have proven themselves to be reliable, affordable, and competitive in comparison with the existing infrastructure.[11]

From Frontal Assault to Entrepreneurial Judo

If we are to realize the full potential of the Green Leap, however, we need to shed the mental models and strategies that have brought us to this point. "We can't solve problems," Albert Einstein observed, "by using the same kind of thinking we used when we created them."

Figure 3-3 summarizes my interpretation of our current mental model regarding global development. Most would agree that the world's two "mega-challenges" are 1) reducing the environmental footprint (over-consumption) at the top of the pyramid and 2) combating poverty and inequity at the base. For example, the U.S., which is home to only 4 percent of the world's population, accounts for more than 25 percent of its energy consumption, material use, and waste—a massive environmental footprint. In sharp contrast, the developing world—with 75 percent of the population—uses only about 25 percent of the world's resources.

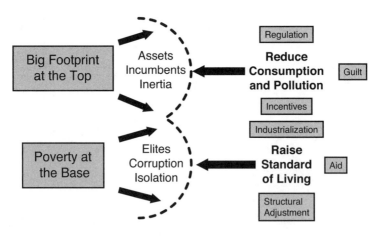

Figure 3-3   Development model: frontal assault

For the past 50 years, we have approached these two global challenges by means of an economic frontal assault. Indeed, to continue the military metaphor, these two mega-problems are much like two very large and well-defended hills. As we have already noted, large investments in yesterday's technology make for tremendous inertia in environmental footprint at the top of the pyramid. Incumbents have war chests filled with cash, enabling them to hire armies of lobbyists to make sure that the rules of the game remain in their favor and virtually ensuring continuing environmental degradation.

The poverty "hill" is similarly well defended. A relatively small number of elites benefit greatly from keeping large numbers of people poor. Corrupt regimes and dictators, for example, depend on keeping the masses ill-informed and disempowered. Ironically, armies of "development" specialists and consultants have built careers—and indeed, an entire industry—on the very existence of poverty.

To capture a well-defended hill, military doctrine tells us, the frontal assault force must be many times stronger than the force defending the hill. Tragically, the strength of our frontal assault has been relatively weak, compared to the forces defending the hills. For example, to combat environmental degradation, we have resorted to regulation, economic incentives, and occasionally, guilt. Regulation and incentives have registered some small wins, including air- and water-pollution controls, acid rain reduction, and the control of ozone-depleting CFCs. On balance, however, lawmakers and government regulators have proven no match for the corporate defenders of the environment footprint hill. Efforts to shame the rich into consuming less have also been ineffective. Indeed, only skyrocketing gas prices seem able to pry Americans out of their SUVs.

Overall, then, the frontal assault to reduce consumption and pollution at the top has been less than successful. The 2005 publication of the first *Millennium Ecosystem Assessment* provided sobering evidence that we are headed for an environmental train wreck on a global scale. More than a thousand of the world's leading biologists and ecologists agreed that the majority of the natural systems supporting life on the planet—soils, watersheds, oceanic fisheries, frontier forests, coral reefs, and the climate system—are in serious jeopardy.

Nor has the frontal assault on poverty through industrialization, infrastructure development, structural adjustment, and foreign aid been up to *its* challenge. As with the environment, one can point to specific accomplishments and encouraging trends: Millions have been lifted from extreme poverty, and life expectancy and literacy are on the rise throughout the world. Overall, however, the effort has not been successful. The most recent *Human Development Report* shows that while extreme income poverty may be declining (those earning less than $1 per day), inequity continues to grow throughout most of the world. Indeed, there are now 4 billion people—fully two-thirds of humanity—who earn less than $4 per day.[12] If present patterns persist, in the coming decade we could see an additional billion people flooding into the already overcrowded squatter communities, urban slums, and shantytowns of the world's megacities. As William Easterly concludes, after 50 years and more than $2.3 trillion in aid from the West, we have shockingly little to show for it.[13]

No, I am not suggesting that we abandon completely the strategies outlined here. Instead, I'm suggesting that we supplement our arsenal with some new weapons, which start from a different premise. To do so, however, will require a new mental model and a new metaphor. My suggested metaphor is *entrepreneurial judo*.[14] Unlike frontal assault, which requires greatly superior force to win, entrepreneurial judo uses the opponents' weight and momentum against them.

This is the essential quality of the Green Leap strategy (see Figure 3-4). The two world metachallenges remain the same—big footprint at the top and poverty at the base—but the approach is entirely different. Rather than taking on the incumbent forces directly, the Green Leap seeks to *avoid* early direct confrontation by seeking out incubation havens out of the mainstream, mainly at the base of the pyramid (Step 1). To do so requires not only business model innovation, but also a new, participatory approach to market creation.[15] In fact, to be successful, Green Leap strategies must work in concert with the poor, co-designing appropriate technology platforms and strategies.[16]

Properly developed and executed, new enterprises based on Green Sprout technologies not only serve to incubate tomorrow's technology, but also generate income and raise the standard of living of the poor (Step 2). It will take thousands of such relatively small-scale business experiments to have a material impact in the world, but eventually, a critical mass will be reached and momentum will grow. I should stress here that taking the "leap" to the base of the pyramid makes sense not only for green tech entrepreneurs, but also for incumbent firms, given that all the early growth involves new customers and market space. Clay Christensen and I have called this "creative creation" because it constitutes new growth that does not come at the expense of incumbents' current core business.[17]

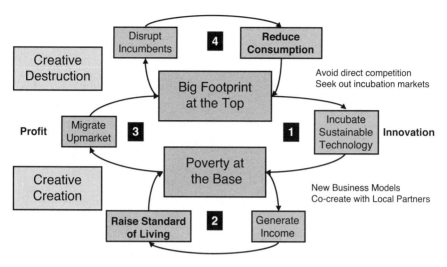

Figure 3-4 Green Leap: Entrepreneurial Judo

For example, if Philips, GE, or Osram-Sylvania were to incubate new household-scale solar lighting systems for the poor using energy efficient LED light bulbs (which they are), early LED sales would not come at the expense of their existing light bulb business at the top of the pyramid. Indeed, the Green Leap buys time and enables incumbents to be deliberate in how they phase out their existing core businesses, rather than giving new entrants an opportunity to attack and displace them.

Given the size, growth, and green technology potential of the BoP, it offers the perfect "laboratory" for incubating the Green Leap Revolution. The challenge is to combine the advanced technology of the rich world with the entrepreneurial bent and community focus of the BoP. As other authors in this volume have noted, *learning how to build upon, and not over, ancient foundations and local knowledge is key*. Unfortunately, a growing number of such ventures seek merely to penetrate the BoP with "green" products, such as smokeless cook stoves, water filters, and solar lights (to name a few), as though distribution were the fundamental challenge. Worse, many of these technologies are designed in the U.S., Europe, or Japan based on demographic data and quantitative "needs assessments." While these efforts are mainly well-intentioned, imposing "green" solutions from the outside is highly unlikely to be effective. To avoid becoming the latest poster-child of corporate imperialism, it is therefore crucial that

Green Leap strategies be co-created with those living in the BoP communities. This is the only way to embed those strategies in those communities.[18]

Ultimately, some of the low-cost, green-tech platforms developed with the base of the pyramid will migrate up-market (Step 3). It turns out to be relatively easy to add cost and features onto a low-cost platform for sale to more affluent customers. (Contrast this with the difficulty involved in trying to squeeze cost out of a high-cost platform to make it available to lower-income segments.) As a result, up-market migration can be enormously profitable. In fact, with enough experience and development at the base of the pyramid, Green Sprout technologies like small-scale solar and point-of-use water treatment can become so effective, reliable, and cost-competitive that they can compete directly with incumbent offerings at the top of the pyramid—even with all the perverse incentives and subsidies that have enabled those outmoded incumbent technologies to remain dominant (Step 4). As incumbent positions based on yesterday's technology succumb to the gales of creative destruction from the new green technologies, consumption of nonrenewable resources will also be reduced, and unsustainable practices eliminated, finally starting to shrink the massive environmental footprint of the rich world. When this happens, the cycle of entrepreneurial judo will be complete.

There is evidence that the Green Leap has already begun to occur. In a 2009 article in *Harvard Business Review*, General Electric's CEO Jeff Immelt and his co-authors stated emphatically that the future of the company depends on becoming adept at what they call "reverse innovation"—that is, the ability to incubate low-cost innovations in the developing world and then migrate them up-market to the developed world.[19] Most of their early efforts at reverse innovation are focused in China and India, where innovations in rural health care, transport, and energy are coming at breakneck speed (see Exhibits 3-1 and 3-2). Similarly, Microsoft has created a new "Trickle Up Innovation" group, focused on the incubation of a new breed of easy-to-use, inexpensive applications. Their initial focus is India, where they are looking to generate applications that bring together the Internet, software, and mobile phones for use by the underserved.

Exhibit 3-1 China's Mega-Migration

After "opening up" in the 1980s, China became a manufacturing and exporting juggernaut—the Workshop to the World—experiencing astounding, often double-digit annual economic growth. That growth, however, was limited largely to the eastern coastal cities, where the country's factories and manufacturing capacity were concentrated. It has been slower to reach the rural areas and the central and western regions of China, where hundreds of millions of peasants still live in poverty.

The economic boom has also resulted in massive environmental problems, including toxic contamination, choking air pollution, and a solid waste nightmare, including deforestation, ecosystem destruction, and an impending water crisis. In addition to China's mounting domestic environmental problems, the country's carbon footprint has also been expanding—with global implications. With a new coal-fired power plant coming online every eight to ten days, China has now become the world's largest greenhouse gas emitter.

To make matters worse, China's rapid economic growth has depended primarily upon growing consumer spending in the United States. Put simply, Americans borrow money (often from China) so they can buy more cheaply produced goods so the Chinese can build more coal-fired plants to make those goods. This co-dependency was a vicious circle destined to collapse. Sure enough, when the American real estate bubble burst with the subprime debacle in 2008, "Chimerica" came tumbling down, with both the U.S. and Chinese economies taking a beating.

Since the bubble burst in 2008, thousands of Chinese export factories closed, and tens of millions of unemployed migrant workers returned home to rural areas in search of work—that is, where 700 million-plus peasants still struggle to earn a livelihood. This reverse migration runs directly counter to the central government's policy, which seeks to accelerate the urbanization process by moving 15 to 20 million peasants to towns and small cities each year. To head off social chaos, the Chinese government has proposed a 4 trillion RMB "stimulus package" to create jobs in infrastructure development and public works.

In the long run, however, the only way to keep the Chinese economy growing at a rate fast enough to absorb the urbanizing population is to increase domestic consumption. Fortunately, China enjoys a high savings rate and a low current level of consumer spending (less than 30 percent of GDP, compared to nearly 70 percent of U.S. GDP). With 200 million rural people moving to China's nearly 20,000 towns and small cities over the next ten years, the challenge of our time is to create an environmentally sustainable form of production and consumption for this growing internal market.

It is here that Green Sprout technologies might readily take root through Green Leap strategies. The opportunity is to create the sustainable communities (and industries) of tomorrow in China's rural, central, and western provinces, at the same time growing local economies and building the internal market. The same logic applies throughout most of the underserved communities of the world.

Exhibit 3-2 India's Rural Renaissance

When liberalization took root in India in the 1990s, the Indian economy embarked on a period of rapid growth. As a consequence, tens of millions of people were lifted out of poverty, and India's information technology and business service industries became the envy of the world. Cities like Bangalore and Hyderabad experienced building booms, and the country's business hub, Mumbai, joined the ranks of the world's elite financial capitals.

But despite the rapid growth in many of India's sophisticated urban centers, the countryside continued to lag behind. Fully two-thirds of India's population —in excess of 700 million rural villagers—had yet to see the benefits of economic globalization. Growing dissatisfaction and unrest in the rural areas had direct political consequences, including the recent change in government. The pace of urban migration increased, leading to an explosion of squatter communities, tent cities, shantytowns, and urban slums.

The new government has made rural development a focus. But without opportunity-creation on a massive scale in India's 600,000 villages, it will be difficult to achieve a truly sustainable form of development, and it will be difficult to avoid having the nation's population divide into 200 to 300 million "haves" and 700 to 800 million "have nots."

India's recent growth has also caused massive environmental problems. Rapid urbanization and industrialization has resulted in rising toxic contamination, choking levels of air pollution, and mountains of solid waste. With more and more automobiles on the roads, India's cities have become mired in gridlock. And with dramatic increases in energy use, India's contribution to climate change is on the rise. In rural areas, ecosystems and natural capital are increasingly endangered by population pressure, resource extraction, and industrial development. It is simply not possible to project the current form of development into the future: Attempting to provide livelihoods for all of India's 1.1 billion using the current approach will ultimately lead to environmental collapse.

As with China, the recent global economic slowdown had a profound effect on India. The information technology and business services sectors took a beating. The Indian stock market was down by more than 50 percent, and real estate prices in the cities collapsed. Even though Indian banks were not impacted by the subprime meltdown, investment capital in India decreased by half.

Ironically, the 700 million rural Indians now represent the country's "silver lining." With a good monsoon in 2008, farmers reaped a bumper crop. Largely "decoupled" from the global economy, Indian farmers are eager to improve their quality of life. Most would prefer to stay in their villages if there were viable options for generating livelihoods there, rather than migrating to the urban slums in search of non-existent jobs. As in China, the challenge—and opportunity—is to create an environmentally sustainable way of living that is affordable and that builds livelihoods in India's rural villages. Green Leap strategies represent one potential way to "kill two birds with one stone," that is, fostering economic opportunity in the rural areas and at the same time leapfrogging to an environmentally sustainable form of development.

A Case in Point: The Water Initiative

The logic of Green Leap also applies to start-up ventures—a point that is well-illustrated by The Water Initiative. Fully 2 billion people worldwide lack dependable access to clean drinking water. In 2006, serial entrepreneur Kevin McGovern decided that he wanted to devote the rest of his professional life to the development of a company that could address the growing world water crisis—specifically, the lack of affordable clean drinking water for the underserved.[20] The new venture, which McGovern dubbed The Water Initiative (TWI), would focus on developing a commercially and environmentally sustainable way to serve the drinking-water needs of those at the base of the pyramid. It would focus on distributed, "point-of-use" technologies, embrace a co-creation-based approach to business development, and, ultimately, seek "trickle-up" solutions.[21]

Centralized water treatment plants are inherently inefficient and environmentally unsustainable. It takes tremendous amounts of energy, chemicals, and money to purify water to drinking-water standards. Meanwhile, less than 2 percent of water is actually used for drinking and cooking; most is used in less demanding applications like washing, bathing, and irrigating. At the same time, nearly half of the purified water from treatment plants leaks out of antiquated pipe networks before it reaches its final destination. (Leaky pipes also provide opportunities for recontamination, thus negating much of the investment up to that point.) Given these realities, it became clear to McGovern that point-of-use systems, offered through enterprise-based models, showed the greatest promise to make clean, convenient, and affordable drinking water available to underserved households and communities.

McGovern observed that most existing water ventures focused almost exclusively on marketing specific technologies—such as filters—to the world's poor and under-served, usually without great success. TWI therefore began with two premises that represented departures from conventional wisdom. First, TWI asserted, there can be no single solution or "magic bullet" to the clean-water crisis. Water problems and challenges vary multi-locally, from one region to the next, and any successful company has to take this reality into account.

Second, rather than seeking merely to market existing products, TWI would engage people from local communities in the co-creation of its business concept. Using a methodology called the "BoP Protocol" as the foundation for this approach, TWI aimed to develop a business that would combine the knowledge and resources of the company with those of the local community.[22] In so doing, TWI would focus on building "community pull," rather than "product push," as its basis for BoP market development. This strategy would clearly set TWI apart from other water ventures.

TWI's leaders chose Latin America—specifically, Mexico—as the initial location for incubating the new business, in part because of its geographic proximity to the U.S. and company principals. (Making it easy for principals to be onsite, where possible, almost always makes good sense.) TWI launched the BoP Protocol process in Chapala, a poor community in North Central Mexico near the city of Torreon, where arsenic contamination was the most pressing drinking water problem. Government-supplied water also contained excessive amounts of chlorine (used to kill pathogens), so local people preferred to buy expensive bottled or *garrafon* (jug) water because it tasted better. Neither of these preferred water sources, though, was consistently free of arsenic or pathogens. TWI's R&D team thus set out to develop an affordable, point-of-use technology to remove arsenic and excess chlorine, while providing protection against pathogen contamination when needed.

The TWI team recruited a number of interested partners, or *socios*, from the immediate community to join in the co-creation effort.[23] Home stays and trust-building exercises produced a committed group of local partners intent on helping to build a successful business. Ultimately, a business concept was developed that embedded TWI's platform technology in a wider community-based process of Healthy Dialogue Groups (HDGs), which engaged mothers and families to encourage healthier lifestyles.

Initially, TWI had assumed that any in-home water purification device would have to be as "bare-bones" as possible to make it widely affordable. By engaging the community in the co-creation process, however, TWI quickly learned that local residents did not want a "cheap" device on the roof to remove arsenic from their water. (In fact, most people were not particularly concerned about arsenic contamination because they couldn't taste or smell it in the water.) Instead, people aspired to have something in their homes that they could be proud of. And yes, they wanted "healthy" water, but they also wanted cold and good-tasting water.

It was through this process that the design of the "WATER-CURA" purification product came about—again, a more elaborate product than TWI originally anticipated creating. Even with its added functionality, however, the WATERCURA can still be operated without any external energy source, thus reducing both its cost and its environmental footprint. The device also permits disassembly and remanufacture, which again holds down long-term cost and waste.

In addition, ideas for complementary products using TWI's healthy water were developed by the socios. One such product was "FruTWI"—a line-up of healthy fruit drink concentrates made with purified TWI water and various fresh fruits. Some socios launched their own microbusinesses selling FruTWI, thereby offering a good-tasting and healthy alternative to Coke and other soft drinks and also creating welcome opportunities for income-generation. Finally the business model also included a set of activities focused on community greening, such as TWI-sponsored events at schools, neighborhood clean-ups, and so on. Thus, the co-creation process produced a business concept that added value at several levels, creating "community pull," with TWI's point-of-use water treatment technology at the center.

By early 2010, the business had begun to take root in Chapala, with more than 100 socios involved and hundreds of WATERCURA units in place. Of course, many challenges remain, but through small-scale experimentation and co-creation, TWI is poised to take the business to the next level in the coming years, pending second-round financing. A second site has been established, with FruTWI and other similar complementary products (such as salsa and soup concentrates) providing the early revenue for socios. The company also receives frequent inquiries from more affluent individuals and organizations voicing interest in the WATERCURA. Eventually, TWI will develop a model focused specifically on the needs and requirements of this higher-income demographic ("trickle-up"), but for now, the focus remains on scaling out the business across the Mexican BoP. In time, the company aspires to expand throughout Latin America and ultimately, the world.

As it does so, it almost certainly will adapt and evolve. Like water poured into a glass, TWI takes the shape of the communities in which it does business.

The Wisdom of the Hive

As the TWI case demonstrates, distributed green technologies lend themselves to small-scale experimentation and learning, thereby minimizing the effects of the law of unintended consequences. Failed approaches can be killed quickly, thus minimizing any negative consequences. By "failing small" (at times) and "learning big," such commercialization strategies generate the learning necessary to rapidly evolve viable and locally embedded strategies and business models.[24] Yes, Green Leap business experiments tend to start small, but many have the potential to evolve and grow into large enterprises. Given their distributed character, when Green Sprout technologies "scale," they do so modularly, retaining their local focus, even as they expand to serve thousands or millions of communities around the world.

Success, moreover, breeds imitation. Take the case of rural telephony. What began as a small and discrete experiment in rural Bangladesh in the mid-1990s (Grameen Phone) has morphed into a world-wide cornucopia of wireless telecommunication enterprises, all focused on serving the BoP.

In his wonderful book *The Wisdom of the Hive*, Thomas Seeley demonstrates that the uncanny ability of bees to locate the resources crucial to making honey—pollen, nectar, and water—has little to do with the queen, who almost never leaves the hive. Instead, that collective ability is the result of each worker bee's and drone's forays—call them his entrepreneurial experiments—to scout out the needed resources. Most fail, and they return to the hive empty-handed to rest and regroup. Those few bees that *do* locate resources communicate this welcome news to the others back at the hive by performing a "waggle dance." Almost incredibly, the enthusiasm and length of the dance is directly proportional to the amount and quality of the resources that the individual explorer has found. The next time the successful scout leaves the hive, he is followed by hoards of others who follow him to the mother lode.

In a similar fashion, successful Green Sprout entrepreneurs will be mimicked by many others, accelerating the spread of the most adaptive models.[25] We should remind ourselves that no central authority "planned" the Industrial Revolution; it was the result of thousands of small players and entrepreneurs each trying their own particular variations on a larger theme. Winners emerged, based on market tests and experience. I see no reason to think that the ongoing transformation to green technologies, a similarly revolutionary departure, will be any different. The successful, sustainable corporations of the twenty-first century may well be forged in the vast and dynamic crucible of the BoP.

Taking the Plunge

If history is any guide, most of the growth opportunities in the vast, underserved space in the base of the pyramid will be seized by entrepreneurs in the developing countries themselves, just as the opportunities in impoverished postwar Japan were captured by innovators such as Sony, Matsushita, Honda, and Toyota. Indeed, countries such as China and India already appear to be making a version of the Green Leap one of their primary strategies for national economic development. We may be witnessing the birth of the next generation of "sustainable" multinational corporations, nurtured in the base of the pyramid through bottom-up innovation and ready to take on the high-cost structures and rigid management models of top-of-the-pyramid incumbents.[26]

The Green Leap, however, is by no means a foregone conclusion. As we have seen, there are substantial headwinds that serve to slow or even deter effective venturing in this space—from unrealistic expectations and inappropriate metrics to incumbent inertia and perverse government incentives. The following portfolio of actions and initiatives should therefore prove useful in accelerating the Green Leap Revolution around the world:

- *Create protected "white space."* For Green Leap ventures to get out of the starting gate, it is crucial to create the necessary organizational "white space" to enable them to develop, whether as an initiative within an existing company or as a new venture. What does this mean? Traditional metrics and time-lines for evaluating new products do not apply to the incubation of new ventures at the base of the pyramid. It takes time and patient capital to develop sustainable Green Leap businesses that are embedded and have "community pull." Transplantation to new geographies also takes time and patience. Creating a protected envelope in which the new business can take root is thus key to its long-term growth and success.[27]

- *Exploit "shelf technology."*   Many corporations and universities today have substantial stocks of unused (or at least uncommercialized) green technology literally "sitting on the shelf." Frequently these technologies are disruptive to current core businesses or at least do not fit easily into existing business models. GE, for example, has dozens of small, distributed solar and water technologies on the shelf, in part because the company's core business for the last half-century has been focused on large-scale infrastructural technologies (such as power plants) sold to governments or other large players. Even today, the company's "Ecomagination" initiative focuses on Green Giant technologies like big wind rather than Green Sprout applications. For most Green Leap ventures, therefore, expensive R&D and new invention is often unnecessary; instead, the first step is to take a careful inventory of what relevant Green Sprout technologies already exist, assembling a small portfolio of the best of these as candidates for an alternative route to market—the BoP "bottom-up" route.

- *Innovate from the bottom-up.*   To be effective in the BoP, green technologies need to be optimized in new and unexpected ways, based on the experience on the ground in the community. The technology and the business model being developed on the ground must thus co-evolve as the process unfolds. This may well produce innovations that the company had never imagined, as GE found in its medical device business. Indeed, a whole new suite of small-scale, "point-of-care" medical technologies (such as hand-held ultrasound devices) has resulted from the company's efforts in "reverse innovation."[28]

- *Build regional ecosystems.*   Green Leap ventures can also be nurtured through regional ecosystems of entrepreneurs,

NGOs, universities, and government partners, which can collectively catalyze new business development that encourages spreading of the strategy.[29] Over the past two years, for example, with initial sponsorship from the William Davidson Institute, we have launched the *Green Leap Global Initiative*. With an initial focus on China, the initiative is dedicated to building the capacity for university and government partners to help shape business experiments focused on the commercialization of Green Sprout technologies with companies, both domestic and multinational. These commercialization experiments provide the empirical, on-the-ground platform for scholars to research the topic and practitioners to derive strategy guidance for accelerating the Green Leap around the world.

- ***Remove the bias against distributed solutions.***   Innovation in public policy could also greatly accelerate the Green Leap. In addition to the perverse incentives for the consumption of fossil fuels and other unsustainable practices in the developed world, there is also a clear bias in favor of large-scale solutions. Indeed, throughout the world, centralized solutions are favored, while distributed solutions are discouraged. In India, for example, distributed solar is hampered by a massive kerosene subsidy for the rural poor, while purchasers of solar equipment must pay a steep sales tax. In the U.S., point-of-use solutions for safe drinking water are blocked by the legal requirement that drinking water be "clean" (as defined by regulators) when it enters buildings. New policies that "level the playing field" for distributed solutions would thus help enormously.

- ***Create Green Leap seed funds.***   Finally, governments could create seed funds to catalyze investment in Green Leap business experiments throughout the world. Such policies would be especially important in the rich countries, where few green technology entrepreneurs look beyond their own borders for commercialization opportunities. If it's true that Green Sprout technologies will form the basis for entirely new industries in the coming decades, then developed-world governments need to create incentives for their technologists and entrepreneurs to get "on the ground" in the developing geographies where the Green Leap will happen first.

Again, none of this is easy or as obvious as this summary might sound. As is always the case in pursuing disruptive innovation, companies need to manage these new Green Sprout opportunities independently from their mainstream incumbent businesses. They will have to build new business models that include strategies, organizational structures, and management processes that have proven themselves "on the ground" at the base of the pyramid.

Perhaps most important, they will have to learn a new approach to innovation: an approach based upon humility and partnership. In the end, the Green Leap means innovating *with,* and not *for,* the base of the pyramid.

Notes

[1] I would like to thank my colleague Ted London for his excellent feedback and constructive criticism on this chapter. The final product that you see is much better as a result of his thoughtful suggestions.

[2] A working paper by the two of us entitled "Raising the bottom of the pyramid" was first circulated in 1998. It took four years for it to be published as C. K. Prahalad and Stuart Hart (2002). "The fortune at the bottom of the pyramid," *Strategy+Business*, 26:1-15.

[3] Peter Menzel (1999) *Material World: A Global Family Portrait* (San Francisco: Sierra Club Books).

[4] Tom Friedman (2009) *Hot, Flat, and Crowded* (New York: Farrar, Strauss and Giroux).

[5] National Research Council (1999) *Our Common Journey* (Washington, D.C.: National Academy Press).

[6] For further discussion, see Stuart L. Hart (2010) *Capitalism at the Crossroads* (Upper Saddle River, NJ: Wharton School Publishing).

[7] Clayton Christensen (1997) *The Innovator's Dilemma: When New Technologies Cause Great Firms to Fail* (Boston, Harvard Business School Press).

[8] C.K. Prahalad and Allen Hammond (2002) "Serving the poor profitably," *Harvard Business Review* 80 (9): 48-57.

[9] C.P. Snow (1959) *The Two Cultures and the Scientific Revolution* (Cambridge, UK: Cambridge University Press).

[10] See www.cornellglobalfourm.org.

[11] This idea was first articulated in Stuart Hart and Clayton Christensen (2002) "The Great Leap: Driving disruptive innovation from the base of the pyramid," *Sloan Management Review*, 44: 51-56.

[12] Allen Hammond et al (2007) *The Next 4 Billion* (Washington, D.C.: World Resources Institute).

[13] William Easterly (2006) *White Man's Burden* (New York: Penguin Press).

[14] I believe that Peter Drucker was the first person to coin this term in his 1985 classic book *Innovation and Entrepreneurship: Practice and Principles.*

[15] See Erik Simanis's chapter in this book.

[16] Much more detail about specific tools and methods for codevelopment can be found in this book in the chapters by Madhu Vishwanathan and Patrick Whitney.

[17] Stuart Hart and Clayton Christensen (2002) "The Great Leap: Driving disruptive innovation from the base of the pyramid," *Sloan Management Review*, 44: 51-56

[18] See Erik Simanis's chapter in this book for more on the importance of market creation in the BoP.

[19] Jeffrey Immelt, Vijay Govindarajan, and Chris Trimble (2009) "How GE is disrupting itself," *Harvard Business Review*, October: 3-11.

[20] This section on The Water Initiative is adapted from Stuart Hart (2010) *Capitalism at the Crossroads* (Upper Saddle River, NJ: Wharton School Publishing).

[21] In the spirit of full disclosure, the author became involved in this new venture early on, and worked with McGovern to assemble the management team and develop the strategy.

[22] The BoP Protocol is a business co-creation methodology, developed at Cornell University and the University of Michigan in collaboration with several companies. For details on the process, see Erik Simanis and Stuart Hart (2008) *The Base of the Pyramid Protocol: Toward Next Generation BoP Strategy*. www.bop-protocol.org. See also Erik Simanis's chapter in this book for more information about market creation.

[23] My doctoral student, Duncan Duke, led the field team in the co-creation process for TWI.

[24] See Ted London's chapter in this book for a more in-depth discussion of how to minimize the negative impacts associated with failed BoP ventures.

[25] Due to the importance of trust and social capital to BoP venture success, first movers can still retain an enduring competitive advantage.

[26] Stuart Hart (2010) *Capitalism at the Crossroads* (Upper Saddle River, NJ: Wharton School Publishing).

[27] See Robert Kennedy and Jacqueline Novogratz's chapter in this book for more insight into the importance of appropriate metrics, timelines, and "patient capital" to BoP venture success.

[28] Jeffrey Immelt et al. Op cit.

[29] Al Hammond's chapter in this book develops the idea of BoP venture ecosystems in greater depth.

4

Needs, Needs Everywhere, But Not a BoP Market to Tap

by Erik Simanis, Center for Sustainable Global Enterprise, Johnson School of Management, Cornell University

Market creation, argues author Erik Simanis, is fundamentally different from market entry. And although the BoP is a "basket of compelling needs," it is not yet a "market" in the traditional sense of that term. As a result, entrepreneurs in the BoP context have to think in terms of market creation—and understand how to achieve that end in a uniquely challenging context. The wise venturer in the BoP space, Simanis writes, learns how to frame the value proposition and manage the innovation process (through seeding, base-building, and growth and consolidation) in ways that align business strategy with BoP opportunity. Through a sustained case study involving a soy-protein product, Simanis illustrates how to stay on track while building markets with the BoP.

Numbers, as they say, don't lie. But they can definitely send you down the wrong path. Consider the following: Something like 2 billion people worldwide suffer from vitamin and mineral deficiencies. Perhaps 1 billion people globally are without clean water. More than 2.6 billion people are without access to basic sanitation. Another 1.6 billion live without electricity.

Over the past decade, such daunting statistics have been used to make the case for the existence of an untapped, multi-trillion dollar market in the base of the pyramid (BoP). The world's most technologically adept and marketing-savvy corporations have aimed to address the seemingly pressing basic needs of this demographic, from Procter & Gamble and Coca-Cola to Johnson & Johnson and Phillips.

But time and time again, there has been a strange disconnect: Low-income consumers have shown little interest in companies' basic-needs products. This happens even when companies send anthropologists and R&D teams into slums and villages to create products and business models tailored to local conditions. Take clean water, for example, an area that has attracted enormous attention. One of the most rigorous efforts involved consumer products giant Procter & Gamble (P&G).[1,2,3]

P&G, in partnership with the Centers for Disease Control and Prevention (CDC), developed and marketed a revolutionary chemical treatment called PUR that converts murky, pathogen-contaminated water into pure drinking water. A skunk-works style product development team committed to getting close to the customer drove this $10 million initiative. The team sought input from thousands of low-income consumers, visiting the homes of slum dwellers and villagers to understand their needs. Key design variables identified during the research phase included 1) visible signs that the water was clean, 2) affordability, and 3) at-home convenience.

Based on the findings, a product and a business model were developed. PUR's powder-based technology was packaged in single-use sachets, a packaging format to which low-income consumers in many developing countries were accustomed. One sachet, which could purify 10 liters of water, retailed for $0.10—a price point that was thought to fall within the means of those in the BoP. The product was "shelf stable"—an important factor, given the anticipated challenges of distributing to rural villages. The purification process demanded little more than stirring in the packet's contents and waiting five minutes before filtering the water through a clean cloth.

The business model included a social marketing campaign conducted with local health ministries, village health workers, and the CDC's field research stations, with the goal of educating consumers about the negative health impacts of dirty water. Local manufacturing was also investigated. P&G identified and pursued test markets in Guatemala, the Philippines, Morocco, and Pakistan to gain additional insights and to adapt the business model.

In short, P&G's effort was a textbook example of deep consumer listening, disruptive technology development, and holistic business model innovation. Yet despite hitting on all of the innovation buzz-words that are supposed to deliver success at the BoP, P&G's PUR was a resounding commercial failure: Three years of test marketing in the four countries produced consumer adoption rates mostly below 5 per-cent.[4] Even a large-scale coordinated marketing push in Pakistan involving government health officials—the one test market where P&G initially achieved a 25 percent penetration rate—soon saw con-sumer adoption fall back down to 5 percent. Recognizing the potential social benefits of PUR, P&G shifted its efforts into a philanthropic arm of the company. Since 2004, the P&G-supported Children's Safe Drinking Water Initiative has donated or provided at cost hundreds of millions of packets of PUR to relief efforts and nonprofits.[5]

P&G's experience is not unique. Few "clean water businesses" have profitably tapped into the supposed wellspring of BoP demand, despite the philanthropic capital and media hype bestowed on water-purifying technologies such as the LifeStraw.[6] The same pattern can be seen in other "needs-based initiatives" in sectors ranging from nutrition to energy to healthcare. To date, most such initiatives have quietly fizzled out, migrated up the economic pyramid to serve higher-income consumers, or—like PUR—shifted into a nonprofit mode.

Why have global corporations had such a hard time building lucrative businesses to serve the needs of billions of people—needs that are considered basic to human life? I believe that this seeming paradox can be resolved. The answer I point to, however, fundamen-tally recasts the business-innovation challenge presented by the BoP.

From Needs to Markets

I don't dispute the statistics regarding global poverty and need. I *do*, however, disagree with what they have been assumed to repre-sent. Why? Because the BoP, even with its basket of compelling needs, *is not actually a market*.

What do I mean by this? A consumer market, in the simplest terms, is a lifestyle built around a product. Members of a consumer market—be they at the very top or very bottom of the economic pyramid—have two defining characteristics.

First, the idea and practice of paying money for a value proposition is second nature to them. There exists a reflexive, intuitive understanding that a value proposition is, in fact, a value worth purchasing. In many Indian villages today, the idea of handing over money for clean water is as unthinkable an idea as buying bottled water was to the majority of Americans in the 1970s. It is worth recalling that almost two decades elapsed after the introduction of Perrier and Evian into the U.S. (in 1974 and 1978, respectively) before a large number of American consumers accepted the idea of buying a product you could get for free out of a faucet.

The second defining characteristic of a consumer market is that its members have "embedded" a product and its value proposition into the fabric of their lives—lives that are shaped by limited budgets and hours in a day. Consumers embed products by adapting behaviors and habits of thinking, reprioritizing routines and budgets, and adjusting relationships to other products and objects that make up their environment. It may even require creating and learning altogether new habits and routines. A working parent embedding something as simple as a morning Starbucks coffee into her life may have to set the alarm clock back an additional fifteen minutes, shepherd the kids down to breakfast earlier, learn a new commute route to work, and ultimately purchase a vehicle with a suitable coffee cup holder. The lives of low-income people are just as structured and just as full of priorities and boundaries that must be renegotiated to adopt a new product.

This distinction between needs and markets is more than semantic. It underpins the BoP paradox reflected in experiences like P&G's and PUR's. For a business to serve a need—be it clean water or high quality coffee—*a company must first create a new consumer market, a new lifestyle*. It must transform that need into a value proposition worth valuing, and it must embed the product into people's lives. But here's the catch: My research indicates that *innovation strategies effective in serving or entering existing consumer markets are ineffective in creating new consumer markets*. Market creation, it turns out, poses an entirely different kind of innovation challenge from that of market entry.

Market Entry Versus Market Creation

Take market entry. When a corporation or solo entrepreneur looks to enter an existing market in which they do not presently operate—be it the Chinese cell phone market or the carry-out pizza market in my home town of Ithaca, New York—they face an *information deficiency*: gaps in knowledge about the local environment, the local competition, and the preferences and particularities of the targeted customers.

Those information gaps, however, can be effectively overcome through partnerships and joint ventures; industry analysis and competitor benchmarking; and various "get close to your customer" innovation strategies and marketing tools, such as human-centered design, ethnography, and the traditional focus group. All of that market research can be translated into localized business models and tailored products that outperform the competition and deliver greater value to the consumer. With market entry, managers know the questions that need to be asked and can get the answers. As entrepreneurship researchers have argued, there is literally a market code just waiting to be cracked.[7,8]

What managers and researchers often overlook is that the same situation exists on the consumer end of the equation. Once consumers have embedded a product and value proposition into their lives, they too have mental schemas and benchmarks that let them assess the oftentimes subtle changes in value that a new product presents. As anthropologists who study the role of consumption have observed, we live our lives *through* the products and objects that surround us.[9,10] Why we buy what we buy is, therefore, a complex, frequently subconscious calculation that cuts across economic, psychological, and social factors. So in one case, the monetary savings of a less-expensive shampoo may not offset the fact that the bottle's taupe color reminds one of the sterile office cubicle where he or she works. In another case, the opportunity to chat and swap stories with a long-time friend and owner of the local electronics store may trump the better picture quality of a television brand sold exclusively through a retail chain. The central point is that once a market exists and a particular product/service has been embedded in their lives, consumers have an internal value compass that allows them to intuitively map any change in value derived from switching to a newer or competing product.

Now let's look at a very different activity: market creation.[11] When there is no market and product nonconsumption is the issue, companies confront an information condition of *ambiguity*. There are no competitor products against which to benchmark; there are no customers to observe. Without any frames of reference, any and all data companies gather about the local context and consumer needs and wants—regardless of whether the data comes from a World Bank survey, from grass-roots marketing teams using empathy-based methods, or from participatory poverty assessments with villagers—are random predictions about an *unknowable* future. As *The Tipping Point* author Malcolm Gladwell poetically points out, "A prediction, in a field where prediction is not possible, is no more than a prejudice."[12]

This same conundrum is found on the consumer side. Outside of a consumer market, there is no *a priori* price point or product design that makes a product inherently appropriate to any class of consumer, be they in Kansas City or Kibera (Nairobi). Lacking the reference points that anchor products in daily lives, consumers have no basis for predicting the changes and shifts in their existing routines, ways of thinking, and sense of self that may come with embedding a new product into their lives. BoP consumers can no more reliably say whether and how much they would pay for a liter of clean water than American consumers can say whether they would pay for the mobility value of a $5,000 Segway (which to date, they have not).

My conviction on this matter comes from a personal experience much like P&G's PUR. In 2005, while working at Cornell University, I led a field team in Kenya on behalf of the global consumer-product company S.C. Johnson with the goal of developing a BoP business serving the slums of Nairobi.[13] Our novel innovation approach was built on the belief that by understanding deeply the true needs of the community, we would be able to create a business that delivered appropriate and desired products and services.

Yet despite an intensive process aimed at understanding local needs and building local insights and knowledge into the business concept—including a several-week immersion in the community, the use of various participatory development tools such as community transects and participatory workshops, multiple ideation sessions together with community members, and months of extensive consumer surveying (more than 1,000 across three slums) and product/service testing—our business launch was met with almost no consumer demand. Neither grass-roots marketing techniques, such as community theater, nor intensive awareness building efforts within the slums' various neighborhoods succeeded in moving the needle.

Yet the business, which was a direct-to-home cleaning service called Community Cleaning Services (CCS) that offered to rid homes of insect pests such as cockroaches, mosquitoes, and bedbugs; clean and sanitize carpets (many of the Muslim families in the slum had carpets), furniture, hard surfaces, and latrines; and freshen the air, certainly seemed to address salient, even pressing, needs. The slums' residents, people who took enormous pride and care in their homes and dress, had confirmed it verbally and through their actions. In one test application of S.C. Johnson's Raid in a Kibera home, some 40 cockroaches emptied out of the one mud wall on which it was applied; mattresses were often seen positioned out in the direct sun on the tin-roofs of Kibera homes in an effort to get rid of bed bugs that afflicted many residents; mosquitoes were very active at night, interrupted sleep, and were potential carriers of malaria (my home stay host in Kibera left a kerosene lantern burning on low to keep them away); and the odor of the open-pit latrines wafted around and into the houses, particularly those living along the streams into which the latrines emptied.

The fact was, residents of Kibera, Nairobi, and the other slums where we launched the project had never before been presented with a direct-to-home home cleaning service. They simply didn't know what to make of CCS. It was as odd and out of their range of experience as the Segway was to U.S. consumers when it was launched, despite the unprecedented media hype and awareness generated around it.[14] Our innovation approach, as was the case with most others, was geared to understanding local needs, translating them into an offering, and then communicating out those benefits. It was classic *market entry*. What was needed, however, was a *market-creation* approach—one built for instilling the slum residents with the new consumer mindsets, routines, and habits that would make the CCS offering a valued part of their lives.

Were it not for S.C. Johnson's steadfast commitment to the communities where the project was launched and its willingness to invest in the project as a means of building the company's capabilities for serving the BoP, it is very likely that CCS would have come to an ignominious end at that point. Instead, the business—which has been repositioned to focus exclusively on cleaning communal latrines and public toilets in the slums—now has some 40 entrepreneurs working in more than a half-dozen slums in Nairobi. As of this writing, S.C. Johnson continues in its efforts to transform CCS into a profitable business model.

Market Creation: Why Bother?

A business leader reviewing the CCS saga recounted here might well be discouraged. Maybe "market creation" seems to be just too far outside of the company's experience. He or she might well decide to stick with the more traditional practice of market entry and to simply target company R&D and business development efforts at existing BoP markets.

That is certainly one option, and it is has borne fruit for some companies. Hindustan Lever's (HLL) often-cited success developing its Wheel brand detergent for India's BoP demographic illustrates this point.[15] Responding to a competitive threat from an Indian competitor, HLL used ethnographic methods to redesign its detergent to better match the unique needs of low-income purchasers, who in most cases were washing clothes by hand. The company reengineered its supply chain to reduce costs and reach the prevailing market price. With Wheel, HLL innovated against an existing customer value proposition and for an established BoP market. Wheel was a commercial success.

So yes—sometimes existing BoP consumer markets can be tapped without turning upside-down the company's existing routines and business models. Arla, a $9 billion global dairy company operating in more than 100 countries, is a case in point. The company's Nigerian sales and marketing team sensed an opportunity in the very low-end segment of the milk powder market. Arla conducted extensive consumer research over several months, identifying color (bright white) and solubility (lump-free) as key product attributes for this low-income segment. Milk-fat was replaced with vegetable fat to hit the target price of 10 naira (approximately seven cents) per packet. Arla's Dano "Power Cow" milk powder was launched into the Nigerian market and proved an immediate hit with BoP consumers.

Unfortunately, focusing solely on the kinds of mature BoP markets that HLL and Arla successfully penetrated may not be enough, because it effectively seals corporations off from the majority of the estimated trillions of dollars of economic value that circulates within the BoP demographic. Why is this so? As development economists have noted, developing-country economies are far from homogeneous landscapes. Instead, they consist of small islands of mature consumer markets within a vast sea of informal and nonmonetized economic activity.[16] In other words, despite the economic *potential* that exists within the BoP demographic, only a small portion of it sits in existing BoP markets that can be tapped using standard market-entry strategies.

Let's remind ourselves at this point that *nonconsumption of products and services is the defining condition of the BoP.*[17] Some companies may not even find a single existing market. For this reason, turning that economic potential into bankable returns—the elusive fortune at the bottom of the pyramid—requires the creation of new consumer markets.

This is far from a new challenge to would-be entrepreneurs. In fact, it's a challenge as old as business itself. At the end of the day, the core business challenge of selling clean water in the urban slums and rural villages of developing countries is essentially the same one faced by Silicon Valley entrepreneurs aiming to commercialize radical new technologies in the developed world. So taking the leap to serve BoP consumers lands companies in a business development challenge that—although *appearing* to be very different—actually sits very close to home.

Making Sense of Consumer Market Creation

To understand what's different about managing an innovation process effective in creating a new consumer market, we first need to step into the shoes of the consumer and consider the process of market creation from their point of view—what cultural anthropologists call an "emic understanding."

The definition I use for a "consumer market" is drawn from such an anthropological viewpoint: It is a community of people for whom the idea and practice of paying money for a value proposition is second nature and who have embedded a product into the fabric of their lives. Embedded products, much like stage props to an actor, become part of the tapestry of objects through which we live out and perform the diverse roles and identities we take on every day—from parent, spouse, and brand manager on the weekdays, to junior-league soccer coach and amateur cyclist on the weekends. Viewed from this angle, a consumer market is the end result of a successful collective sense-making effort that has infused a product with personal meaning and significance.

As economic anthropologist Stephen Gudeman points out, markets derive their meaning and significance from a "community base."[18] The community base consists of norms and traditions held by friends and family; people's daily routines and habits; close relationships as well as transactional interactions with people; images on television and programs on the radio; man-made things, from roads and art-work to durable goods and daily consumables; and even experiences with the natural environment, including rivers, forests, and wildlife. The community base provides the raw material that gives shape to new markets and enables consumers to breathe life into an otherwise sterile, abstract product.

A great example of the birth of a consumer market through the interplay of a sense-making process and a community base is captured in the 2001 Sundance documentary, *Dogtown and Z-Boys*. The documentary provides a retrospective account of the rise to skateboarding stardom in the 1970s of a group of mostly poor, borderline-delinquent teenage surfers living in the South Los Angeles "beach slum" of Dogtown. The Z-Boys—so named because they surfed and skated for the local Zephyr surf shop team—gave rise to a global skateboard market that still today reflects the unique community base of Dogtown.

When the Z-Boys picked up the skateboard, they brought with them the aggressive, risky surfing techniques cultivated at their locals-only surf cove located under the piers of the abandoned, half-collapsed Pacific Ocean Amusement Park. The Z-Boys skated like they surfed, speeding down South LA's asphalt roads in deep crouching positions, and making daring turns while touching the pavement with their hands, much like surfers touching a wave.

This sense-making process took an interesting turn when a severe drought led to the draining of swimming pools throughout LA's suburbs. The Z-Boys sneaked into backyards to skate the emptied pools, developing radical "vertical" techniques that heralded the half-pipe skate parks of today. Thanks in part to a series of magazine articles that contained edgy photos of the Z-Boys in action, along with accounts of skateboarding tournaments frequented by the Z-Boys, consumers across the U.S. and beyond were motivated to try out this new lifestyle and to initiate their own sense-making process.

As the Z-Boys example suggests, the sense-making process behind consumer market creation doesn't follow a linear pattern. Rather, as with other complex systems comprised of many interdependent and moving parts, a consumer market is what complexity scientists refer to as an "emergent property." Emergent properties are novel properties that cannot be reduced to the component pieces that gave rise to it. There's something *more* there than what you began with.

The trouble with managing emergent properties, as complexity scientist Kevin Kelley has written, is that they present a "causality problem." When and why a collective sense-making process gains critical mass and crystallizes into a mass consumer market is unknowable. Consider, for example, some of the potential changes that might be required to persuade one village woman to embed PUR in her daily life. It may require her to reassess age-old "folk knowledge" and home remedies in order to assimilate new knowledge regarding microscopic bacteria. It may require her to jettison long-held beliefs about what clean water looks and tastes like. It may create conflict with her husband or children when money spent for PUR sachets can no longer go toward a weekly Coke or other treat. And the time taken to purchase the sachets and filter water may interrupt an informal weekly chat with friends.

The list goes on, but you take my point. What's more, this is only one (hypothetical) woman's list. The relevant personal factors will most likely vary for the other 250 women living in that one Indian village, as well as for those living in India's 600,000 other villages.[19]

Once we recognize the individual-level contingencies that come with embedding a new product and value proposition, it becomes clear why creating new consumer markets—whether in the suburbs of the U.S. or South African shantytowns—will not happen simply by delving more deeply into people's needs or by searching for so-called holistic solutions to those needs. Market creation requires a different innovation logic and approach.

In the remainder of this chapter, I discuss the different treatment under a market creation scenario of two key components involved in any new business development effort: first, *framing the value proposition*, and second, *defining the strategic innovation process*.

Framing the Market-Creating Value Proposition

Let's begin with the value proposition. The objective from a market-creation perspective is to create an offering that encourages people to "try it on" and thereby initiate the sense-making process. For this to happen, the value proposition must have a special kind of "stickiness," as Malcolm Gladwell would have it, and as Chip and Dan Heath explore further in their book, *Made to Stick*.[20,21] The kind of stickiness that helps spread a message and generate awareness, however, isn't what we're looking for. Rather, what's needed is a kind of stickiness that gets consumers open to learning new mindsets and new behaviors. For market creation, an initial value proposition should be what I call "value open."

Value open means that a value proposition is open-ended and does not define specifically a product's value. Instead, value-open propositions focus on the wide range of applications in which a product can be used. Think of those late-night infomercials that show the dozens of exciting and different things you can do with a new gadget for the home. Martha Stewart, the guru of homemaking, amusingly demonstrates this concept as well. Stewart's trademark approach to showcasing creative alternative uses for products—a talent of hers spoofed in a celebrated American Express commercial that depicted Stewart using discarded credit cards to tile her swimming pool— unleashes her viewers' own zest for experimentation with novel product applications.

Value-open propositions have the effect of enlisting the consumer in "filling out" a value proposition, as it encourages him to work out in practice, and on his own terms, how a product fits in his life.[22] The idea has its roots in the work of pioneering community organizers like Myles Horton and Paolo Freire. Horton and Freire have long held that traditional educational methods that are designed to simply transfer information to people are ineffective in bringing about social change, as the ideas remain abstract. The popular education techniques they champion—techniques that get people to learn about an issue through the lens of their own personal experiences and connect it to their particular life situations—ensure that people take ownership of the social meaning around that issue. That ownership brings with it a personal commitment, and personal commitment is the key to sustained mindset and behavior change.[23]

Conventional marketing wisdom leads managers toward *value-closed* messaging. Explicitly defining and communicating a product's value is believed to remove customers' uncertainty, thereby enabling them to make informed choices. But until a product is embedded in the community base, precise messaging of a product's value combined with efforts to educate the consumer about that value counterproductively "lock in" the product's social meaning and create a "take-it-or-leave-it" decision framework that blocks sense-making.

Starting with a value-open proposition has even more positive potential in low-income markets. Why? Because it prevents the product offering from becoming boxed into a single consumer budget category, such as "health care" or "food," which necessarily puts an artificial ceiling on the size of the target market and on consumers'

willingness to pay. Straddling numerous consumer budget categories—health, entertainment, socializing, personal care, and so on—
expands the range of people that would find relevance in the offering,
as well as the proportion of the pocketbook that consumers will direct
toward the sale.

Work I conducted in India with the Solae Company helps make
the point. Solae, a DuPont subsidiary headquartered in St Louis, Mis-
souri, is a $1 billion global manufacturer of soy protein isolate for the
food and nutrition industry. In 2006, Solae launched business-development initiatives in three sites across India to reach low-income consumers. While there was coordination among the sites, the two-person
field teams at each of the sites were given a lot of independence and
room to experiment, including setting the local sales price for the soy
protein. The highest-priced site offered their soy protein at a price
point almost *50 percent higher* than that set in the lowest-priced site.
They used, however, a value-open positioning, creating a wide range of
food-based events and socializing opportunities for women that
blended fun, food, camaraderie, women empowerment, family unity,
and health. In sharp contrast, the team in one of the lower-priced sites
fell into a value-closed framing, focusing their communications and
sales pitch almost exclusively on the health benefits of the soy protein.

The result? Despite their significantly higher price point, the site
using value-open framing had *higher* demand for their soy protein, as
well as a higher customer-retention rate.

I return to the Solae story in subsequent pages. For now, I submit
that Solae illustrates the strategic implications of a value-open framing; such a framing can boost gross margins and, by extension, reduce
the geographic reach needed for a business model to have a sufficient
population base to sustain operations. One only need spend a few
days traveling between the villages of almost any developing country
to understand how critical both of these factors are to the viability of
a business aiming to serve the rural poor, who constitute the bulk of
the BoP demographic. The low-margin, high-volume logic that has
taken root in BoP strategic thinking may make sense in urban slums
and shantytowns where hundreds of thousands of people (or even a
million, as in the case of the largest slums such as Dharavi, Kibera,
and Soweto) live in close quarters and can be accessed by simply

walking door-to-door. It's no coincidence that a main case study used as proof-positive of a low-margin, high-volume strategy—HLL's successful market entry with Wheel detergent—was serving largely urban Indian populations through the dense networks of mom-and-pop shops that predominate in these areas.

But in the rural areas, where an equivalent population size might be spread across a 30-mile radius in dozens of villages connected by poor roads, with no lighting, and with only sporadic bus and rickshaw service, the same business's cost structures are inherently higher. (Among other things, it takes more people at a greater travel cost to serve the same number of people.) Using value-open positioning to boost gross margins and customer conversion rates—that is, the percentage of a target population that actually becomes customers—is vital under these circumstances.

Defining the Market-Creating Innovation Strategy

Value-open positioning increases initial traction with individual consumers and gets the ball rolling. Keeping that ball rolling to ensure the emergence of a market requires an innovation strategy built around the contingent nature of the consumer sense-making process.

Embedded innovation is one such approach.[24] *Embedded innovation* is built on a simple observation about human behavior: When people feel that they have themselves defined a want and the way to satisfy that want, they are likely to make the necessary changes and sacrifices in their lives to get it. The implication for market creation is that the most effective way to get someone to desire a value proposition and consumer offering and to then invest the time and effort to learn new routines and behaviors is to have him or her feel a sense of ownership for it.

Embedded innovation creates that sense of ownership—and by extension, consumer demand—by marrying business development with community organizing and the popular education methods noted earlier. In other words, the business-development process itself is structured to generate demand, rather than relying on marketing and awareness-building campaigns carried out at the point of commercialization or at the "go-to-market" stage. The latter often come across to consumers as efforts to convince them of a need the company believes they have, and for which the company—no surprise!—has a solution. It is a sequence that is bound to generate skepticism.

How does it work, in practical terms? Embedded innovation creates a sense of ownership by vesting an initial target community with varying levels of responsibility and ownership for imagining, piloting, and evolving a new value proposition and business, making sure that the company's own products and technologies play a central role in that business offering. As in the case of Z-Boys and Dogtown, getting the business offering embedded into an initial community base is the key, as it establishes a concrete reference point and benchmark that kick-starts the sense-making process for other consumers.

Like good community organizing, embedded innovation can be pictured as a snowballing process that continually grows the scope of community engagement and sense of ownership, thereby building the proverbial "base." Based on my experiences as a project field lead on both the S.C. Johnson and Solae initiatives mentioned earlier, and also as a consultant to additional corporate ventures in Mexico and the U.S., I recommend breaking the process into three main phases to make it manageable:

- Seeding
- Base-building
- Growth and consolidation[25]

The *seeding phase* involves building an initial buzz and base of trust in the community and then developing a strategically grounded business concept together with a community business team using the company's products and the skills of the community team. The goal is to integrate the company's products into a broader business idea that excites the community team, tapping into their visions and aspirations of running a successful business. The company's products ride the wave of emotional commitment and enthusiasm the community team has for the broader business concept.

One important point: creating this concept does not require the kind of in-depth needs assessment that typically comes with consumer research for market entry. In fact, that kind of exhaustive survey can be counterproductive. Needs assessments, because they tend toward cataloging problems, often lead to "negative" business concepts—that is, businesses aspiring to rid the community of an alleged "problem." Ironically, this can make the new business (and the company by extension) appear opportunistic, even exploitive. And from the standpoint of market creation, the elimination of something bad—whether it is carbon-dioxide emissions or cases of water-born illnesses—has a narrower and less sustained emotional appeal than that of growing the impact of good things, a message framing that McDonough and Braungart call "eco-effective" in the case of the environment.[26]

In the *base-building phase*, an initial product/service offering and basic management systems are co-developed by the company and community team through events conducted with close friends and family of the community team—what sociologists call a person's "strong-tie networks." This isn't a prototyping exercise, where consumers are engaged for their feedback on a test product. Rather, friends and family are brought together to engage in "make-and-model" workshops that turn the high-level business vision into a practical, grounded consumer offering.

Make-and-model workshops are structured as fun, socializing events at which participants provide their knowledge and experience to generate a tangible output that will form part of the product offering (the making), while engaging in the kinds of routines and behaviors that the business concept will require of consumers (the modeling). This extends the feeling of ownership and the sense of personal identification for the business offering, and gets people over the initial hump that comes with trying something for the first time. Working with strong-tie networks is important, as they are much more likely to enter with a supportive and open mindset and be willing to give their time. Contrast this approach with, for example, paying people for their involvement, which tends to undermine the forming of personal commitments to the business and risks tainting the broader community's expectations.

In the third and final phase, *growth and consolidation*, the legally registered business is launched with an initial customer base already in place, and the full value proposition and business model are evolved through the same kind of make-and-model events, through targeting the friends and family of the community team (their strong-tie networks). This leverages the goodwill in the community one step further out and expands the base of personally vested consumers.

The key things to focus on at this stage are 1) maintaining the social connections among the various participants by creating tangible markers or "badges" of their involvement and 2) visibly showcasing to the broader community the growing mass of people using the consumer offering. In anthropological terms, this "normalizes" the consumer offering and makes it appear as a natural part of the community base.

For an example of embedded innovation, I turn again to my work with the Solae Company in India. In 2006, as noted earlier, Solae (in partnership with Cornell University) created a new business to bring soy protein to low-income consumers in India. Keep in mind that soy protein isolate is not an inherently attention-grabbing consumer product like an iPhone. On the contrary, it is a bland-tasting, off-white powder. Furthermore, it's not a plug-and-play product; it requires learning new cooking habits and skills, as the protein isolate's performance is affected by the acidity and temperature of foods into which it is incorporated.

The Solae case isn't a textbook example of embedded innovation—some of the elements in the process I outlined earlier were successfully implemented in-field, whereas other elements of the process were in fact derived from the challenges we experienced and, in some cases, had the opportunity to test out in other projects. But it should give the reader a good, intuitive feel for the different flow and focus of the approach.

We launched the Solae project in two urban slums and a rural village in India. The field team and I began the process with weeklong home stays, during which we participated in the host families' livelihood activities, such as rice harvesting and operating a local retail kiosk. Our intent was to show that we were committed to being part of the community. Afterward, we began recruiting a community business team, holding dozens of small group meetings in people's homes to share our goal of finding partners who would be committed to growing a new business with Solae that could serve the community. In the end, a group of some 20 women in each location stepped up.

Rather than jumping into brainstorming sessions of how to sell soy protein, the Solae team and I spent several weeks with the women exploring how they could work together as business partners. Both sides shared personal stories and experiences on topics like unique customer value, complementary products, business models, and strategic drivers. The work built a sense of camaraderie between Solae and the women and at the same time created a shared business language linked to the women's personal experiences.

Over a period of a month, we converged on a business idea that integrated the soy protein within an offering that tapped into the women's vision of owning a bakery and being chefs. (Cooking talent is a highly respected and prized skill among Indian housewives.) The concept combined a direct-to-home cooking consulting service—akin to Avon—that would help housewives cook great-tasting, healthy meals using soy protein, along with a line of packaged and prepared foods fortified with the soy protein.

From there, the team spent an entire month cooking with Solae's soy protein in their homes, testing out and sharing recipes with family and friends, as well as together at the team office. Daily debriefs were held during which the women shared their experiences, findings, and personal anecdotes. The women and their family members became believers in the soy protein.

The team then reached out to the wider community, hosting "neighbor cookery days" with friends they considered to be expert cooks. These local gurus, as they were called, were asked by the women to share the personal skills and secrets that made them such good cooks and to prepare their specialty dishes with them using Solae's soy protein. Organized tasting sessions brought together the neighbor's family and friends and community leaders—some 80 people at a time—to give other community members a stake in the process. A recipe booklet of the community-inspired dishes was created.

The team progressed to daily "cooking outreach," meeting up with several housewives at one person's home to jointly cook a healthy dish incorporating the soy protein. The focus was on fun and socializing, as well as getting people to model and practice cooking with the protein. In the rural site, the women did their own version of home stays in neighboring villages, staying with relatives and spending the day doing cooking outreach activities. Before the businesses had been formally registered, they were receiving daily requests from other community women to sell them the soy protein.

After launch, the business introduced the soy protein in branded, refillable plastic containers for repeat customers. These customers became part of a "container club" of housewives. The housewives were often invited as a group by the women business team to present with them at local schools where their children were enrolled. In less than a year of formal business operations, the business was generating enough take-home profit, driven by the sale of soy protein to housewives, to meet almost one-half of the women's targeted incomes. And Solae's margins on the soy protein (the price at which Solae sold the soy protein to the community businesses) were on par with what it got from its traditional business-to-business customers.

Despite this encouraging start, the recent worldwide economic downturn delivered a body blow to the initiative. The additional investment required to scale the business, together with the time to reach break-even on this incremental capital outlay, couldn't be sustained. The community businesses have continued to function and purchase protein from Solae, though the absence of the Solae field teams' management guidance has been hard to replace.

Interestingly, in the haste to grow sales quickly in light of Solae's departure, the tendency by the women teams in all three sites was to revert into a market-entry approach with the soy protein: They turned to value-closed messaging emphasizing nutrition in an effort to rapidly create awareness and interest among housewives. The strategy backfired, and sales growth flattened. In response, the women teams have refocused their efforts on protein-fortified packaged and prepared foods for which there do exist consumer markets in the slums and villages. The margins on these products, however, are less than half of what they were receiving for the soy protein.

Time will tell if they can sustain their businesses on a low-margin offering, particularly in the rural site.

Aligning Business Strategies with BoP Opportunities

My main objective with this chapter has been to parse out the BoP opportunity space, outlining different kinds of business challenges that exist and, by extension, the different kinds of business strategies they require. One of the key fault-lines that subdivides the BoP opportunity space—and one that I've tried to emphasize here—is the distinction between *market-entry* and *market-creation* opportunities. The focus is on BoP consumer market entry and BoP consumer market creation because they represent endpoints of a continuum.

As I've suggested, entering existing BoP consumer markets (as did HLL with Wheel and Arla with Power Cow) presents much the same business challenge and, therefore, requires much the same project management structure as extending one's product into a new country. It requires getting on the ground and doing rigorous consumer and competitor research, followed by some degree of product redesign and repositioning in line with those findings (should they look promising). Participatory consumer research and design capabilities are valuable in this context, whereas nontraditional partnerships tend to be less so.

These are projects that can be driven by country and or regional-level management, with payback targets somewhere between one and three years. So from the perspective of getting started at the BoP, entering existing BoP markets presents the least organizational disruption and investment. The downside, as I've noted, is that these opportunities are limited in number and size. There is no fortune to be gained by *entering* BoP consumer markets.

Conversely, *creating* new BoP consumer markets—just like creating new, blue-ocean industries in developed countries—carries enormous upside potential. But the degree of management complexity is much higher, the investment cost much greater, and the payback periods much longer. Creating an initial seed market and taking it to a scale sufficient to pay back invested capital and deliver shareholders a return is every bit of a five- to seven-year proposition—and maybe more.[27] Grameen Bank—an excellent example of an organization that created a new BoP consumer market around micro-credit—spent six years on the ground before an initial consumer base was installed and the business model was in a position to be scaled.[28] KickStart, a well-known nonprofit that created a new consumer market in East Africa around its micro-irrigation pump, took a similar amount of time to get going.[29]

A BoP market-creation effort needs to be owned and driven at the level of the country manager but with the full support and involvement of corporate-level top management. Country-level managers are unlikely to have the necessary financial flexibility to make such long-term investments unilaterally. Furthermore, the churn that happens among country-level managers—particularly in developing markets, where many managers earn their stripes—makes it difficult to maintain the necessary continuity and focus on the ground. And as I've suggested, the process of market creation effectively requires outputs and milestones that are different from the traditional go/no-go decision criteria used for product development. Top-level management sign-off is needed to work outside of operational norms.

The management implication of this final discussion can be summed up in the following adaptation of a well-known adage: "Look before you do a BoP leap." Targeting BoP opportunities whose investment profile and organizational capability needs align with what the company can do and is prepared to do sets the stage for a successful BoP venture that can then serve as a springboard for creating a portfolio of BoP-targeted investments—and, not incidentally, serving the world's low-income populations.

Notes

[1] Hanson, M. and K. Powell, Procter & Gamble PuR Purifier of Water (A): Developing the Product and Taking it to Market. 2006, INSEAD.

[2] Hanson, M. and K. Powell, Procter & Gamble PuR Purifier of Water (B): A Second Chance. 2006, INSEAD.

[3] Simanis, E.N., "At the base of the pyramid," *Wall Street Journal*. October 26, 2009. Dow Jones and Co.: New York City.

[4] See also Allen Hammond's discussion on BoP scaling challenges, in his chapter in this book, which also cites the PuR experience.

[5] For more on the Initiative, see http://www.csdw.org/csdw/home.shtml.

[6] For more on the LifeStraw, see http://www.vestergaard-frandsen.com/lifestraw. htm.

[7] Sarasvathy, S.D., "Causation and effectuation: a theoretical shift from economic inevitability to entrepreneurial contingency." *Academy of Management Review*, 2001. 26(2): p. 243–263.

[8] Alvarez, S. and J. Barney, "The entrepreneurial theory of the firm." *Journal of Management Studies*, 2007. 44(7): p. 1057–1063.

[9] Turkle, S., ed. *Evocative Objects: Things We Think With*. 2007, MIT Press: Cambridge, Massachusetts and London, England.

[10] Miller, D., *The Comfort of Things*. 2008, Cambridge, U.K.: Polity Press.

[11] For more on the opportunity (and approaches) to create markets with the base of the pyramid, see Ted London's chapter in this book.

[12] Gladwell, M., "Most likely to succeed: the trouble with spotting talent," in *The New Yorker*. December 15, 2008. p. 36–42.

[13] I led this work as part of the BoP Protocol Initiative, a multi-year action research project centered at Cornell University and conducted in partnership with the William Davidson Institute, the Ross School of Business at the University of Michigan, and World Resources Institute that aimed to test out and refine an innovation approach appropriate for sustainably serving the BoP demographic. For more information on the BoP Protocol Initiative, see: www.johnson.cornell.edu/ sge/research/bop_protocol.html.

[14] Kemper, S., *Code Name Ginger*. 2003, Boston, MA: Harvard Business School Press.

[15] Prahalad, C.K. and S.L. Hart, "The Fortune at the bottom of the pyramid," in *Strategy + Business*. 2002. p. 1–14.

[16] DeSoto, H., *The Mystery of Capital: Why Capitalism Triumphs in the West and Fails Everywhere Else*. 2000, New York: Basic Books.

[17] Hart, S.L. and H.K. Christensen, "The great leap: driving innovation from the base of the pyramid." *MIT Sloan Management Review*, 2002. Fall: p. 51–56.

[18] Gudeman, S., *The Anthropology of Economy*. 2001, Cambridge: Cambridge University Press.

[19] Here's an interesting perspective: in the entire U.S., there are something less than 20,000 governing entities—villages, towns, and cities.

[20] Gladwell, M., *The Tipping Point: How Little Things Can Make a Big Difference*. 2000, Boston, New York, and London: Little, Brown and Company

[21] Heath, C. and D. Heath, *Made to Stick: Why Some Ideas Survive and Others Die*. 2007, New York: Random House.

[22] And, of course, the solutions arrived at through the "value-open" approach can eventually be incorporated into product and service design. See, for example, Patrick Whitney's description of the evolution of the concept of the Chotukool in his chapter in this book.

[23] Pyles, L., *Progressive Community Organizing*. 2009, New York and London: Routledge.

[24] Simanis, E.N. and S.L. Hart, "Innovation from the inside out." *MIT Sloan Management Review*, 2009. 50(4): p. 77–86.

[25] These three phases have evolved from the initial three-phase innovation sstructure—consisting of Opening Up, Building the Ecosystem, and Enterprise Creation—that I and colleagues developed through the BoP Protocol Initiative (see Simanis, E. N., S. L. Hart, et al. (2008). *The Base of the Pyramid Protocol, 2nd Edition: Towards Next Generation BoP Strategy*. Ithaca, New York, Center for Sustainable Global Enterprise, Johnson School of Management, Cornell University). As noted earlier, the underlying strategy behind this earlier model was based on a market-entry logic.

[26] McDonough, W. and M. Braungart, *Cradle to Cradle: Remaking the Way We Make Things*. 2002, New York: North Point Press.

[27] See Robert Kennedy's and Jacqueline Novogratz's description, in their chapter in this book, of "philanthrocapitalists," social entrepreneurs, and "patient capitalists"—and the extended time horizons that they commonly need to accept.

[28] Yunus, M., *Banker to the Poor: Micro-Lending and the Battle Against World Poverty*. 1998, London: Arum Press.

[29] Simanis, E.N. and S.L. Hart, "Expanding possibilities at the base of the pyramid." *Innovations*, 2006. 1(1): p. 43–51.

Part
Three

Effective Implementation

5

A Microlevel Approach to Understanding BoP Marketplaces

by Madhu Viswanathan, University of Illinois,
Urbana-Champaign[1]

"The devil is in the details," as the old saying goes. In this chapter, Madhu Viswanathan makes the case that BoP markets have to be understood at the ground level—from the bottom up—if a venture is to succeed in those marketplaces. What are the marketplace-relevant characteristics of poverty? In the one-to-one interactional marketplaces of the BoP, the boundaries between "human" and "economic" issues tend to get blurred, long-term relationships tend to trump short-term ones, "rich networks" make up for resource constraints, and consumption and entrepreneurship can be two sides of the same coin. BoP entrepreneurs, therefore, have to concretize, localize, and "socialize" their products and services.

This chapter presents insights about base of the pyramid (BoP) consumers, entrepreneurs, and marketplaces, derived from research, teaching, and social initiatives spanning more than a decade.[2] The focus developed through that work—and the organizing theme of this chapter—is that a bottom-up orientation, beginning with microlevel insights, is critical to learning from and designing solutions for BoP contexts. I use this orientation to understand buyer, seller, and marketplace behavior, which allows for the drawing out of key implications for practitioners.[3]

Consistent with a bottom-up orientation, the voices of BoP consumers and entrepreneurs have served as my starting point, and two individuals in particular are interspersed in the discussion for illustrative purposes. In other words, rather than beginning with the study of commercial and social organizations in BoP contexts, I begin with individuals and communities living in poverty and with the study of BoP consumers, entrepreneurs, and marketplaces in their own contexts. Using insight developed at this microlevel, I then derive implications from the bottom up, for commercial and social enterprises. These implications relate to developing understanding of BoP contexts, as well as designing economically, environmentally, and socially sustainable solutions—including the design of goods and services.

I believe that this perspective is not only germane, but urgently important. We have seen the multiplication of ecological disasters at higher levels of the income pyramid. If production and consumption at the BoP begin to mimic production and consumption at higher strata in the pyramid, and if the environment sustains parallel damage as a result—*at the BoP's much larger scale*—the consequences for the planet are likely to be disastrous.[4]

An enterprise seeking to engage with the BoP needs to understand and learn from preexisting marketplaces as they are and also envision how they can become sustainable marketplaces as they move up the income pyramid. We need to learn, therefore, how the subsistence marketplaces that characterize the BoP can become sustainable marketplaces. With this bottom-up orientation, BoP contexts are viewed as more than parallel markets to sell into. They are also seen as preexisting marketplaces from which we can learn valuable lessons and for which we can then design appropriate solutions.

The chapter is divided into three broad sections. The first focuses on the *what* of BoP marketplaces, through microlevel insights about the unique characteristics of BoP consumers, entrepreneurs, and marketplaces. The second discusses *what this means* for understanding BoP marketplaces. The third discusses *how* practitioners in the commercial and social realms can design solutions. The discussion is summarized in the following sidebars.

A Bottom-Up View of BOP Marketplaces

The BOP and Multifaceted Deprivation

- Multifaceted Deprivation—Low Income Compounded with Low Literacy
  - Thinking concretely and pictographically
  - Coping and maintaining self-esteem

The BOP Marketplaces

- Products and Consumption—Making or Buying (or Forgoing) to Better Immediate Life Circumstances
- Marketplace Interaction—Relationships Versus Transactions
- Marketplace Transactions—Fluidity and Constant Customization
- Dispersed, Fragmented Markets and Myriad Group Influences—Negotiation of Social Milieu
- The Resource-Poor but Network-Rich One-on-One Interactional Marketplace—Development of Socio-Culturally Embedded Marketplace Literacy
- Entrepreneurship—Consumption and Entrepreneurship as Two Sides of the Same Coin
  - Strengths and vulnerabilities
  - Adaptivity across different realm

Local Sustainability

- Consuming to Survive the Near Term and Conserving for the Medium Term

Developing Bottom-Up Understanding of BOP Contexts

Learning from BOP Contexts

- Overcoming Lack of Personal Connections and Identifying Complementary Strengths
  - Mindset of mutual learning
- Understanding Preexisting Marketplaces
  - Understanding strengths and vulnerabilities

Researching and Understanding BOP Contexts

- Holistic Immersion in BOP Contexts
  - Development of authentic, deep-seated understanding
  - Understanding product, relationship, and marketplace levels
- Considerations Regarding Research Methods
  - Cognitive, emotional, and administrative considerations
  - Insights from opinion leaders in 1-1 interactional marketplaces
  - Solution testing in realistic situations
- Broader Research Recommendations
  - Communication on an equal plane
  - Understanding broader life circumstances
  - Understanding product consumption and individual and community welfare

Designing Bottom-Up Solutions for BOP Contexts

Designing Sustainable Solutions for the BOP

- Identification of Basic and Aspirational Needs
- Design for Broader Life Circumstances, Multiple Usage Situations, and Multiple Purposes
- Engenderment of Trust and Respect for Inherent Dignity

- Design for Low Literacy
- Design Leveraging Existing Products and Infrastructure
- Design for Customization at Point of Delivery
- Design for Local Sustainability

Communicating and Delivering Sustainable Value

- Communication of Cost-Benefit Tradeoffs
- Provision of Informational and Educational Product Support
- Concretized, Localized, and *Social*ized Communications
- Communication Designed for 1-1 Interactional Marketplaces
- Pricing and Delivery Leveraging Social Networks

Implementing Enterprise Solutions for the BOP

- Diverse Partnerships
- Decentralization or Externalization of Functions

Ingraining Social Good in Organizations

- Deep Understanding of Individual and Community Welfare Related to Product Offerings
- Centrality of Enhancing Individual and Community Welfare in Business Processes, Outcomes, and Assessments
- Inculcation of Product-Relevant Social Good in Organizational Culture

The "What" of BoP Marketplaces: Context and Characteristics at the Micro Level

I highlight some key aspects of the BoP context here that provide microlevel insights stemming from our bottom-up approach, with particular emphasis on marketplace interactions among consumers and entrepreneurs. To provide granularity and concreteness, I include brief profiles of a BoP consumer and a BoP entrepreneur, whose stories provide key elements of the context.

The BoP and Multifaceted Deprivation

In the world of the BoP consumer and entrepreneur, activities that are mundane and predictable in an affluent context can be rife with uncertainty. For example, cooking a staple such as rice for a central consumption event—in other words, the day's one square meal—may involve uncertainties associated with the availability of cooking fuel, the quality of the generic rice, or the quality of the cooking water.

Beyond a single consumption event, other uncertainties may include (for example) unreliable electricity supplies, intermittent public transportation, and uncertain seasonal income. These create the ongoing need to plan from challenge to challenge, whether small or large. A shopping trip to a nearby town may be facilitated or thwarted by the availability and timeliness of public transportation. The successful operation of an enterprise is very likely to depend on the reliable delivery of supplies and a more or less constant supply of electricity.

"Poverty" touches almost every aspect of life—a point that is made eloquently elsewhere and upon which I do not elaborate here. Rather, the focus is on marketplace-relevant aspects of poverty.[5]

Thinking Concretely and Pictographically

A key facet of deprivation arises in the informational and educational arena. Low literacy deserves our special attention, given that it has been associated with difficulties in making abstractions, leading to thinking styles that tend to be both distinctive and often counterproductive.[6]

Concrete thinking implies a focus on single pieces of information, often without abstracting across other information—for example, choosing to buy based on lowest price without adequately factoring in size. Concrete thinking manifests itself in a variety of ways, such as getting overly focused on isolated pieces of information (price, expiration date) without understanding the full meaning (that is, what exactly the expiration date means or what "maximum retail price" refers to); seeking familiar contexts (the same store); accounting by storing money in different places; or focusing on the immediate term, due to the difficulty abstracting across time (agreeing to pay exorbitant interest rates because they are presented in terms of seemingly modest daily payments, such as "Rs 10 per day").

Another thinking style is pictographic thinking—in other words, in the face of symbols that require a certain degree of literacy to read, falling back upon a rudimentary form of processing information that depends on a one-to-one correspondence with reality. Such thinking goes well beyond simply "depending on pictures" (which, in fact, individuals at all levels of literacy do). Typically, it involves viewing text such as brand names as images; "adding" or "subtracting" by manipulating imaginary currency bills; matching patterns to identify the right bus to board or medicine to buy; and buying goods by visualizing their potential uses and picking package sizes that match (for example, the amount of sugar needed for a particular dessert).

Compounding low literacy is *low income*, which can require a focus on day-to-day necessities—that is, securing the next meal. This lack of resources combined with the concrete thinking that arises out of low literacy means both BoP consumers and entrepreneurs do not consider much beyond the immediate term. Envisioning the future—whether in the form of searching for better products or dreaming up new ideas for enterprises—ranges from difficult to impossible in the BoP context.

Exhibit 5-1

Sumitra, a 46-year-old woman with no formal education, represents a BoP consumer. Unable to read, she identified the numbers of buses to travel on by matching patterns. She often travelled by the wrong bus and reported being treated rudely by strangers when asking for help:

> I would show it (the number written on her hand) and ask the people in the bus stand, and then I would catch the bus. I didn't want to enquire of anyone in the middle of the journey...I wouldn't ask anyone who was standing in the bus stand. First, I would judge the people around, whether they were good, and then I would ask them. I could identify the right people from their face and appearance...They wouldn't

tell or guide, but criticize. So I would decide that we should not ask such people; instead I should catch whatever bus comes. I would catch the bus and enquire from the bus conductor in the middle of the travel. Suppose he was a good person, he would say that this bus wouldn't go on the route I asked and he would guide me to get down and show the proper stop to catch the right bus. Sometimes, the conductor was not in good mood or was an irresponsible person, and he would shout at me in anger with filthy words and ask me to get down from the bus.

Her experience illustrates the constraints of low literacy and the interdependencies it creates.

And yet, even within these limitations, people find ingenious ways to negotiate around their lack of literacy and their low income (refer to Exhibit 5-1). For example, they resort to oral counting skills (referred to in the local South Indian language as "mouth arithmetic"), pattern-matching (to match prescriptions with the names of medicines), or "concrete accounting" (that is, physically partitioning money). Consumers and entrepreneurs also adapt to new technologies, such as cell phones, often finding innovative ways to use "missed" calls to communicate based on a predetermined code. (For example, phone users who are not charged for missed calls sometimes use them to signal their arrival at a destination. Others close deals based on the number of rings they allow before "hanging up.") Reusing products and using products for multiple purposes are part and parcel of the resourcefulness that arises from necessity—that is, using detergents to kill ants or reusing newspapers and plastic bags in a myriad of creative ways. Similarly, entrepreneurs find ingenious ways to serve customer needs and engage in innovative business practices under extreme resource constraints—for example, developing installment payment plans for big-ticket items, managing communications to customers, and maintaining general business procedures and prices in the face of constant demands for customization.

Coping with Self-Esteem Issues

The low literacy often associated with poverty hugely complicates the challenge of self-esteem. Even in a context of widespread low literacy, low-literate individuals may feel apprehensive about starting or sustaining a conversation—say, with an unfamiliar shopkeeper—for fear of being asked a question they cannot answer. In fact, low literacy may create a more acute stigma than low income, given that low literacy can be seen as the cause of one's poverty.

Low literacy serves as a special sort of trap for BoP consumers. They may be fully conversant in their native language and yet be strangers in their own land when having to deal with banks or stores that require knowledge of, say, English. BoP consumers may navigate a potentially hostile marketplace—and defend their self-esteem—by avoiding unknown products or unfamiliar stores or by seeking help from their children, friends, acquaintances, and even strangers. Low-literate BoP consumers may conclude that it is futile to question product price or quality, assuming first, that they will not be able to express themselves convincingly, and second, that the available products and prices are the best that can be expected in light of their condition in life and their limited purchasing power.

Although the superimposition of Maslow's hierarchy of needs on BoP contexts might seem to point toward the predominance of basic needs—survival needs—the truth is often far different. In a setting characterized by scant material resources, human relationships tend to trump other considerations. The upper tiers of Maslow's pyramid, including psychological needs and self-actualization, may actually become paramount. When one has little else, a strong sense of self-worth motivates subsistence and survival in the face of long odds and sustains one's role in the social network. Thus, individuals have "everything to lose" when their good name is tarnished.

For the same reason, the nuclear and extended family, social groupings, tradition, and religious beliefs take on great significance in the BoP context. People who have desperately little in a material sense lean all the more heavily on their families, traditions, and social surroundings—and in turn, support them as well.

Exhibit 5-2

Sumitra, the BoP consumer introduced earlier, describes how she suffered public humiliation—a particular kind of enforcement—when she fell behind on repaying a loan:

> We had borrowed 30,000 rupees when my husband was ill. The moneylender came once and shouted with filthy words. We felt sad and worried much. My husband felt that the person who came up well (in life) with his (her husband's) support shouted at him because of the credit. So, he instructed that I should not go to him (the moneylender), whatever the family situation is in the future.

Self-esteem issues are not restricted to the upper strata of the economic pyramid. Quite the contrary: Poverty accentuates the need to maintain self-esteem and to minimize the harsh emotional consequences of privation. The quote just given reflects the role of self-esteem and the centrality of group influences in such settings with frequent 1:1 interactions. Sumitra also related to us how her husband was abusive and controlling until his death. Although her husband's death liberated her in many ways, she still lives the way he would have wanted her to, by and large. She is apprehensive of others' perceptions in various circumstances, like eating at a hotel:

> We visited, when my husband was alive. Suppose I go now, there are chances that my neighbors would notice it. If someone noticed me in the restaurant, they would come and tell others that so-and-so's wife is eating in the restaurant. They wouldn't say that I was in the restaurant to have food because I was hungry. But, they would pass sarcastic comments like, "Look at her, she goes to the restaurant instead of cooking in the house." I would get angry if I hear such comments. So, I won't even buy and have a snack from the shop nearby here. You could check with others. Even when I am hungry, I prefer to prepare rice porridge and eat it. I don't have the habit of eating in hotels.

The Reality of Tradeoffs in the BoP Marketplace

Individuals living in poverty regularly face stark and difficult—even impossible—tradeoffs in the marketplace. One basic choice for individuals living in poverty is among *buying*, the cheaper (and more customizable) option of *making* (buying things such as packaged soaps, spices, and medicines versus their homegrown/homemade equivalents), and *foregoing*.[7]

A second basic and sometimes agonizing challenge is to choose between two equally compelling types of consumption. Is it more important to get health care for a family member or pay for a child's education? There is no "right" answer; there is just an implacable question.

The drive to better one's immediate life circumstances, however, can have significant implications for products and consumption. In the BoP marketplace, consumers are sometimes willing to pay a little more for better products, particularly for central consumption events that take on greater significance due to the chronic inability to consume. This may mean, for example, purchasing higher-quality rice for the day's one square meal. It may mean purchasing symbolic products or brands that the consumer is proud to own (such as a silk sari or a brand of cell phone with certain features). Even beyond what is experienced in more affluent settings, goods and services can take on immense importance in contexts of deprivation. For instance, a cell phone can be a lifeline when a parent in an isolated village seeks advice on treating a sick child in the middle of the night. A food that includes an important nutrient can be more than a "nice to have"; it can be life-saving.[8]

Beyond the press of immediate circumstances, individuals living in poverty also aspire to a better life, which again may take the form of owning certain products. Many also share the basic motivations that drive wealthier consumers elsewhere, including—most powerfully—wanting a better future for their children above all in the realms of education and healthcare.

Marketplace Interactions: Relationships Versus Transactions

When it comes to marketplace interactions in the BoP context, individuals often have a primary economic relationship with one store—say, the neighborhood retail store in an urban area or the large reseller farther away (see Exhibit 5-3).

Exhibit 5-3

Velamma is a 45-year-old woman who studied up to fifth grade in a village. She ran her household in conditions of abject poverty for many years. Her family often substituted meals with inexpensive beverages, rich in carbohydrates. She never borrowed through these very difficult circumstances, and she lived within her very limited means.

After about 15 years of running her household, her husband became dysfunctional. Thrust into the role of the primary bread-winner, she started a business where she resold utensils in her community bought from stores a few miles away. She developed an installment plan for customers to buy large utensils over many months, rotating the money advanced to her for other loans. She provided free samples of small utensils for those who signed up and held a monthly lottery where winners received the large utensil earlier than expected.

Velamma educates customers about the benefits of products for important life-events such as marriage. She counters their husbands' likely objections, discusses the marriage of a child, and emphasizes the gratitude and respect the potential consumer will receive for having saved despite adversity in the family—a key element in a world of one-to-one interactions. She discusses such issues at length with individual customers, while maintaining confidentiality. She expects reciprocation from potential customers, that is, business in return for counseling. Economic and human elements are blurred, with counseling and consumption in a reciprocal relationship. She illustrates how being an entrepreneur and being a consumer are two sides of the same coin in BoP contexts.

There are compelling reasons to develop these kinds of relationships. The neighborhood store may offer credit in times of need and keep records (and of course, charge more) for credit purchases. The store owner may also offer vital peripheral services, such as holding money safely (again, for a fee). With uncertainty in so many aspects of their lives and with the next crisis always just over the horizon, individuals tend to forge strong ties with vendors. "Solutions" that would otherwise seem rational—such as stocking up at the beginning of the month through purchases from large resellers—actually entail pitfalls, such as reducing liquidity that may be needed to deal with medical crises and other emergencies.[9]

Additionally, overcoming the next crisis may require maintaining a relationship with the neighborhood retailer, who extends invaluable credit in times of need. Thus, the *relationship*, rather than the *transaction*, often takes precedence for individuals who negotiate the marketplace under extremely uncertain conditions. For BoP consumers and entrepreneurs alike, coping with and riding out uncertainty requires developing trusting relationships through a medium- to long-term perspective, which multiplies their economic value as buyers or sellers. Ironically, survival in the immediate term requires investment in relationships in the medium term. When the immediate and near terms are not at risk—that is, in more affluent contexts—a short-term perspective on marketplace transactions becomes affordable.

Marketplace Transactions: Fluidity and Constant Customization

In the one-to-one interactional marketplace just described, transactions can be fluid, as price and payment plan are negotiated face-to-face between buyer and seller. Weighings may be "adjusted" based on the price negotiated ("That's the weighing you get for the price you bargained" being a common refrain). Installments may not be paid when products are faulty (such as when the color on clothing fades). A central feature of such fluid transactions is *customization*, whether in price or product configurations. Sellers constantly have to navigate the tensions between adhering to general procedures and making exceptions.

Exceptions make for sales, but when word gets out about a special deal or the waiver of a payment, other customers are likely to make similar demands on a scale that is detrimental to the business. Hence, sellers have to manage word of mouth. Sometimes, for example, they must insist on a "symbolic" payment to prevent news of differential treatment spreading out across the customer base. Given a reasonable rationale, however—for example, regular patronage or extremely poor or elderly consumers—certain kinds of differential treatment may be justifiable and even essential.

In this one-to-one interactional marketplace, characterized by constant demands from customers based on personal preferences, Velamma resists providing a costlier item in exchange for a returned item. She is fully aware that negative consequences would follow quickly, as word got out and similar demands from other buyers followed. In her words:

> Few people are like that…I would ask them to check the products that were given to others. I would tell them that I gave them the same products that I gave to others. Some may accept what I said and leave quietly, some may shout. I may have to adjust to both situations.

> I would invite them to check the quality of products supplied to other customers. The other customers would say that the product given was good and useful. This feedback would cool down their temper and they would leave quietly.

> If they don't want, they can choose any other product available with me. But I won't return the money. At any cost, I won't give the money back.

> We can't encourage this; others may follow it. They may go and announce to others that she got the money back from the chit woman (herself). So the others would follow suit. Hence, I would give the product only. Whatever item, they can ask, but no money. I would not give the money back.

Marketplace Relationships: An Emphasis on the Human Dimension

In a marketplace characterized by minimal resources, buyers and sellers place a special emphasis on *relationships*. In a sense, this multiplies the economic value of small transactions, and committed relationships serve as the basis for credits and discounts. Thus, as noted earlier, the long-term relationship—rather than the short-term transaction—is often the relevant unit of analysis in gauging value between exchange partners.

Due to these complex dynamics in the one-to-one interactional marketplace, the line between the "human" and the "economic" is inevitably blurred. Personal judgments are central in negotiating the marketplace, such as in finding trustworthy buyers and sellers or in gauging credit-worthiness. Appeals to empathy are often made in a larger context of shared adversity, with pleas for mutual benefit and fairness being common. This presents a sharp contrast to the arms-length transactions that characterize more affluent settings. In the BoP marketplace—in which skills develop and word-of-mouth influences are strong—the human dimension and issues of fairness and trust simply overwhelm abstract notions of markets and competition. Intuitive and interdependent relationships that are viewed as fair and trustworthy—and therefore likely to lead to individual and community welfare—prevail.

Although an intensely relational environment can lead to many benefits, such as making many BoP contexts network-rich, at the same time that they are resource-poor, substantial downsides to these relationships exist as well. Inevitably, parties take advantage of trust and engage in cheating and abusive behaviors. Fluid transactions are exploited to the benefit of one party and the detriment of the other. Consumers choose to make unreasonable demands for customization. Thus, the one-to-one interactional marketplace has unique and double-edged characteristics and often comprises some very harsh realities.

I should reiterate that these rich social networks can cut both ways. People can be hurt as well as helped. Pleas for help in the marketplace from strangers or acquaintances may be rejected. Public humiliation may be used as the means for enforcing payment of non-collateral loans. Consumers may unfairly target entrepreneurs to settle personal differences. Individuals may be ostracized from social circles for not maintaining traditions surrounding birth, marriage, and death that involve unaffordable monetary expenses. My intent here is not to put a gloss on what can be an extremely harsh reality but, rather, to emphasize that certain aspects of this reality are beneficial to consumers and entrepreneurs alike. Yes, social networks hold the potential for abuse and exploitation, but in many cases, they also can be leveraged for positive outcomes.

Fragmented Markets and Group Influences: Negotiating the Social Milieu

Also noteworthy in many poverty contexts are the highly fragmented, geographically dispersed markets. This certainly applies to many rural villages, but it can also extend to "isolated" urban areas.

Poor infrastructure and limited resources, for example, restrict physical mobility. Thus, rather than finding the huge and relatively homogeneous markets that characterize the world's advanced economies, in the BoP context we find heterogeneity and fragmentation. Languages, dialects, and social structures vary by state, region, district, and even neighborhood. Compounding the challenge of these fragmented markets are myriad and diverse group influences, including local governing bodies, social strata, nongovernmental organizations and community-based organizations (such as self-help groups buying and selling goods and services), and many others.

Many such markets are characterized by a widespread mistrust of outside entities. Thus, negotiating the social milieu involves understanding differences across contexts and working with diverse organizations and groups. Again, this state of affairs is markedly different from wealthier contexts, where greater resources, state-of-the-art infrastructure, pervasive communications channels, and other factors combine to inoculate affluent communities against strong local influences.

Developing Socioculturally Embedded Marketplace Literacy

As noted, resource-poor poverty contexts can be network-rich, characterized by complex (and both satisfying and disappointing) face-to-face interactions. It is ironic that such a personal and idiosyncratic marketplace helps individuals in poverty learn about economic and marketplace fundamentals, both as consumers and entrepreneurs. Constant interaction with sellers and other consumers leads to the development of highly valuable skills, including negotiating tactics, and such orally-based interactions allow consumers of different literacy levels to participate and benefit. As they develop confidence, consumers may seek advice from other consumers, sellers, friends, acquaintances, and even strangers. Individuals may attain numeracy and acquire other skills as a result of being entrepreneurs themselves (see Exhibit 5-4).

Exhibit 5-4

Although having minimal skills as a consumer when her husband was alive, Sumitra, the BoP consumer discussed earlier, became the primary decision-maker after his death. Taking some adult-oriented classes, together with increased experience, have transformed her into a consumer with *marketplace literacy*:

> Nowadays I am asking with a commanding tone. He (shopkeeper) would say that the drumstick is two rupees I would ask him whether he is ready to sell it for one rupee, otherwise I would go to next shop. I would ask everything very assertively and in high tone...

> He had exploited me (previously)...I wouldn't have calculated...I wouldn't know the price. It was just what he told. I just followed the same for the past 36 years. I was 13 years old when I got married. Now my age is 46. I had been buying for the same price that he fixed and stated. I paid the same. I wouldn't ask the price.

> Now, it is okay for the past one month. I would check and verify as they coached me. I would verify the bill. I know all this. I would ask him why he cheated me. It is in the wholesale shop too. They (local shopkeepers) asked why I am not like I used to be earlier. They realize that I am changed...He is selling the soap for 11 rupees, which is sold for 10 rupees at the wholesale stores. I would ask how he could sell like that. I would ask him to justify. He would ask me to pay the wholesale price and not to shout there. He cheats well. It is the place for cheating. We earn hard money. Here, we could earn good money if we know cheating.

They (shopkeepers) are cheating. They cheat, even the weighing is not correct in the local shop. The person here has bought a new machine. I would check the weight because, sometimes, it was wrong.

What emerges is a socioculturally embedded form of what might be called "marketplace literacy," which should be distinguished from the "literal literacy" of reading and writing skills.[10] Marketplace literacy brings together consumer and entrepreneurial skills, an awareness of rights, and a measure of self-confidence. It enables low-literate consumers to negotiate the marketplace through verbal counting, bargaining, and switching stores and low-literate entrepreneurs to manage consumer interactions and maintain rudimentary accounts. Finally, marketplace literacy in a context of one-to-one interactions and strong word-of-mouth provides a counterweight against unfair selling practices.[11]

BoP Consumption and Entrepreneurship: Two Sides of the Same Coin

In the one-to-one interactional marketplace, consumption and entrepreneurship are two sides of the same coin, illustrated by the way Velamma, the BoP entrepreneur in Exhibit 5-3, runs her enterprise. To a far greater extent than in wealthier economies, they are interwoven phenomena.

Why is this so? The two roles of consumer and entrepreneur reinforce each other. Negotiating, counting, and closing a sale as a seller, for example, improve one's skills as a consumer. Many consumers themselves possess experience running microbusinesses. Individuals learn about the marketplace by sharing knowledge with others as consumers or sellers and engage in face-to-face interactions with both buyers and sellers. The intertwined roles of consumer-entrepreneur form a symbiotic relationship, with the two parties sharing adversity and empathizing with each other. In day-to-day life, the two roles can be blurred, as entrepreneurs juggle supplies and resources between their enterprises and their families.

At a more macrolevel, these two roles feed off each other in fostering economic progress. A case in point is the cell phone market, as consumers' needs for communication are served by entrepreneurs selling cell phones or cell phone minutes, who, in turn, are consumers with enhanced buying power. In the best of worlds—again, not always attained!—it is a virtuous circle.

Strengths and Vulnerabilities

BoP consumers and entrepreneurs (like Sumitra and Velamma) possess both strengths and vulnerabilities—an assertion that is surprising only because some of the BoP literature has emphasized the latter over the former. Consumers and entrepreneurs *do* have considerable expertise in navigating and surviving in poverty contexts. At the same time, with low literacy and low income compounding the effects of concrete thinking, individuals are constrained in their ability to envision.

As a case in point, a poor woman—having learned how to cook in the family context—starts a food shop near her home. Her goal is to survive and subsist and perhaps improve the lot of her family. She begins with a concrete reality: her own. But this may be the wrong business to be in, it may be the wrong location, or it may not be the best part of the value chain for her to operate in (that is, there may be opportunities to sell specific food ingredients, like dough, to commercial establishments).

Adaptivity Across Different Realms

Entrepreneurs start businesses as a way to subsist and survive or—depending on their luck and pluck—to escape from poverty. As noted and illustrated by Velamma the entrepreneur, they operate in an environment of fluid transactions and constant customization, managing communications and customizing products and prices to different customers. Not surprisingly, the *human* and the *economic* tend to become blurred in these contexts. Entrepreneurs juggle a range of different roles: as buyers from suppliers, sellers to consumers, and breadwinners for their families. Again, this is in contrast to the arm's-length transactions and compartmentalized functions that characterize more affluent contexts.

Given this reality, analyzing any single element of their market-place interactions—such as their selling or buying behavior—without an understanding of its interconnections with their family and larger life circumstances is incomplete and potentially misleading. For instance, entrepreneurs may support their families in part by allowing them to consume unsold perishables—or they may demand that their family forego consumption to help the business survive.[12]

Local Sustainability: Near-Term Consumption, Medium-Term Conservation

The microlevel perspective also provides a window into what "sustainability" means for individuals in the BoP. What do low-liter-ate, low-income individuals strive to sustain, beyond themselves and their families? Do their priorities extend to comprise the local cul-ture, the local environment, or the local economy?

The answers can be surprising. For individuals living in poverty, ecological issues are not distant, but *immediate*, with disease and death resulting from degraded local environments. Whatever form the pollution takes—be it noise, dust, garbage, soil contamination, or water pollution—there is very little that individuals in the BoP can do to protect themselves. Degradation of the local environment tends to have harmful effects on health, quality of life, relationships, and social networks—for example, the high-rise building erected in a crowded urban setting that isolates parts of a community from each other, cuts off their sunlight, reduces their access to cooling breezes, and so on.

So for BoP consumers and entrepreneurs alike, "sustainability" extends into several realms. There is, first and foremost, *subsistence*, in terms of basic physical needs ranging from food to water and air, health and sanitation. There is also *connectedness*, in terms of com-munity and local ecology and growth or progress in terms of educa-tion, livelihood, and poverty alleviation. Additionally, there is *conservation*, albeit in a somewhat narrow definition of the term. Poverty almost always involves tradeoffs between consuming and conserving. The family needs firewood to cook its next meal (the immediate term), but it also needs forests (versus deforestation) in the medium term.

BoP consumers and entrepreneurs respond to these trade-offs. They adapt by under-using, reusing, and recycling. Through inventiveness and coping, they maintain a semblance of control over their immediate environment. So they *cope*. They invent makeshift solutions aimed at conserving resources: reusing plastic containers for storage, using clothes to screen against pollution at home or during travel, using public transportation, making rather than buying to save money and enhance nutrition, harvesting rainwater, producing products locally, using innovative cooking methods to retain nutritive ingredients, and many more.

This microlevel understanding of BoP contexts underscores how poverty and the environment are deeply intertwined issues that cannot be compartmentalized, as may be assumed in affluent settings. Thus, solutions have to be socially, environmentally, and economically sustainable to address the many facets of deprivation, as well as their interconnected nature.

In sum, we need to *learn* from these consumers and entrepreneurs. We need to understand their behaviors at a microlevel, and devise solutions that both reflect realities on the ground and positively impact individual and community welfare.

What This Means: Developing Understanding of BoP Marketplaces

Given the microlevel insights presented in the previous pages, how do we leverage this bottom-up perspective to develop a greater understanding of business development in BoP marketplaces?

First, we need to acknowledge our own weaknesses in understanding BoP contexts. Most managers cannot personally relate to poverty and particularly the poverty that characterizes the BoP.[13] Added to this are preconceptions that need to be unlearned, such as the presumed "dependence" of the poor when, in fact, dependence is relatively unusual. (There is too little to depend on.) Middle-class or lower-middle-class individuals not deeply exposed to the BoP context tend to have their own preconceptions that prevent visualization of solutions and may even lead to dismissal of innovative approaches.

Perhaps most counterproductive is the attitude that solutions need to be imported from advanced contexts.[14]

Second, we need to acknowledge that those living in subsistence have significant experience in surviving it, either as consumers or entrepreneurs or both. That learning can serve an invaluable foundation. At the same time, we have to understand their limitations, including their (understandable) difficulties in envisioning beyond the challenges of the moment. It is important to understand both strengths and vulnerabilities, without romanticizing the former or exaggerating the latter.

A somewhat paradoxical insight is that those who cannot personally relate to poverty and low literacy, but have an openness and willingness to learn, are ideally positioned to envision new and innovative solutions. Herein lies a strength of managers and researchers that complements the weakness of those close to the BoP context. With a willingness to learn from BoP contexts, managers and researchers can complement the strengths and weaknesses of BoP consumers and entrepreneurs. Indeed, a mindset of mutual learning can lead to the customized adaptation of ideas from advanced economies, as well as learning that is transferable to advanced economies.[15]

Researching and Understanding BoP Contexts

If we seek to undertake a fundamental shift in thinking about the BoP, a holistic immersion in that context is extremely important. Such an immersion would help overcome individual and organizational deficits in BoP contexts, including the lack of knowledge, expertise, and personal connection. It would help us unlearn prior notions—such as what appears to be rational decision-making and efficient problem-solving in affluent settings—that may not be applicable in the BoP.

Holistic immersion in the daily lives of BoP consumers and entrepreneurs should aim for authentic, deep-seated understanding of a number of specific issues. For instance, at the product level, issues would include how a portfolio of products fit into consumers' life circumstances, what the usage situations are, and whether such usage can lead to individual and community welfare.[16] At the relationship level, issues would relate to the nature of one-to-one interactions, the role of opinion leaders, word of mouth effects, and the development of consumer skills. Issues at the marketplace level would include the sociopolitical structures, varied group influences, and livelihood opportunities that can sustain the local economy and create wealth.[17] The need for holistic immersion should not be viewed as being in contradiction with gaining general understanding of BoP contexts, as reflected in the earlier discussion. Rather, holistic immersion should aim to gain nuanced understanding of specific BoP contexts, given the myriad differences across these contexts (see Exhibit 5-5).

Exhibit 5-5

A real-world example from the social realm that I have been involved with is the development and dissemination of market-place literacy education. A key need was identified through extensive immersion and research, such as in-depth interviews and observations of subsistence consumers and entrepreneurs. The initial listening process, which occurred over the course of a year, led to identification of a critical need for individuals learning to participate more effectively in the marketplace as consumers and as entrepreneurs—that is, marketplace literacy—in addition to other elements, such as market access and financial resources. This marketplace literacy enables subsistence consumers and entrepreneurs to negotiate the marketplace, bargain, verbally count, and so on.

Marketplace literacy was categorized at three levels; a concrete level of livelihood skills, a more abstract level of know-how as consumers or as entrepreneurs, and a meta-level of "know-why" that provides deeper understanding of marketplace dynamics—and, by extension, adaptability to changing circumstances (that is, how and why do exchanges work, how do exchanges add up to a value chain, why should enterprises be customer-oriented, and so on).

This immersion provided a window into both the strengths and vulnerabilities of subsistence consumers and entrepreneurs.

In addition to reviewing recent literature,[18] learning about the BoP marketplace should incorporate the insights of BoP "experts," ranging from small vendors and retailers to self-help group leaders, nongovernmental organizations, and community-based organizations. The network-rich nature of the BoP context emphasizes the need to gain insights from opinion leaders and to understand how word of mouth works in specific marketplaces.

At the same time, we need to avoid relying exclusively on "filtered" views of the BoP, such as those that may be presented by middle- or upper-income individuals working for NGOs or nonlocal companies. This can't be overstated: Direct interaction with BoP consumers and entrepreneurs is essential.

In many respects, the missing insights have to be stitched together from the bottom up—that is, through localized studies from select communities—rather than through top-down sampling methods that tend to be based on unrealistic assumptions about homogeneity in these marketplaces.[19] They have to be gleaned in ways that reflect the BoP reality. For example, in the realm of product testing: given the reliance that low-literate consumers have on holistic experience with a product, the use of actual products is likely to be far more effective than the testing of products along the kinds of abstract attributes common in product testing in affluent contexts.

And to extend the example further, product testing may have to take on dimensions rarely seen in affluent settings. For example: How can the consumption of this product enhance individual and community welfare? How does it foster a constructive interplay between marketplace activity and social good?

How else should we think about the "missing" BoP research? One answer, also implied in previous pages, is the need to engage in interactions with our research participants on a more or less equal footing. We can't see ourselves as possessing solutions for what are fundamentally unfamiliar problems and settings. More so than many research settings, this requires empathy and the ability to engage in a sincere conversation. It also requires a sincere focus on individual and community welfare.[20]

Also important is "big-picture" thinking, that is, an understanding of the rich contextual setting in which BoP marketplace exchanges and consumption tend to play out. In contrast to a transaction in a context of affluence—the purchase of a single product, in isolation, using a small proportion of one's discretionary income, in impersonal settings—the BoP marketplace and life circumstances are inextricably intertwined. *Solutions succeed and fail based on the extent to which they are based on a deep understanding of life circumstances.*[21] And such understanding requires a bottom-up orientation that relies on microlevel insights as a foundation for designing solutions.

The How: Designing Solutions for BoP Marketplaces

Given a microlevel orientation to understanding BoP contexts, how do we build on what we know and design for a better future? My recommendations, not surprisingly, emphasize designing solutions from the bottom-up, delivering sustainable value propositions, implementing enterprise solutions, and ingraining social good in organizations.

Designing Sustainable Solutions

At the risk of stating the obvious, the biggest challenge for an enterprise that seeks to operate in the BoP niche is identifying a central need that can be met affordably. It is a universe of far too many needs and far too few resources.[22]

But people in this world *do* consume. They meet their basic needs. They seek healthier alternatives for their children. They aspire to own (or at least have access to) higher-quality products that won't fail them. The ubiquity of cell phones in the BoP context attests to the centrality of one vital need—communication—which sometimes helps overcome isolation and at other times may provide a literal lifeline in a medical emergency. Other aspirational needs revolve around the driving motivation to create a better life for one's children—for example, through education—or acquiring skills for themselves to improve their life circumstances.

The fundamental challenge is to envision life circumstances and, more specifically, flexible product-usage situations. Rather than responding to a fixed set of usage conditions, the effective "BoP design" allows for the many different and unanticipated ways in which the product will be used, depending on situation and need.[23] Again, this is made possible by a rich understanding of the household activities of consumers and the kinds of fluid point-of-sale conditions faced by BoP entrepreneurs (for example, on bicycles and carts). The nature of usage in harsh conditions needs to be factored in as well.

The transactional context of constant customization discussed earlier suggests the need for product design to allow for different configurations and perhaps determination of final configuration by local entrepreneurs. Communications solutions may call for different local language and dialect interfaces, which may best be done at the local level. Food products may call for value addition at the point of purchase by local entrepreneurs, who may customize the product by adding different ingredients for different segments, such as the elderly versus children. Such localization may sound like heresy to those in charge of standardization and quality control in large organizations, but nevertheless, relinquishing control in this way may be essential to success.

Solutions should address livelihood opportunities and explore potential partnerships to cocreate products through business relationships. Solutions should sustain the local economy, the local ecology, and the local culture.[24] Solutions need to address the myriad of differences among fragmented small markets, and the demand for customization in an intensely one-to-one environment. Solutions have to grow out of transparent and fair processes that both engender trust and respect the inherent dignity of BoP consumers and entrepreneurs.

I emphasize the need to concretize, localize, and *socialize* solutions.[25] For example, packaging, communication, and education should be concrete in light of the low-literate audience. Localizing solutions range from using local language in designing product interfaces to involving local entrepreneurs. In the one-to-one interactional/relational marketplace, the socializing of solutions entails both involving the community and leveraging the inherent social and oral language skills of BoP consumers and entrepreneurs. This means, for example, community-level interaction in informational and educational products; involving local entrepreneurs in final assembly and communication of value and benefits to low-literate consumers; and packaging, communication, and education that can be disseminated through word of mouth.[26]

Product interfaces and packages should be designed for concrete thinking and pictographic thinking. Also central to the design is the need to visualize and communicate benefits. Equally, the design of solutions should address the issue of multifaceted deprivation. For example, educational aspects can be a central aspect of the packaging, covering topics like benefits or proper usage.

Existing products can serve as vehicles for important add-ons (that is, staples serving as vehicles for nutritional additives or cell phones serving as platforms for educational and informational products). Leveraging existing infrastructure and products and services is also important, rather than thinking in terms of a unique device and a microfinancing plan for every seemingly discrete need. Leapfrogging the lack of infrastructure is another important facet, as with cell phones in the absence of landlines.[27] Solutions should show sensitivity in sustaining local culture in an intensely social world—for example, in the realm of cooking products and associated cultural beliefs.

At the broadest level, designing solutions calls for a *microlevel, bottom-up* approach, wherein each step in the process involves immersion in the field. It also draws upon insights from nonprofit organizations, small vendors and retailers, and self-help group leaders, thus deriving expertise from those most experienced in the context.

Delivering Sustainable Value Propositions for the BoP

Communications must help potential customers *visualize benefits*. Despite their limited resources, BoP consumers are sometimes willing to pay a small premium for quality products that serve core needs (communication, staple food, and education) and better their life circumstances. It is therefore critical to design and communicate the value proposition to emphasize costs and benefits in a context where consumers may undervalue or even ignore nonmonetary resources such as time, costs and benefits beyond the immediate term (interest rates, for example), or hidden outcomes such as enhanced health.

In marketplaces with lacking informational and educational resources, communications should be envisioned and initiated from the bottom up, rather than relying on top-down, mass media-based approaches, and aim to provide product-related support. Communication strategies can leverage the intensely social interactions, through word of mouth, partnerships with opinion leaders to share information and obtain feedback, and dialogue with the community. Social networks should be integrated with communications to maximize impact and adoption through product trials (see Exhibit 5-6).

Exhibit 5-6

The marketplace literacy educational program discussed earlier was designed entirely around low-literate audiences, using concrete materials, localized content, and methods that leveraged participants' inherent social skills, using role-plays, pictorial tasks, and other such means. Thus, this program represents an illustration of the need to concretize, localize, and *socialize* communication.

The program was designed around cultural sensitivity, given the unfamiliarity of educational settings for our participants. It addresses aspirational needs of individuals to seek (nontraditional) education to better themselves and find a way up and out economically. The ongoing process to scale these programs to reach larger audiences is based on using existing infrastructure, audio-visual media, or community-based television, depending on different situations.

The educational program serves multiple purposes, with the potential to be customized more narrowly to emphasize employability training in areas such as customer service, entrepreneurial opportunities in specific arenas, or consumer education on nutrition, or more broadly as a stepping stone for advanced education.

What about distribution? As noted, the one-to-one interactional marketplace is characterized by trust and patronage between small, local retailers or service providers and local customers. An effective distribution model draws upon these social networks. The distinctive services offered by local vendors—such as extending credit to consumers in times of need—creates loyalty, and there are parallels in the relationships between entrepreneurs and their suppliers. Pricing and distribution practices can be designed to build on these relationships, allowing for retailers to extend credit, adjust prices, and offer different product configurations. The broad point about communicating value propositions also applies here: the most effective distribution methods are those developed from the bottom up, rather than from the top down.

Implementing Enterprise Solutions for the BoP

Enterprise solutions for the BoP require the successful negotiation of widely diverse conditions and sociopolitical environments across small geographic regions and along such challenging dimensions as language and culture. Enterprises should therefore consider decentralizing, working with diverse organizations, and even "externalizing"—in other words, forming partnerships with local entities and empowering them to make decisions.[28] These approaches are likely to bring several benefits, including increased access to marketplace knowledge, high responsiveness, livelihood creation, the involvement of local communities, and a more symbiotic relationship between enterprises and BoP consumers and entrepreneurs (see Exhibit 5-7).

Contrast this approach to the extended transactional relationships that characterize affluent markets. Through these economic-centered relationships, enterprises can work within and across different communities. But the assumption that dominates in affluent markets—that certain types of institutions (such as credit bureaus) are required to facilitate marketplace exchange—generally does not hold with the BoP. Nor are the types of institutions that play a role in exchange necessarily clear-cut or fixed. Family, neighborhood, and village play a subtle but important role in exchanges. Children may help run enterprises; neighborhoods may come together to establish savings plans; villages may organize marketplace activities.

> ### Exhibit 5-7
>
> An interesting and illustrative example of a small company working with the BoP is provided by Sun Oven International Inc., which makes solar ovens around the world.[29] The company has considerable experience in subsistence contexts, having spent time understanding the life circumstances in these contexts. Its CEO, Paul Munsen, adopts the view of understanding how business can fit into preexisting traditions in a profitable manner that also sustains the local economy, culture, and environment.
>
> The product is designed to address a lack of firewood and high fuel prices. Portable solar ovens are produced by local entrepreneurs, with a key component being licensed. The company works with diverse organizations—including local NGOs and entrepreneurs—to reach their customers. The product is priced carefully to enhance affordability, with innovative financing schemes also part of the package. Along the way, of course, a number of local challenges have to be overcome, given the culturally ingrained nature of cooking and eating.

Ingraining Social Good in the Organization

Another key implication is that "social good," in a product-relevant sense, is essential for economic success in the BoP.[30] Why? An overriding characteristic of BoP marketplaces is that traditional boundaries become permeable. In a context of severe resource constraints, product needs become intertwined with the betterment of basic life circumstances. Economic relationships overlap substantially with human relationships. The larger social milieu blends into marketplace activities and vice versa.[31]

The prescription? Enterprises have to run in a similarly nuanced way, reflecting the permeable border between commercial purpose and social good.[32] A compartmentalized approach to products and functions—in other words, one that puts the business in one box and the social context in another—is unlikely to work. In most cases, a holistic approach holds far more promise. Products and related communications have to go beyond their (necessary) focus on the betterment of immediate life circumstances. They also have to provide support that improves individual and community welfare.

Such a focus on individual and community welfare may be a prerequisite for BoP consumers to spend their scarce resources. Similarly, an emphasis on the human dimension in relationships—a key aspect of life for the BoP—can help make the organization and its product offerings a more credible "community member." Enterprises that develop a reputation for enhancing individual and community welfare and for reinforcing individual relationships and the social fabric are likely to succeed.[33]

Negotiating a complex social milieu also entails working with diverse organizations, often through the common denominator of "social good." Geographically dispersed and fragmented markets come under a wide variety of influences. In an era of increasing connectivity, the small groups that focus on compelling issues—ranging from women's rights to ecological concerns—provide both a connection to BoP marketplaces and a counterweight to unfair or exploitative practices that harm individual and community welfare.

This is rarely easy. Embedding an organization into a community through embracing social good requires a deep understanding of individual and community welfare as they relate to product offerings. That thinking must be ingrained in the organization. With such ingraining, product-relevant social good becomes a fundamental orientation for the enterprise, affecting its knowledge, processes, outcomes, performance, and culture. Again, it is not easy; but it may be an essential for economic success in the BoP.

Implications for Commercial and Social Enterprises

Entrepreneurs and consumers in intensely social networks use the relationships they develop to engage in marketplace exchanges. A rejection or heavy-handed overhaul of such systems, based on a top-down mentality, is not likely to succeed. To cite just one example, invoking the credit bureau as "the solution" for BoP contexts is an example of a top-down prescription that ignores the social richness of these marketplaces, as it would bypass the rich social networks that enable and sustain exchanges. At the same time, exploitative practices *do* need to be confronted and realigned for mutually beneficial exchanges. So the pertinent question becomes, *how can social relations be used to encourage and enforce credit-based transactions?* A bottom-up approach using microlevel insights is ideally suited to answer such questions.

Such an approach also illustrates the need to develop deeper understanding of these phenomena, including the social networks. Labels and categories go only so far in this regard. In a very real sense, such labels and categories are imported from a different context—the context of affluence—and their misapplication can lead to the compartmentalization of phenomena that should be viewed holistically.

Through a microlevel, bottom-up approach, the primacy of life circumstances—of reality—is brought home in many concrete ways. Envisioning how BoP consumers actually live and how they actually use products will change the way we think about "optimal design." Childproofing is a case in point. Product designers in an affluent context can safely assume that gas stoves are inaccessible to children. In the BoP context, that gas stove may be put into service on the floor of a hut, with many children nearby. We can't change that reality; what "optimal" design now comes to mind?

This microlevel approach also emphasizes that BoP contexts are preexisting marketplaces. Social and commercial practitioners must begin by understanding existing dynamics. They must also, however, realize that BoP contexts are much more than parallel markets for existing products or solutions. This means there are many opportunities for learning. What, exactly, then should we try to learn? We can learn how appropriate solutions can be designed within the context of rich, existing marketplace dynamics. We can learn how such solutions can enable these marketplaces to become ecologically, socially, and economically sustainable, while also generating profit for the outside enterprise. And finally, we can learn how solutions that arise in these adverse settings can be transferred, profitably, to other contexts.

But—going full circle—before we can create solutions for subsistence marketplaces, we must first *understand* those marketplaces—at the microlevel. Yes, this is true in any context, but it is even more true in the BoP context, for all the reasons articulated in the preceding pages. The typical researcher or manager who has not spent much time in that context—and to date, only small numbers have—has a great many preconceptions to set aside and a great deal of learning to do. That learning requires communication on an equal footing. It requires a mindset of *learning from* in order to *design for.* Almost certainly, it will reflect an inescapable truth: that individual and community welfare are deeply intertwined with effective solutions.

Notes

[1] "I gratefully acknowledge the support and involvement of various nongovernmental organizations and community-based organizations in India, adult education centers in the United States, and commercial enterprises in several countries. Projects described in this chapter were supported by the National Science Foundation, Washington, DC, (Grant No. 0214615; any opinions, findings, and conclusions or recommendations expressed in this material are those of the authors, and do not necessarily reflect the views of the National Science Foundation); the Center for International Business Education and Research at the University of Illinois, which is funded by the United States Department of Education (Nos. P220A6000398, P220A020011, and P220A060028); the Social Sciences and Humanities Research Council of Canada (No. R3414A05); the Association for Consumer Research through a Transformative Consumer Research Grant; and the Department of Business Administration, the College of Business, the Campus Research Board, the Cooperative Extension Program, and the Academy for Entrepreneurial Leadership, all at the University of Illinois.

Many individuals and organizations have been co-travelers on parts of this journey, and deserve immense credit. I am indebted to R. Venkatesan and S. Gajendiran, who have been core members of my team for almost a decade. I am grateful for the opportunity to work with Avinish Chaturvedi, Roland Gau, Kiju Jung, Robin Ritchie, Jose Rosa, Srinivas Sridharan, and Srinivas Venugopal, coauthors in a number of research initiatives. I thank John Clarke and Robin Orr, who have encouraged and supported my educational initiatives at the University of Illinois. I thank Verghese Jacob of Byrraju Foundation and Tara Thyagarajan of Madura Micro Finance Limited for their invaluable support of our endeavors. And finally, I am deeply grateful to Stuart Hart and Ted London for giving me this invaluable opportunity, as well as for creating an editorial team that led to a most careful, thoughtful, and thorough process every step of the way, with special thanks to Jeff Cruikshank for his extraordinary efforts in copyediting the chapter.

[2] See, for example, the summary of the Subsistence Marketplaces Initiative at http://www.business.illinois.edu/subsistence. It should be noted that while BoP marketplaces are a preexisting context, markets for specific products or services (as discussed in Erik Simanis's chapter) may not exist.

³ A number of caveats should be noted. BoP contexts around the world range from war-torn areas to those with relative stability. They include contexts in which the assembly of groups is restricted and also those where social groups are pervasive. These are only two of many such differences that could be cited. And although the insights presented here are largely based on work in India, I believe they provide a useful point of departure for comparison and contrast across BoP contexts.

⁴ See Stuart Hart's chapter in this book for a more in-depth treatment of the environmental implications of BoP strategies.

⁵ The contents of this chapter draw on a number of articles in this program. However, relevant articles are cited a minimum number of times to maintain flow and minimize repetition. They include Viswanathan, Madhubalan, "Understanding product and market interactions in subsistence marketplaces: A study in South India," in *Product and Market Development for Subsistence Marketplaces: Consumption and Entrepreneurship Beyond Literacy and Resource Barriers*, ed. Jose Rosa and Viswanathan, Madhubalan (Amsterdam: JAI Press, 2007), 21–57 and Viswanathan, Madhubalan, S. Gajendiran, and R. Venkatesan, *Enabling Consumer and Entrepreneurial Literacy in Subsistence Marketplaces* (Dordrecht: Springer, 2008).

⁶ Viswanathan, Madhubalan, Jose Antonio Rosa,. and James Harris, "Decision-making and coping by functionally illiterate consumers and some implications for marketing management," *Journal of Marketing*, 69(1) (2005): 15–31.

⁷ Viswanathan, Madhubalan, Anju Seth, Roland Gau, and Avinish Chaturvedi, "Ingraining product-relevant social good into business processes in subsistence marketplaces: The sustainable market orientation," *Journal of Macromarketing*, 29 (2009): 406–425.

⁸ We should note, however, that many BoP consumers either don't know or may not be able to envision some of their needs, particularly as they relate to health-related essentials or longer-term considerations.

⁹ And for those living in rural settings, travel to larger resellers that offer lower prices may simply be impractical.

¹⁰ Viswanathan, Madhubalan., S. Gajendiran, and R. Venkatesan, *Enabling Consumer and Entrepreneurial Literacy in Subsistence Marketplaces* (Dordrecht: Springer, 2008).

¹¹ Discussed in research, which includes the study of low-literate, low-income consumers in the United States is the contrast between the U.S. marketplace with large chain stores, technology that computes for the consumer, and a plethora of symbolic labels that assume a certain level of literacy, and the BoP contexts in South India with direct bargaining and counting in dealing with vendors, experience as vendors, and the one-to-one interactional marketplace (Viswanathan, Gajendiran, and Venkatesan, 2008). Speculating on this comparison in research settings, the BoP consumers studied in India may possess relatively higher marketplace literacy than the low-literate, low-income consumers studied in the U.S., although lack of basic literacy is widespread in BoP contexts.

[12] Viswanathan, Madhubalan, Jose Antonio Rosa, and Julie Ruth, "Exchanges in marketing systems: The case of subsistence consumer merchants in Chennai, India," forthcoming, *Journal of Marketing* (2010).

[13] See Ted London's chapter in this book.

[14] See Stuart Hart's chapter in this book.

[15] See Erik Simanis's chapter in this book.

[16] Ibid.

[17] See Patrick Whitney's chapter in this book.

[18] Cognitive considerations relate to using realistic, concrete stimuli (e.g. pictures of products or actual products) and tasks, using straightforward, verbal language, minimizing need for reading or writing, verbalizing all instructions and questions, and recording answers on behalf of participants. Emotional considerations relate to immersing oneself in the environment being studied, engaging in a sincere conversation, developing rapport, being transparent about purpose and engendering trust, avoiding exploitation of vulnerabilities, emphasizing abilities not deficiencies, and avoiding settings that create anxiety (say, through artificial tasks or test-taking scenarios). Administrative concerns relate to developing relationships with organizations—NGOs or community-based organizations—that provide access to and expertise about BoP consumers and entrepreneurs. Madhubalan Viswanathan, Roland Gau, and Avinish Chaturvedi, "Research methods for subsistence marketplaces," in *Sustainability Challenges and Solutions at the Base-of-the-Pyramid: Business, Technology and the Poor,* ed. Prabhu Kandachar and Minna Halme (Greenleaf Publishing, 2008), 242–260.

[19] See Patrick Whitney's chapter in this book.

[20] See Robert Kennedy's and Jacqueline Novogratz's chapter in this book.

[21] See Erik Simanis's chapter in this book.

[22] See Robert Kennedy's and Jacqueline Novogratz's chapter in this book.

[23] For a complementary perspective, see Erik Simanis's discussion of "value-open" innovation in his chapter in this book.

[24] See Stuart Hart's chapter in this book.

[25] Viswanathan, Madhubalan., Srinivas Sridharan, Roland Gau, and Robin Ritchie, "Designing marketplace literacy education in resource-constrained contexts: Implications for public policy and marketing," *Journal of Public Policy and Marketing,* 28 (1) (2009): 85–94.

[26] Our experience in designing a marketplace literacy education program mimics a new product development process in a number of ways, central here being the need to concretize, localize, and *socialize* our approach.

[27] See Stuart Hart's chapter in this book.

[28] Ritchie, Robin and Srinivas Sridharan, "Marketing in subsistence markets: Innovation through decentralization and externalization," *Product and Market Development for Subsistence Marketplaces: Consumption and Entrepreneurship Beyond Literacy and Resource Barriers*, Vol. 20. ed. Jose Rosa and Madhubalan Viswanathan (Oxford, UK: Elsevier, 2007), 195–214. See also Ted London's chapter in this book.

[29] See http://www.sunoven.com.

[30] Viswanathan, Madhubalan, Anju Seth, Roland Gau, and Avinish Chaturvedi, "Ingraining product-relevant social good into business processes in subsistence marketplaces: The sustainable market orientation," *Journal of Macromarketing*, 29 (2009): 406–425.

[31] My arguments here are closely aligned with those of Erik Simanis, Stuart Hart, and Robert Kennedy and Jacqueline Novogratz in their respective chapters in this book.

[32] I see congruence with Ted London's idea of "co-mingled competitive advantage," as described in his chapter in this book.

[33] For more on this idea and importance of social embeddedness, see Ted London and Stuart Hart, "Reinventing strategies for emerging markets: Beyond the transnational model," *Journal of International Business Studies*, 35 (2004): 350–370.

6

Reframing Design for the Base of the Pyramid

by Patrick Whitney, Institute of Design, Illinois Institute of
Technology

*By enabling breakthrough products, issues of design have come to the fore
in the industrialized world, which is leaving behind economies of scale for
economies of choice. Contrasting the Apple iPhone with the Chotukool
refrigerator, author Patrick Whitney explores the provocative question of
whether strategic design techniques that have proven themselves at the top
of the economic pyramid might also prove useful—in identical or modified
forms—when applied to base of the pyramid markets. His answer is
"yes"—albeit with some important caveats.*

On the morning of June 29, 2007, early-bird commuters arriving
on the streets of San Francisco, Chicago, and New York discovered
lines of people up to one-quarter mile long.[1] Those at the front of the
line had secured their spots by arriving more than 30 hours earlier. All
of this commotion was for Apple's iPhone—a product in a moribund
category that was already filled with commodity products from other
long-established companies.

The remarkable promise of that first day was surpassed by subsequent wild success in terms of customer satisfaction, market share,
and profit. The product and its related software were integrated with
the iTunes platform that had previously transformed the recorded
music business. Even with its many functions, the iPhone was much
easier to use than any other smart phone, and it went well beyond the
industry standard by being an exceptionally useful—and even fun—
way to manage one's photographs, music, and other media.

A little less than two years later, in early 2009, on a hot and dusty morning in a village 450 kilometers east of Mumbai, India, six hundred villagers crowded into a tent to get a first glimpse of the "Chotukool"— a forty-three liter refrigerator designed for base of the pyramid (BoP) users.[2]

This product, too, had a phenomenal debut. Eight women—who represented the new sales force for Chotukool ("little cool" in Hindi)—carried it into the tent on a palanquin covered with garlands of marigolds. They sang devotional songs to the onlookers about how "Chotu" had given them hope and about how people now looked at them with respect because, for the first time, they were earning money to support their families. Next, a local politician addressed the crowd, extolling the virtues not only of buying a Chotu, but also of becoming a salesperson for this refrigerator—and, by extension, for the group that had launched it.

Even an onlooker from the other side of the world could see that something extraordinary was happening. The team at Godrej & Boyce (G&B)—an Indian conglomerate based in Mumbai—had introduced more than just an innovative product and a new business model tailored to the BoP. They also had created partnerships and jobs for the women in the area. This, in turn, would grow the local economy, enhance people's well-being, and increase the chance that they could buy labor-saving appliances—perhaps even a refrigerator.

When G&B started the project, interactions with their consumers were much more complex, confusing, and lengthy than they expected, but those interactions led to surprising insights that caused the company to *reframe the problem*. After gaining an understanding of how the people lived—rather than just what those potential customers expected from new products—the original goal of selling a cheap refrigerator to people in poor villages was replaced by a bigger, more general goal that G&B eventually called the "3-L vision." The 3-L vision provided a new framework: creating a better *living standard*, *lifestyle*, and *livelihood*. The result was gratifying on many levels: Not only were the sales and profitability of the refrigerator increased, but G&B wound up selling a product that was better and less expensive than the one imagined at the beginning of the project.

Although both the iPhone and the Chotu launches attracted enthusiastic crowds, the offerings couldn't have looked more different. The markets into which these products would be sold were at opposite ends of the economic pyramid. On first blush, the refrigerator for low-income rural Indian families might seem entirely unrelated to the phone that became an icon and changed the mobile phone category. When one looks behind the surface of each success, however, strong similarities in approach and result become visible. With respect to approach, neither team accepted the industry norms; instead, they reframed the problem and the requirements for the product. Both teams designed solutions that went beyond what users said they wanted. Both designed a systems solution that included changing the business models and services. Both projects are clear examples of the use of emerging *strategic design principles* that, while not formalized into a detailed protocol like Six Sigma, are being adopted because they help companies decrease the risk in meeting people's real needs, often even before they know they have them.

The iPhone and Chotukool, like many breakthrough innovations, were surprising in several ways, including the fact that they were not created earlier—especially given how obvious they seem after their surprising success. Neither depended upon inventing new technology. In both cases, the design team went beyond industry conventions and saw user needs that were not being met. Apple envisioned that people would buy a phone that was merely acceptable for the normal services of voice mail and e-mail if their offering delivered a great user experience around their photos, movies, music, and the Web. The G&B team hypothesized that the large group of consumers who had no notion of buying a refrigerator might well become loyal customers if they were brought into the value web not just as consumers, but also as entrepreneurs generating income for themselves. How did the team in each of these companies make the right decision, given that the mobile phone market was moribund and the market for refrigerators for poor people did not exist at all? Neither Chotukool nor the iPhone would likely have happened if the respective teams followed the normal ways that companies frame their innovation projects.

Why are some companies consistently better than other companies at creating offerings that resonate with people who use them? It turns out that there are a few general principles based in the field of design that lie behind the creation of the iPhone, Chotukool, and other breakthrough innovations. A general characteristic of these principles is *not accepting the problem as given* and *using insights about the users to reframe the problem*. Reframing is a catalyst for new ideas that, while unusual within their industry and not expected or requested by the consumers, will seem later to be perfectly natural to users because they fit how they want to live. Some ideas that seem risky in the standard industry framework are actually less risky when the problem has been reframed and is truly grounded in the patterns of the users' daily life, regardless of their income.

One useful lens is that of *complexity*. The cause of complexity in the developed world is the increasingly varied patterns of daily life enabled by unprecedented consumer choice. In sharp contrast, the complexity faced by companies selling to the BoP results from a sometimes bewildering array of factors: language, culture, family relations, religion, food, and many others, all of which may vary from block to block or valley to valley, and all of which need to be understood and dealt with if a company is going to win its prospective customers' loyalty.

Regardless of where in the pyramid their consumers reside, the challenge for decision-makers is heightened because many of the factors driving complexity are soft, value-laden behaviors. These human-centered factors make planning difficult because they are hard to count—and often hard to even *see*—until after a product or service has failed.

It is exactly this type of fuzzy problem that design processes are best able to solve, no matter whether the complexity arises from people having too much choice or too few opportunities. In this chapter, I explore the following two questions:

- Can the new design principles adopted to create breakthrough innovations at the top of the economic pyramid be used to create successful innovations at the base of that pyramid?
- Do these methods have to be adapted for use in the BoP?

My contention is that using design to increase a company's innovation success rate works equally well at both the upper and lower strata of the economic pyramid. In both cases, and for different reasons, companies are faced with less knowledge than they would like about the people who buy and use their offerings. This lack of knowledge causes the design and development problems to have unusual complexity—which emerging design methods can help mitigate and overcome. I argue that the design processes that help solve fuzzy problems are not the well-known techniques that determine the style of the product. Instead, they are from lesser-known aspects of design, which focus on what the offering *should* be.[3]

From an Economy of Scale to an Economy of Choice

During the twentieth century, one of the major successes in the developed world was the escape of large numbers of people from poverty and their elevation into the middle class. To a large extent, this was enabled by the phenomenal growth and efficiency of mass production. Factories like Henry Ford's River Rouge plant set the stage for a continuous growth in efficiency—a growth that within 50 years turned a society in which most people were in need to one in which most people were living a comfortable middle-class life with many choices.[4]

Through most of the twentieth century, companies competed based on an economy of scale paradigm. Those with the best and biggest factories tended to win. This argued against giving consumers real choices, as exemplified by the iconic quote of Henry Ford: "Any customer can have a car painted any color that he wants so long as it is black."[5]

As the ever-more productive factories enabled people to live abundant and comfortable lives, companies invented platform strategies, segmentation models, focus groups, product styling, and planned obsolescence to help stimulate demand. Taken to the extreme in industries like the American automobile industry, it led to artificial choices.[6] Trying to mitigate the "one size fits all" ethic of mass production, industry leaders turned to designers to change the appearance of their products and communications, even though the performance remained the same. For example, streamlining was applied so pervasively that trains, staplers, refrigerators and entries into almost every other category of product looked as if they were going 90 mph, even when the product was meant to sit on a table.

By the middle of the century in America, how to market and sell a product had become as important as how to make it. We witnessed the rise of respectability of management science and business schools. The model preparation for the future executive became an engineering degree followed by an MBA: a perfect base for learning how to analyze a situation and optimize toward an answer. The general belief about management was that companies should be run with a balance between manufacturing and emerging business principles in marketing, finance, and operations. Business planning and production technology were inextricably linked. Furthermore, the principles and methods of manufacturing and of business were continuously being formalized and quantified. This made perfect sense because the data being gathered—for example, the efficiency of an assembly line or the items purchased in a supermarket—were stable enough to be counted with growing precision. The result was reduced risk and a heightened ability to make plans.

But these techniques have their inherent limits. Today, because the major players in every industry have adopted Six Sigma, TQM, and other processes that have stripped every unnecessary expense from their production operations, there simply aren't many more costs to reduce. If all companies have efficient production systems, then executives have few options but to design higher-quality and more innovative offerings: products that fit the patterns of how people live.

Today's consumers are much more sophisticated. The abundance of choice created by domestic manufacturers, as well as the growing number of imported products and services, have expanded consumers' expectations of what is possible and desirable. Stores and media have served as a real-life classroom that has created a population of sophisticated super-consumers.

Innovation teams making consumer products and services have found the rules of the game have changed. They find themselves trying to decide which option, from among a large number of ideas that all seem equally good, will capture the hearts and minds of the users. People in the developed world are now living more varied, less predictable lives than did people during the age of mass production and mass media. The need for top-line growth is propelling executives to adopt new design strategies in order to create innovations that pleasantly surprise these consumers, not just with new styling, but with offerings really in touch with their lives, determined by employing deeper user insights.

Flexible production systems, global trade, and a host of other influences constantly increase the number and variety of services and products available to people. We have shifted from an *economy of scale* to an *economy of choice*, in which the dominant voice is not that of Henry Ford, but that of the anonymous consumer who says, "Give me what I want, in the style I like, via the channel I want—and I want it at a lower price than yesterday."

Corporate decision-makers have been dragged away from that relatively secure world in which competition was centered on optimizing known production processes and reducing known costs.[7] Now they live in a world in which technology and new business models enable them to make almost anything, yet this new overabundance of consumer choice creates new risks. As consumers live ever more varied lives, it becomes more and more difficult for producers to know what those consumers need and want.

This divergence between having *increased* knowledge of how to produce almost anything and *decreased* knowledge of the patterns of users' daily life is called the *innovation gap* (as depicted in Figure 6-1). It is one of the main reasons companies are increasingly adopting principles of design. Gaining an understanding of what people need enables executives to reframe the original problem in a way that is more likely to lead to their creating offerings that are both different and better than those currently available.[8]

It turns out that paying attention to users' desires is a different class of problem than those they faced before. Companies must now be able to gain an understanding of the user that complements their understanding of technology and business, creating *balanced innovation*. In the twentieth century, business leaders dealt with big problems, and they were able to get a clear view of what to do by using quantifiable phenomena like performance of factories, flow of supply chains, channels of distribution, demographics, and segmentation models. Information technology, automated factories, systems planning, financial modeling, and other innovations helped them determine the clearest course of action and make reliable plans. The future seemed sufficiently clear that executives were comfortable with making long-term plans, such as investments in factory efficiency that would take ten years to pay back.

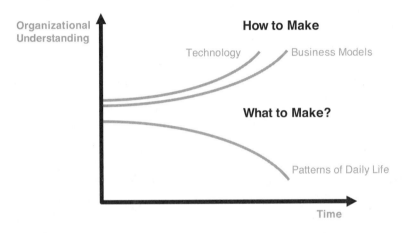

Figure 6-1   The innovation gap

Today, executives have to rapidly respond to the fast-changing lives of their consumers. They are faced with problems that have what is frequently called a "fuzzy front end." The factories that had been major assets in the economy of scale have become liabilities in the economy of choice. They had once been a company's main source of stability but now, with their lack of flexibility, are the main source of risk. As they outsource their manufacturing and supply chain to enable more flexible production, they are still faced with the prerequisite question: *What to produce?*

Addressing the BoP Innovation Gap

The same question faces corporate decision-makers when they consider entering emerging markets and particularly when they contemplate engaging with the BoP. Most executives realize that to grow they will eventually have to enter BoP markets, but they are not sanguine about the prospect. They suspect that it won't be easy to deal with unfamiliar distribution channels, partnerships, or low prices—or with consumers who are very different culturally from those they currently serve. They suspect, too, that offerings that have been designed for their domestic markets will not be desirable or affordable, even if they remove features and lower prices; others before them have tried that and failed. Unfortunately, *they don't know what to do instead.*

When they employ standard methods such as consumer segmentation and business models, the BoP markets seldom seem viable. Lacking a clear path toward the BoP consumer, companies conclude that the BoP is too difficult, so they either stay home—ignoring a future major growth market—or they focus their work in emerging markets on the smaller but more familiar growing middle and upper classes. As in the developed markets, they are faced with the vexing problem of not knowing what to make.

This state of uncertainty about what to make cannot be totally removed, but it can be mitigated with the help of design. At the top of the pyramid, the iPhone, like the iPod/iTunes combination before, transformed its category and is a compelling example of Apple's use of design to create breakthrough products. At the heart of Apple's design competency are 1) a stubborn refusal to accept the status quo of the industry, and 2) a drive to create great products that surpass what users ask for or can even imagine. Simply stated, Apple recognizes users' needs and desires not only before they are recognized by the competition, but before they are recognized by the users themselves.

Is this approach only relevant in developed economies? I argue, strongly, that it is *not*—and we don't have to go far to find the evidence. In the same industry, but at the low end of the market, the Nokia 1100 has steadfastly maintained its ranking as the best-selling consumer electronics product *of all time*, with more than 200 million units sold. This phone—also called the "ka-torchi" because it has a built-in flashlight—was designed on the assumption that BoP users (among others) would find its features particularly useful. It is rugged, simple, and dust-resistant and has a built-in flashlight that can be invaluable to those living in places with unreliable power supplies. The idea of the embedded flashlight came from Nokia designers watching people use the illuminated screen on their mobile phones when their electricity failed. Of course, a sturdy, reliable phone with an embedded flashlight also appeals to many people in the developed world, and that has helped contribute to the extraordinary success of the 1100.

In summary, the success of Apple in top of the pyramid markets and Nokia in base of the pyramid markets illustrates the power of developing user insights that help reframe problems as a way to create offerings that go beyond what people request or expect. How can this become the norm, and what does it have to do with design?

From "What Should It Look Like?" to "What Should It Be?"

Sometimes the word "design" conjures up images of a mysterious, genius-driven, black-box process. In this chapter, I argue that such is *not* the case. While it may be helpful to have a creative genius close at hand, a design process that *reframes the problem* is actually a straightforward and replicable activity. Furthermore, because of design's ability to cope with ambiguous problems—indeed, often using ambiguity as an aid to creativity—design is particularly well-suited for business problems that do not have clear answers or don't lend themselves to standard methods based on optimization.

Teams practicing traditional design and development processes accept a problem as it is given, conduct research to determine what customers say they like and dislike, and then choose a direction and work toward an optimal solution. Optimizing current knowledge is key. In this "direct design" approach, teams move directly from analyzing the current reality to creating a predictable solution (see Figure 6-2).

Direct design works well for creating incremental changes in known markets. These changes often focus on improvements of usability and appearance. It is less effective, however, as uncertainty increases—for example, when creating a new offering for known markets or even more difficult, when developing a new offering for unfamiliar markets.

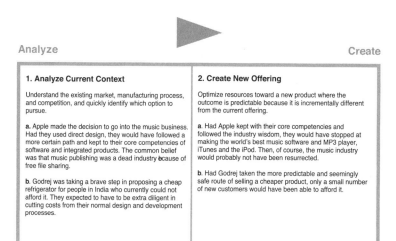

Analyze   Create

1. Analyze Current Context	2. Create New Offering
Understand the existing market, manufacturing process, and competition, and quickly identify which option to pursue.	Optimize resources toward a new product where the outcome is predictable because it is incrementally different from the current offering.
a. Apple made the decision to go into the music business. Had they used direct design, they would have followed a more certain path and kept to their core competencies of software and integrated products. The common belief was that music publishing was a dead industry because of free file sharing.	**a.** Had Apple kept with their core competencies and followed the industry wisdom, they would have stopped at making the world's best music software and MP3 player, iTunes and the iPod. Then, of course, the music industry would probably not have been resurrected.
b. Godrej was taking a brave step in proposing a cheap refrigerator for people in India who currently could not afford it. They expected to have to be extra diligent in cutting costs from their normal design and development processes.	**b.** Had Godrej taken the more predictable and seemingly safe route of selling a cheaper product, only a small number of new customers would have been able to afford it.

Figure 6-2   Direct design

The set of design methods needed to cope with the uncertainty inherent in the economy of choice is very different from methods focusing on styling relevant to the stability and predictability in the economy of scale. (Of course, it is a given that a company's products still need to "look good," but now this is often achieved as a free service in China done by the contract manufacturer.) To answer the question "What should we make?" companies need to take two more steps. The first is to incorporate user understanding as part of balanced innovation. Looking at what people actually do, rather than what they *think* they do, proves to be very valuable, especially when users have unprecedented choice.

The second step is to look at the problem from the point of view of *what the users are trying to achieve*, rather than what products and services they currently use. The team needs to define the problem at a higher, more abstract level that is determined by the activities and related values that surround the product. Adding the dimension of abstraction to the design and development process is necessary if a company is going to create innovations that make a difference to the users. It changes the process from optimizing toward a predictable solution to deciding what should be made. It helps a company cope with the complexity of creating new offerings for changing markets, and it is at the core of a set of frameworks and methods called strategic design.

Strategic design has four general stages.[9,10]

- Understanding current context
- Reframing the problem
- Prototyping options
- Developing a roadmap stating the ultimate goal and where to start

Strategic design seeks *a broader context* than is normally looked at in the standard design and development process, often looking at factors missed by the normal company view. In particular, a team using strategic design will look at the users' activities and desires, not just the direct use of a product, and take the problem to a level of abstraction that is more open to innovation.

For example, if they were planning laundry appliances, they would look at the activity of "taking care of clothes," not just the use of the machine they sell. If planning a new snack food, they would look at "family gathering" or "putting on a party," not just the packaged snacks. If planning new housing for the urban BoP, they would look at the activity of "running a business," not just the operation of the home. After all, the one-room dwelling of a person living in Daravi (the slum in Mumbai reputed to be Asia's largest) might be a bedroom at night, a kitchen before each meal, and during other daylight hours a tiny factory for whatever products the family is selling. In all of these cases, the strategic design process reframes the problem at a higher level of abstraction by defining the problem as the activity the user cares about rather than by the product the company sells. Of course, this requires that the team gain a deeper understanding of what users really care about, which helps the company create products that exceed what the users expect.

Using user insights to create a more abstract view of the problem frequently leads to innovations that go beyond product, sometimes suggesting modifications to the business model or even a whole new business. The results often surprise the team (and the competition) and usually create a better total user experience. For example, had Apple used the direct-design approach, they might well have stopped at developing the world's best MP3 player and associated easy-to-use software. Instead, they reframed the problem, going beyond the standard industry framework that valued low cost and more features, and created not just a great product but also services, a phenomenal retail presence, and a new business model. They analyzed the whole user experience around music, including how users bought it, shared it, and listened to it, as well as how the industry devolved to the point where the publishers were suing their customers. Their reframed problem, therefore, was not about making a better MP3 player; it was far more expansive and abstract than that. The problem now was *"how to better enjoy music."* By abstracting the problem, the company freed itself to explore multiple options that would consider consumers as people with real-life needs, thus enabling Apple to transform the music industry. Abstraction, or finding the essential nature of an offering, is key to design's contribution to successful innovation. At its core, abstraction is about unbundling an existing product from the essential activities and goals users are trying to accomplish. This enables teams to explore more ways of achieving what users really care about without being burdened by the existing orthodoxies surrounding a specific existing product.

The *reframed problem* describes what users really need and want, which provides a phenomenally rich base for creating options that reflect balanced innovation. Options are descriptions of what *might be created*, described in the forms of a *prototype* of innovations that may improve users' experience, a simple business model or value web, and a statement identifying technological requirements or challenges. The goal in this stage is to create as many viable options as possible and then choose one or more for more detailed work, including a sense of the ultimate goal and the first steps (see Figure 6-3).

At this point, the selected options still need more work before going into development. In addition to adding details to each of the three dimensions of balanced innovation, a *roadmap* is created, indicating the general set of offerings to create the desired user experience, as well as a proposal for a first step that is easily enacted and yet is grounded in users' desires and patterns of daily life. This "grounding" reduces risk by ensuring the company goes far enough to be relevant to the users' desires even when they do not ask for them. The small, fast start reduces risk by ensuring the company does not excessively stretch its operational ability or brand authority. The mantra is "think big, start small, move fast."

Abstract

2. Reframe

User insight enables the redefinition of the problem to one that is based upon the user's activities instead of the company's product. This more abstract view enables a broader exploration of options.

a. Apple set the goal to help people enjoy recorded music again. The music industry thought the opportunity was to stop music sharing and get people to pay.

b. Godrej partnered with their customers to grow the local economy and help people afford refrigerators. The industry thought that 80% of Indians could not afford a refrigerator.

3. Create Options

Options are based on the reframed project statement and are prototypes of innovations and related business models.

a. Apple explored creating a repair shop, a shop-in-shops in mass retailers, and a variety of models for pricing and selling music.

b. Godrej prototyped with the users, explored public buses as a delivery channel, and considered different business relationships with the local women.

Analyze   Create

1. Context

Understanding the opportunity with a balanced viewpoint of technology, business, and user desires sets the stage for innovations that are grounded in the lives of users.

a. Apple noticed MP3 players were complicated, music-sharing software was enabling piracy, music retail was miserable, and everyone was losing money.

b. Godrej noticed an opportunity for selling cheap refrigerators to the poor.

4. Road Map

It is useful to clearly identify the desired user experience and then create a fast, low-risk first step and a path that maintains the integrity of the final solution.

a. Apple started with iTunes as a modest app on a Macintosh and then followed with the iPod, iTunes that sold music by the song, their own retail channel, and services like the Genius Bar. iTunes eventually became a platform for the iPhone and iPad.

b. Godrej launched a less expensive, more profitable product than planned. They created the 3-L model, focusing on improving living standards, lifestyle, and livelihoods. This established a new way of working that can be extended to other communities.

Real

Figure 6-3   Strategic design

How Does Strategic Design Actually Work in the BoP?

How do these advanced approaches to design relate to design for the BoP—the socio-economic segment that is the focus of this book?

It turns out that corporate design and development teams find that the daily life of the BoP is as complex and as difficult to understand as daily life in developed economies. Most often, their confusion about the BoP market does not arise out of an abundance of choice among users, but rather out of two other factors. First is the variability, often approaching chaos, caused by the demands and limits of being poor: If you are an independent tradesman looking for small jobs each day and cannot afford a mobile phone, you have to walk home after each job to get the message of where you will work next. Or if you can't earn enough to get a bank account, you can't get a loan, and therefore you live in a cash-only situation, with all the attendant challenges. And second, the extremely fine-grained differences in culture and language create many different markets that seem too small to serve using standard business models. Even in big cities like Mumbai, the slums are segregated into groups that share the same home village.

Does this variegated landscape argue against strategic design and the creation of innovation in BoP markets? On the contrary: I argue that just as in the developed economies, companies wanting to create offerings for the BoP can use this process to help them create products, information, services, and new business models. While the general process is as useful to cope with the complexities of the BoP as it is when applied to developed markets, the details of this approach may need to be modified due to constrained budgets and the logistic difficulties you often experiences in BoP markets.

To underscore the point, let's look at an example of the four-part strategic design process—understanding current context, reframing the problem, prototyping options, and developing a roadmap—being used with minor adaptations for the BoP context.

A Case in Point

A project with the Institute of Design (ID), a graduate school within the Illinois Institute of Technology, provides our example. ID was approached by Sam Pitroda, a U.S. telecom entrepreneur and an advisor to several prime ministers in India regarding information technology and communication. Pitroda had seen ID apply the four-part design process in developed economies, was impressed by the results, and asked me to lead a team to address the problem of housing in urban slums in India.[11]

Although there was no current client ready to initiate the project, Pitroda was confident that a vision for new housing would attract the right supporters, ranging from government agencies to commercial companies. Anyone else suggesting such a project most likely would be met with skepticism, but Pitroda knew how to accomplish the seemingly impossible. Prime Minister Rajiv Gandhi had asked him to create India's first national telephone system. This involved far more than simply building switches that could stand up to heat and dust—no small feat, in itself. The real innovation came when they realized they would need telephone booths throughout the country in order to serve the poor villages and slums, but there was no existing model for how to maintain a vast facility like this without creating a huge labor force and bureaucracy. Because that expense was impossible, Sam turned each booth into a small business, where someone living close to the booth could sell phone calls and ensure the booth was maintained.

Context

Anjali Kelkar, then a recent graduate, and Alexis Kinnebrew, a student at the time, joined as team members, and we set about to see if we could apply the strategic design process for BoP communities in India. We began by fully accepting the problem as originally framed by Sam: "If we could design a standardized brick, slum dwellers could create stronger, less dusty, higher-quality homes." The brick could have a way to capture and store fresh rainwater, as well as a surface that would survive the windy dry season, during which conventional mud bricks erode heavily, causing dust to invade eyes and lungs.

Adopting the balanced innovation model and the strategic design process, we began the project. To establish the current context, we conducted a series of interviews to gather high-level information about relevant technologies and business models. We learned about ash brick and other techniques around the world and also about the building materials indigenous to the Mumbai region. We learned about family structure and income and the migration patterns to the cities from the villages. We read about the stratospheric land prices in Mumbai's slums. We learned about the informal cash economy and the related black market and how this is a drag on the thousands of entrepreneurs who live there. Our questions covered most of the issues around housing, and confirmed the assumptions that 1) better homes would make significant improvements in people's lives, and 2) better construction materials and processes were a requirement for building the homes.

Reframe

Secondary research was important, but it could not provide us with sufficiently detailed information about daily life in Daravi and the other BoP communities in Mumbai. To obtain this more granular information, we deployed rapid ethnography processes that have become common in strategic design. Using *self-documentary camera studies*, we gathered many hundreds of photographs showing daily life in BoP communities in Mumbai.

This is where the process was modified for the BoP context and, in turn, where the difficulties of working in BoP markets caused us to modify the methods for more efficient use in the developed economies. The major modification was separating the data gathering in the field from the data analysis at the Institute of Design. Normally, all of this work is performed by the same people, but separating it can reduce the cost so much that it can make the difference between conducting or not conducting observational research. To do this, we had to recruit different people and formalize the way field notes were taken. Such a formalized approach to field notes turned out to be useful for increasing the rigor and speed of the research and has implications for projects in the developed world.

For this project, we recruited social workers and schoolteachers in Mumbai as our local team members. Their job was to give instructions to the people doing the self-documentaries and to conduct the subsequent interviews. Because they were untrained in giving instructions and conducting interviews, and also because they would be on their own due to budget constraints that kept most of the team in Chicago, we had to use a very prescriptive protocol. We chose to use the "POEMS" framework and structured interview books to gather data of the same type and detail.

"POEMS" stands for people, objects, environments, messages, and services. Unlike anthropological frameworks that look at family structure, religion, income, and other demographic factors, POEMS identifies the people to be served and the things designers can change to make their lives better. The anthropological frameworks are for building a science of culture. The categories within POEMS, by contrast, are for designing artifacts and services that will make daily life better.

The combination of the photographs, the POEMS framework, and the interview books gave us a view into people's lives in a way that we could compare aspects of family life without our presence influencing subjects' answers and without our needing a large budget. The photographs and resulting stories told to the interviewers helped us "see" a user's life and break down any assumptions we might have had about their lives as a whole. The images helped us refine our interview questionnaires.

The photos from the camera studies had a secondary use as an icebreaker for researchers who were entering people's homes as strangers. Many of our subjects had never met anyone from outside of their local culture, so they tended to be shy or suspicious when interacting with our interviewers. Talking about their daily lives using photos they had taken themselves quickly created an empathic context.

The value of using local workers, even when untrained, is that they are more available and are more familiar with the people being interviewed than skilled foreign researchers would be. Local people know their way around, understand the cultural mores, and know how to behave appropriately. Because they don't see the poor as "exotic," they help maintain the integrity and objectivity of the data-collection process.

We shared the fruits of our investigation with a varied group of external experts in a series of *rapid-immersion workshops*.[12] The experts came from a variety of backgrounds, including entrepreneurs running an ash brick factory in Africa, researchers investigating retail distribution channels in rural India, marketing scholars running a non-governmental organization (NGO) for women's employment in Daravi, IT entrepreneurs, politicians, and producers of films in Bollywood. The workshops grounded them in our user observations, which enabled them to offer particular relevant yet unusual ideas.

The photographs showed a variety of urban slums, all of which were suffering similar situations such as dilapidated housing, lack of basic infrastructure, a dearth of sewage or drainage systems, and insufficient access to water. Even more revealing than what was visible were the stories that were *behind* the photographs taken in those homes and neighborhoods. We saw and heard about the businesses that exist in almost every tiny dwelling and learned about the multiple uses the one-room homes would support every day. We were told about the new high-rises in their neighborhoods that were empty because they didn't accommodate small businesses, given the nature of the interaction with suppliers and customers required small business owners to be on the street. We discovered patterns that we would not have known to look for in a traditional research project.

The rich data and the insights from the workshops helped us develop the central reframe: While all of what we learned from the research in the context phase supported the need for new homes, and our field work confirmed that the residents of the slum neighborhoods would jump at the opportunity to improve their housing, that was seldom their most urgent need. What they *really* needed was more disposable income, so they could purchase whatever would be of greatest benefit to them at any given point in time. As a result, the project was reframed, shifting from "new bricks for better homes" to "creating higher-value, more profitable jobs."

This may seem like an obvious answer. I would argue, though, that the initial framing "better bricks for better houses" was equally clear—so much so that it seemed obvious that our challenge was to find the optimal way of getting to this solution that had been confirmed by all the research to refine the context. Offerings created by the strategic design process often seem obvious because they are based on the lives of the users. This is true regardless of the economic context of the users. For example, Apple's music business seems like an obvious venture in retrospect. But the music publishers did not see it, and neither did the rest of us. Some answers are obvious only *after* they are stated.

Options

The seven options that grew out of the reframed problem focused on increasing their income, saving them time, and increasing their security. Three examples follow.

One option was a water delivery system whereby canisters could be off-loaded from a large truck and wheeled on carts through the narrow streets to get the water to the users. This could replace the current huge tank on the truck that remained parked outside of the small streets, requiring women to spend hours walking to the truck and carrying water home. The lost value caused by hundreds of neighborhood women walking for water and the cost of the large truck being parked for most of the day while thousands of buckets got filled, could more than cover the cost of an efficient cart system that could employ several drivers.

A second option was the creation of a guild system that would enable day laborers to find work and pool money to create bank accounts. Combined with a mobile payment system, this could reduce their reliance on cash. (A cash economy entails great risk because it encourages theft and, lacking transparency, enables black markets and corruption.)

A third option, related to the guild, was an information exchange for BoP entrepreneurs to share best practices. There is currently no way for people running a small business to learn from experts outside of their local communities—a resource that their entrepreneurial counterparts in the developed world take for granted.

Because this project was initiated by Sam Pitroda as an exploration that would serve as example for other projects by other people, we paid particular attention to which of these three initiatives we would try to develop. Our first choice was the information exchange for BoP entrepreneurs, mainly because it is not capital-intensive and has potential for viral growth. As currently planned, it uses multiple forms of communication, including video stories, local exhibits, village meetings, and other inexpensive low-technology media. At the time of this writing, a pilot for capturing video stories is being conducted with an NGO in Afghanistan that is helping highly skilled carpet weavers rebuild their supply chain and build a new market in the

West. For this to grow, it will likely need other options to be acted upon, such as guilds and the related cashless payment system.

Back to the Chotukool

Let's now return to the Chotukool refrigerator, a useful example of a BoP-based innovation that used the principles of strategic design. The initial goal of the Godrej team was to create a small box cooler that could meet the daily cool-storage and freezing needs of a large population that was, and is, a largely non-consuming segment. The penetration of refrigerators as a category in India is less than 18 percent, so the team's opening questions were, *Why are they not buying? What would fulfill their unmet needs, especially for something they did not expect to buy?*

Price was obviously one issue—perhaps *the* issue. Manufacturer Godrej & Boyce thought it could make cheaper metal boxes, perhaps with a cheaper compressor, and sell them through the direct door-to-door channel that they use very successfully for their other consumer products. They had an ambitious target price range of Rs 2500–Rs 4950 (about $50–$100) in contrast to the typical mainstream low-end refrigerator that costs around Rs 7000. They believed it would be a challenge to meet the normal margins for the global refrigerator business of 4 or 5 percent.

Their first step was to understand the nonusers in the BoP, especially those consumers who would be able to afford a refrigerator if it were a little cheaper. The villagers relayed that the proposed product was still too expensive and that they didn't need to freeze anything.

The team was surprised and recognized they needed to *reframe* the way they tried to gain insights. They decided to get much closer to the villagers and find out how they lived and what surrounded them in daily life. Rather than use self-documentary studies, their ethnographic process involved direct observation. The team spent days with villagers, learning about their food habits and observing the patterns whereby they purchased vegetables. They saw how villagers adjusted their lives to sleeping, eating, and working in a small dwelling. The team came to understand the homemaker in base of the pyramid communities as an astute manager of her household:

Every day she managed her home, her children, and their education while having to reconfigure the kitchen corner into living room and bedroom space on a rolling basis.

Unlike the initial interviews, these close observations and glimpses of villagers' lives provided surprising insights into what their latent needs might be. For example:

- BOP consumers require only limited storage. They buy small quantities to meet their daily needs and only have limited money to spend on more. They do not need small deep freezers for frozen food.

- At the same time, they pay a penalty for buying only a small quantity at a time. Particularly, they would love to purchase low-priced vegetables on sale from the vendor at the end of the day, but they can't because they don't have a cool-storage space to preserve tomatoes and leafy vegetables.

- A reduction of only 20 to 30 degrees from the ambient temperature would suffice to prolong the life of vegetables for a few days.

- BoP homemakers want to increase their productivity, thereby improving their daily lives. If some ingredients could be available readily when it was time to cook, there would be fewer last-minute marketing chores, leaving more time for productive work.

- BoP families have high aspirations for their children. They want to provide them with more "creature comforts"—for example, cool drinks—whenever they can. More generally, they place a high value on being able to provide cool drinks. Anyone can serve hot tea, but only the "wealthy" can serve "fridge cool" drinks.

- Their houses are small. They want things that have a small footprint and ease of mobility. Their furniture—even their kitchen gadgets—get shuffled around at the end of the day as they convert the floor they were using for leisure into a bed for sleeping.

- They live in rented premises and may need to be mobile. They are a migrant population, kept mobile by wage-earning opportunities far from home or, at times, the inability to pay rent.

It was out of these kinds of insights that the reframed concept of Chotukool was born. The traditional image of the cheap metal box refrigerator had disappeared. G&B was beginning to think of Chotukool as a solid-state, mobile, top-opening cooling device. Instead of a cheap box that cooled and froze food, they began imagining in the options phase a good-looking, convenient, easily serviceable, fully plastic-bodied product. They added a moveable shelf that enabled better storage when used in the home and bulk storage for semi-commercial usage.

Meanwhile, they realized that such a distinctly different product category would need a distinctive value delivery. They understood that they would have to sell through demonstration, rather than text and images. Product and benefits had to be seen to be understood.

They came to the realization that the best conversations about the unusual benefits of the product would take place within the community with a neighbor explaining the product. This notion of a new promotional channel triggered new kinds of social-sector thinking, and they began to explore models of alternate channels for promoting, selling, and delivering the product, in large part by working with the very same women who previously had been regarded as potential customers. In other words, *consumers were beginning to be considered partners* in the venture.

The team, drawing on deep user insights as well as women partners, created a system that comprised a product, services, and business model that was dramatically reframed from what they had first imagined. Almost all elements of the system were transformed by user research. Now the main driver of the system was a far deeper understanding of the desired user experience—and, of course, the willingness to explore options once it became clear that the original assumptions were simply wrong. They now had a new approach to the product, associated services, related business model, localization, and training and development of staff.

The Chotukool case is interesting for many reasons, not the least of which is that the first move required a holistic and systemic set of offerings instead of a single product or service. The "3-L" vision (again, improving the living standard, lifestyle, and livelihood) of the consumer on a large scale became a compelling driver and motivator.

To fulfill this vision for any group of people, they could not start with a single part; rather, they would have to launch with a complete system. What kept this from being a first step that was too large and risk-laden was the scalable nature of the promotion and distribution innovations. They could start with the village where they were working and have the subsequent stages be developed region by region.

Ultimately, G&B introduced the product through a special "village fair" called Sakhi Mela. This was a congregation of six hundred women from villages around a small town in Maharashtra, organized by Swayam Shikshan Prayog (SSP), an NGO that agreed to serve as Godrej's distribution partner. Some of these women were potential consumers, and some were potential intermediaries looking for earning opportunities by canvassing for Chotukool.

Sakhi Mela was a platform for co-creation. The women at the gathering gave feedback on the product. They offered insights on colors, price points, and price/value perception and helped define the value proposition that would appeal to their peers. They worked with company executives to evolve the business model—and to define what share of the additional value created they could receive.[13] Interestingly, though, this was not competitive bargaining. It was more of a consensus that evolved, keeping the three stakeholders—end consumers, intermediary entrepreneurs, and manufacturing company—in mind.

Product

As noted, the original idea of an inexpensive basic box was gone. While still small and engineered to work in a hot dusty climate, almost everything else had changed. It opened on the top instead of the front. Instead of using a compressor, it used a solid-state induction plate. Even though it would be priced at Rs 3500—much lower than planned—it had to look much better than originally imagined. It had to be lightweight, mobile, and stand up to major voltage fluctuation (voltage varies significantly in India). Like all good design, the ultimate construction of the product seemed obvious in retrospect, but only through reframing followed by extensive exploration and prototyping did the final design emerge.

Services

Services became critical and drove choices that created the concept of a replaceable lid. The entire cooling engine was designed in one part of the lid. This could be taken off and replaced in case of malfunction due to weather extremes, quality of electrical grid power, or usage conditions, including misuse. The final design made it possible for basic service to be conducted by unskilled women entrepreneurs.

Business Model and Operations

The business model innovations focused on cocreation with a rural NGO and distribution through an entrepreneurial network. The innovations that got money into the hands of these women began improving the local economy. It also helped bring down the cost of post-manufacturing operations in service delivery, logistics, sales, distribution, and marketing. This was a huge departure from the early idea of direct selling through door-to-door canvassing, which had been used in urban markets to promote usage of lesser-known, lower-penetration appliances like vacuum cleaners and water purifiers in their early stages of evolution.

Localization

Promotion and communications were also cocreated and continue to evolve locally. In a vast country with cultural diversity and unique and rich local traditions, one offering would never fit all. The Chotukool took advantage of this diversity to create unique messages. Looking forward, the company plans to leverage this heterogeneous, amorphous market through the emergent process of local cocreation. When Chotukool was conceived, there were somewhat grandiose ideas about nationwide mass media campaigns following in the wake of glamorous launch events. Now the plan is to create variety—through operating processes and business models and, to a lesser extent, through product modifications—that will meet the different needs of the various groups within the 80 percent of the population who do not currently have refrigeration.

Training and Development of Staff

The preparation of the new entrepreneurs for running the delivery channel was driven by local trainers who brought relevant language, culture, and acceptable social norms. The mass training that was originally planned had to be abandoned, and the core ideas for promotion and distribution were transformed; henceforth, they would focus on members of the local NGO.

As of this writing, the Chotukool business is on a path to grow and improve the lives of BoP families. If this indeed happens, it is likely to prove a very positive outcome both for the consumers and for the company.

Transformation

Chotukool turned out to be more than a project. It helped the leadership of G&B connect the often unrelated goals corporate competitiveness and social development. Navroze Godrej, a company director and a leader of the team that developed the new appliance, described it this way

> For us, it was a humbling moment that reassured us that we were on the right track. We were a part of something that would improve people's lives. We were now left with only one option—to stand by our beliefs, constantly searching for new and different ways of doing things and creating more and better products and businesses for these people, because if involving someone in the distribution of a product can give that person respect for the first time, then how could we not help bring to life a hundred such ideas and help the poorest people?[14]

The team discovered that by being "grounded in the daily life" of the villagers, they could improve people's lives, build a market that previously did not exist, and be more profitable than expected. They created a system of offerings that was celebrated by the users, a business model and delivery processes that created a new stream of income for their customers, and the opportunity to use a technology that was less expensive (and more locally appropriate) than the one they originally planned.

What larger lessons can be learned from Chotukool, Ka-torchi, Nokia Money, the Institute of Design's "from bricks to business" project, and even Sam Pitroda's phone system? The commonalities include the central fact that, as is the case in the developed economies, grounding problems in the patterns of users' daily life— patterns that are often unspoken and need to be discovered—can lead to unusual solutions that fit how people live.[15] Many innovations would be killed if they were judged by normal business criteria early in their development; for example, most of the items discussed in this chapter, including Apple's music business, did not have markets to analyze.

Balanced innovation and the four-part structure of strategic design are especially useful when a company needs to solve problems that are unclear or fuzzy due to the ambiguity and complexity inherent in daily life.

As companies in the developed world transition from the relatively predictable nature of an economy of scale into the apparent chaos of the economy of choice, they find they are turning to design to reframe business opportunities and create a variety of options. These same methods can help them design viable innovations for the complex and confusing world found in base of the pyramid markets.

Notes

[1] See footage of the iPhone launch in White Plains, New York, at http://vimeo.com/1322131.

[2] Unless otherwise noted, the author draws in this chapter from his on-the-ground experience including interviewing Jamshyd Godrej, Navrose Godrej and G.S. Sanderama at Godrej & Boyce. I am also grateful to Anjali Kelkar for contributions to this chapter.

[3] Roger Martin has written extensively about abductive logic or the "logic of the possible." For details see Roger Martin, "Design thinking: achieving insights via the knowledge funnel," *Strategy & Leadership*, Vol. 38 #2, pp. 37-41.

[4] Indeed, Barry Schwartz, in his remarkable book *Paradox of Choice*, explains how those at the top of the pyramid are confused and sometimes angered by the number of choices they face.

[5] From Ford's *My Life and Work*, Kessinger Publishing (January 2003): 71-72.

[6] Remember, for example, the Chrysler K cars and similar offerings from other car companies that differed only in terms of minor style changes.

[7] For a current overview of how executives view complexity, see *Capitalizing from Complexity: Insights from the Global CEO Study* published by IBM in 2010 only in terms of minor style changes.

[8] For more details on innovation and user insight, see Vijay Kumar and Patrick Whitney (2007), "Daily life, not markets: customer-centered design," *Journal of Business Strategy* 28(4): 46–58.

[9] The four-part strategic design model has several precursors. I build directly on the work of Chares Owen and Vijay Kumar. See: Owen, Charles, "Structured design planning. Reforming the development process." Conference Board, Conference on User-Centered Design. Session K Paper, Chicago: The Conference Board, June 9–10, 1994.

[10] For more about the design process and strategy, see Kumar, Vijay (2009). "A process for practicing design innovation," *The Journal of Business Strategy* 30(2/3): 91–99.

[11] For more on user research and the BoP see Whitney, Patrick and Anjali Kelkar, Fall 2004. "Designing for the base of the pyramid," *Design Management Journal*: 41–47.

[12] Kelkar, Anjali, "A quick dip at the iceberg's tip"–Rapid Immersion Approaches to Understanding Emerging Markets Book Series Lecture Notes in Computer Science (Berlin-Heidelberg: Springer), 103–108.

[13] See the chapter by Ted London in this book for more on approaches to crafting solutions with the base of the pyramid.

[14] Personal correspondence from Navrose Godreg to me.

[15] See, for example, the distinction that Erik Simanis makes in his chapter in this book between market entry and market creation.

7

BoP Venture Formation for Scale

by Allen Hammond, Ashoka

Social enterprises do good works. But unless they achieve a significant scale, they aren't in a position to serve millions of BoP customers or to help reshape economies. Author Allen Hammond argues for a combination of both bottom-up and top-down enterprise formation to better reach and serve BoP markets, and explains how that productive mix can be accomplished. Additionally, he suggests, BoP entrepreneurs can also build business ecosystems (rather than stand-alone ventures) to support scale. Hammond explains how "hybrid" organizations can serve that purpose— and provides insights from a real-world example.

There are many social enterprises focused on alleviating some aspect of poverty, and more are formed every month. But relatively few of these BoP ventures reach scale—at least, a scale significant enough to have an impact measured in millions of customers or to shape markets nationally or globally.

We need to ask ourselves why this is so.

One answer, frequently heard, is "lack of capital." But that is clearly less true now than a decade ago: There are a growing number of social investment funds, and even venture capital groups, that often find themselves chasing the same deals. Social-impact investing and doing BoP deals have become fashionable, and money has followed fashion.

Nor is there is a shortage of would-be social entrepreneurs. For better or worse, aspirants abound in the BoP space. Today, it sometimes seems that every other MBA candidate has a not-so-secret longing to start a social enterprise. More compellingly, the trickle of social entrepreneurs from emerging markets—often people who know the BoP firsthand—has become a flood. Ashoka counts more than 3,000 social entrepreneurs from more than 60 countries among its Fellows.[1]

Perhaps all the good ideas are taken? Hardly! Those who monitor and mentor social enterprises know that there is no lack of energy and imagination in the field. Indeed, as the field of social enterprise expands, creativity and potentially pattern-changing ideas seem to be on the increase. As argued elsewhere in this book, the BoP may become an essential source of innovation for the world as a whole, driven in significant part by social entrepreneurs.[2]

I believe that the failure to achieve scale, in all too many social ventures, stems from one of several structural flaws—one or more faulty genes embedded at "birth," if you will. One such flaw is a purely top-down approach to BoP enterprises. The failure rate of well-meaning entrepreneurs (and celebrities) from wealthy countries who try to start an enterprise top-down—working to solve a social problem on the ground in unfamiliar turf without deep local connections, be it an urban slum in the rich world or a rural village in the developing world—is very high. The record of large corporations that have attempted top-down BoP business formation is somewhat better, but even with all their resources, many multinationals and large national companies find the going difficult. As C.K. Prahalad has argued, investment capacity is not as important as the ability to collaborate, to build a new ecosystem, and to develop fundamentally different business models.[3] Thus, successful BoP enterprises— especially those organized by local entrepreneurs—are mostly built bottom-up.

But bottom-up venture creation has its own limitations. The simplistic way to explain this limitation is to say that these ventures very frequently do not plan adequately for scale. Perhaps a better way to express the same thought is to say that it's extremely difficult, in a purely bottom-up BoP business, to solve all the problems that must be addressed in order to reach significant scale.

Challenges on Three Levels

What are these challenges? There are at least three broad categories that are often encountered by bottom-up social entrepreneurs. My colleagues at Santa Clara University's Global Social Benefit Incubator (GSBI), who mentor some 18 social entrepreneurs each year in an intensive two-week process, see a lot of challenges that stem from lack of knowledge of the basic tools of business.[4] Social entrepreneurs from the BoP commonly do not have an MBA and may have only limited formal business experience. All too often, they are unfamiliar with balance sheets, income statements, or the basics of a business plan. They have little experience with the basic techniques of raising investment funds—from elevator pitches to more formal "asks"—or they don't understand the need to build teams with adequate depth and expertise to manage rapid growth. Fortunately, these things can be taught. Formal education is one approach; in many cases, mentoring works wonders in relatively short order.

Far more difficult are the kinds of local, microlevel challenges— creating markets where there are none, engaging a community already fractured along caste or tribal lines, nontraditional approaches to marketing, building bridges to governments and other stakeholders that often seem distant and unreachable, managing distribution chains in the face of unreliable transport and power, and so on—for which there are no textbook solutions. Sometimes the challenge stems from launching the enterprise in an unusually challenging geography, whether due to missing infrastructure, unsupportive or corrupt government, or a disaster-prone climate. I mentioned the market-creation challenge in the list just given.[5] To cite just one example, a recent informal survey of half a dozen community-scale water treatment enterprises in rural India found that most of the ventures (both for-profit and nonprofit entities) were able to sign up only about 25 to 30 percent of the households in a village as customers and were consequently unprofitable or only marginally profitable.[6] When Procter & Gamble tried to market its PUR water filters in rural India, it reportedly didn't do much better.[7]

A couple of the water enterprises, however, *have* done well— averaging close to 60 percent household penetration. Partly in consequence, they are not only generating a surplus, but scaling rapidly.

The crucial difference in one of the water enterprises that has been independently studied[8] was an innovative and quite systematic social marketing campaign that raised awareness of the health problems of using dirty drinking water. Through consciousness-raising, it changed behaviors, convincing people to pay for treated water by identifying clean water—and by extension, the facility that produces it—with modern, urban-quality services. This enterprise spent more on its facility than did its competitors: a counterintuitive strategy that seems to be paying off. Another approach, proven effective in a variety of contexts, is to generate "pull" through cocreation of the market with the local community.[9]

The third set of challenges occurs at the macro or global level and are typically encountered after a social enterprise has been launched and as it attempts to scale up. How is a social entrepreneur from a developing country to identify and recruit strategic partners globally; to identify, evaluate, and acquire best-in-class technology for multiple parts of his or her business; or to develop the contacts and access to raise capital globally from commercial investors, social and philanthropic funds, development agencies, and even foreign angel investors? Yes, a few social entrepreneurs do manage all this, but they are among the extraordinary few.

How can we encourage venture creation in a way that is more likely to achieve scale? In this chapter, I discuss two potential approaches (see the later sidebar "Two Models: The Key Attributes"). The first is to construct ventures whose structure is both local *and* global or both bottom-up and top-down—to build in the "genes for scale" at the formation of the enterprise. Arguably, this is what multinational corporations entering the BoP have attempted, and failures here tend to stem from not being sufficiently local or bottom-up, not partnering widely enough to build a diverse ecosystem or not escaping the suffocating embrace of corporate quarterly reporting metrics or capital-allocation hurdles.

For many BoP entrepreneurs, however, the failure results more from the lack of a global or top-down component to their planning. To use the analogy suggested earlier, scalable ventures need to build into their genetic code both local and global DNA (financial structure, management capacity and experience, investor base, and so on).

That gives the ventures a far greater chance of solving the inevitable challenges and thus reaching scale.

The second and related approach to venture creation for scale is to build an entire ecosystem to support scale, rather than just a stand-alone venture. In effect, social enterprises that can borrow ideas, find support, and thus benefit from the far greater genetic diversity of an entire ecosystem—of partners, stakeholders, advisors, and cocreators—have a far better chance at getting to scale. Examples of this approach include partnering broadly to gain access to new ways of thinking about the problem/opportunity and new capabilities; spending time and capital on aspects of the ecosystem outside the traditional boundaries of a firm; engaging many stakeholders in the social mission to which the venture is targeted; finding strategic partners for the venture whose interest is both in the social goal as well as in the commercial relationship; and cocreating solutions with potential beneficiaries.

In effect, this strategy is about *expanding the scope of the venture creation activity* beyond traditional definitions that focus tightly on the business itself in order to gain allies, supporters, innovations, and new solution modes and thus better cope with the difficulties of BoP venture creation. This strategy is distinct from a strategy that focuses on building a local-global structure for the firm itself, but it can be complementary. In other words, one can imagine both local and global partnerships within an ecosystem to support local and global aspects of the venture.

One example of an ecosystem strategy is to consciously build hybrid organizations—genuine partnerships—between businesses and NGOs (non-governmental organizations) or other social organizations (and sometimes between such partnerships and governments) in ways that generate real value for both and that maximize the chances of reaching scale.[10] There has been relatively little research on hybrid models, and there is plenty of anecdotal evidence of 1) the difficulty of forming such relationships and 2) their instability once formed. Moreover, the "hybrid model" term is sometimes used to include relationships that are of a more traditional donor/recipient or corporate social responsibility relationship—which is not what I intend to suggest at all. So I discuss this approach largely via a few examples based on my own or colleagues' experience or on direct observation. Nonetheless, I think the potential for hybrid approaches—in market creation; distribution, sourcing, or other ongoing operations; and financing BoP ventures—is substantial and largely under-appreciated.

Two Models: The Key Attributes

There are two basic models for venture creation in the BoP space that have the potential of enabling new businesses to achieve the necessary scale:

1. To create enterprises that are *both* bottom-up and top-down
2. To build an ecosystem to support scale, rather than a stand-alone venture.

The key attributes of these two models can be summarized as follows:

Bottom-up/Top-down	The Venture in its Ecosystem
Attributes: Global and local business structures, funding and technology sourcing, management teams	Attributes: Business and nonbusiness structures, partnerships, networks, funding sources

Building Global/Local Ventures to Reach Scale

To look at our first approach to achieving scale, let's start with an on-the-ground example. Husk Power Systems is an award-winning green power social enterprise based in eastern India.[11] It gasifies agricultural residues—rice husks—and uses the fuel to generate electric power. It then distributes the power locally to households and small enterprises. Husk Power operates in communities that are off the national grid and which therefore have no access to electric power at all or in which grid-supplied power is so irregular and limited as to be practically non-existent. The enterprise, founded in 2007, achieved profitability early, was strategically well positioned to benefit from the shift to green power and the availability of carbon credits, and seemed scalable. Not surprisingly, its energetic CEO attracted the interest of international investors.

But then a problem arose: The international investors expected to invest in an international holding company. This would send the money to India via a tax-favored Mauritius subsidiary—the conventional route for most foreign direct investment in India. So the company had to scramble to create these global parts of its corporate structure and to rearrange its capital structure. To reach scale, even within India, Husk Power needed to be both global and local.

Global/Local Business Structures

One way to bridge the global/local divide is for the entrepreneur himself or herself to personally become the connection. Bal Joshi, founder of Thamel.com, lives in Oregon part of the time but spends equal time at home in his native Katmandu (Nepal). His enterprise is an innovative model that taps the Nepalese diaspora in the United States to send remittances to relatives in Nepal as locally-produced cakes and other holiday gifts.[12] Joshi has been able to tap global sources of technology and investment, but at the same time, he spends enough time in Katmandu to gain the trust of the local business community and the government and is now spinning off additional businesses.

Joshi is not alone in this approach, of course. A significant number of Indian entrepreneurs live at least part-time in the U.S. but launch businesses in India, thereby leveraging connections in both countries. A growing contingent of Latin and African entrepreneurs is adopting the same pattern.

A second and more common approach is a business alliance between a global organization or company and local enterprise(s). The Grameen Technology Center, a global NGO, partnered with mobile phone company MTN Uganda to create a village phone company in that country. The village phone company, in turn, worked with local microfinance organizations to franchise a village phone model that operated over the MTN network. In effect, the Grameen Technology Center brought its global knowledge of the village phone model to help MTN go downscale—and did this so success-fully, in fact, that MTN Uganda eventually took over operation of the model.

Similarly, multinational BP partnered with multiple local NGOs to build distribution and servicing networks for its efficient dual-fuel cookstove in both India and South Africa. Neither activity would have scaled without both the global and the local components.

Yet a third model is strong personal partnerships between two or more entrepreneurs, some based globally and the others in the target country of interest, who come together to form a global/local enterprise. (One example, Healthpoint Services, is discussed in more detail later.) Mechanisms to enable such partnerships, even if that is not their prime purpose, are correspondingly important. Examples include the Santa Clara GSBI program; the Acumen Fund's Fellows program, which gives its participants in-depth experience both globally and locally; and the Skoll Foundation's Fellows program.

A fourth model is intensive mentoring and technical support for entrepreneurs tied to investment activities, such as is provided by the Shell Foundation's SME investment funds, the Acumen Fund, the Grassroots Business Fund, and a number of other investment funds or organizations. Related to this approach are a number of enterprise development activities run by (mostly) NGOs, which both mentor and attempt to connect enterprises with funders. While such mentoring and assistance mechanisms can provide a global perspective to local, bottom-up enterprises, they do not guarantee that the resulting enterprise will become both local and global; for that, the appropriate structure and outlook must become embedded in the venture's DNA.

Tapping World-Class Technology

A number of bottom-up health entrepreneurs in emerging markets are developing pharmacy/clinic models to fill the huge vacuum created by failed public health systems. They are all interested in using telemedicine and ehealth tools to "import" doctors into communities that have none, and in gaining access to advanced point-of-care diagnostic tests. But most of them have told me they do not feel comfortable sorting through and thoroughly vetting the many competing ehealth choices on offer or have the time to source from among the large number of new diagnostic offerings that are becoming available but do not yet have global distribution. They would prefer, in principle, to buy such technologies as a service—paying a licensing fee—or else work with a neutral organization that did have global surveillance of these technologies.

Their dilemma is a common one. Sourcing technology globally, and doing it *well*, is not easy in a purely bottom-up model. And the consequences of making the wrong technology choices can be enormous. In the pharmacy/clinic example, choosing a telemedicine application for which changes are difficult to make (a common characteristic of most telemedicine software packages now on offer) would likely require a venture to spend far more to customize the application to their changing needs than the apparent first cost.

A related example is Sabbia Telecom, a promising startup that provides phone and data services in small towns in the Oaxaca region of Mexico, which up until now have had no telecom services of any kind. When my GSBI colleagues and I examined Sabbia's business model in 2009, we were struck by the high prices they were charging customers—which turned out to be a direct reflection of the high prices the venture was paying for Israeli wireless equipment. As it happened, I was able to connect the entrepreneur to a friend at Cisco who tracks such equipment, and we quickly pointed the company to suppliers from Taiwan whose prices for comparable equipment were 90 percent lower! As a result, Sabbia's business plan underwent a radical change, with lower prices and a far more ambitious market penetration per town—a shift that may mean the difference between success and failure. If a venture doesn't have the advantages of a local/global structure, then having global advisors in its ecosystem may lessen the chances of such mistakes and may lead to the discovery of helpfully disruptive technology.

A third example comes from the growing interest in biofuels in many developing countries. In the Philippines, for example, when oil prices reached one of their recent peaks, many small entrepreneurs rushed to buy or plant coconut plantations, anticipating that the oil harvested and converted to a biofuel would continue to rise in value.

Not too surprisingly, when oil prices sagged, most of these bottom-up, strictly local ventures failed. There was a second contributing factor: Had these entrepreneurs had access to global biofuel perspectives, they could have learned that coconut oil is vastly inferior to other potential biofuel sources, such as jatropha, and perhaps even learned of new, more productive strains of this rapidly-growing plant that are now being developed in India.

Historically, improved technology is the most important ingredient in improving productivity and enabling fundamentally new approaches. These changes are especially important for BoP ventures because they make possible price reductions that bring products and services within range of BoP consumers. And in a world where technology evolves continually and innovation comes from many regions, sourcing technology globally is increasingly essential. A global/local structure, or very good global advisors, are thus extremely important.

Tapping Global Fundraising Networks

Having recently taken on the task of raising funds for a new social enterprise to be based in India—and having done so at the height of the recent financial crisis—I have a fresh perspective on finding capital. To make a long story short, I encountered a lot of interest but not very many investors who were willing to commit, despite being able to tap many different global networks in my search for funding. In fact, I ultimately talked to more than 70 potentially serious individual, institutional, and multilateral investors in the U.S., Europe, Latin America, India, and even New Zealand. How many purely local enterprises have access to capital globally on a comparable scale?

As it happened, the network that ultimately yielded my initial seed investors was Ashoka, a global network of social entrepreneurs, supporters, investors, and donors. Because Ashoka was the incubator of the venture and, in effect, a cofounder, its ability to open doors and call in favors to help me raise capital was immense, and underscores the value not only of access to multiple global networks but also of a hybrid model, to which we will return shortly.

The rise of social equity and social venture capital funds that themselves can source funds globally certainly increases the pool of capital that is theoretically available to bottom-up enterprises. In fact, there are now dozens of such funds, all looking for deals. But they often have trouble finding enough investable prospects—and conversely, purely local enterprises may have trouble finding and getting access to such investors. A global/local enterprise can much more readily know of, meet, and cultivate such investors, talking to both their local branches and their headquartered investment team.

A potentially important new source of capital for social enterprises grows out of the rapid rise of "impact investing."[13] This is a largely U.S.-based phenomenon, fueled by foundations, including many smaller family foundations, that are increasingly interested in channeling part or all of their philanthropy into social investments that can have potentially larger and more sustained impact than grants.

One illustration of the potential of this new approach is a social debt round recently raised by Healthpoint Services. With help from an investment advisor to a number of wealthy families and their foundations, the company circulated a term sheet for PRI investments in the range of $50,000 per foundation; the investments were explicitly intended to help the venture get to scale and to serve as bridge funding, safety net, and other similar uses. They were structured as unsecured, three-year, very low-interest debt, convertible into equity if and when the venture was in a position to secure a growth equity round of at least $5 million.

Obviously, these terms are extremely favorable for the enterprise, and the company expects to raise more than $500,000 through this kind of funding. For an individual foundation, $50,000 represents a relatively small investment, but one with the potential to return the loaned capital several times over if the venture succeeds. And collectively, across a number of foundations, the investment significantly increases the chances that the venture will get to scale, thus lowering risk for the investors. Again, tapping such new sources of funding is much easier if the enterprise has a U.S. presence and can thus build relationships with such funders.

Building Ecosystems to Support Scale

The second of our two approaches to successfully pursuing and achieving scale involves the creation of new business ecosystems, with the word "business" being as broadly defined as is necessary. Suppose you have a great idea, launch a company, and demonstrate that your model works in a specific country where you have local connections or partners. Now you want to scale it across many geographies. Despite your successes, you are still a small venture. How do you figure out which countries might be good markets for you, and more important, how do you find the right partners and local know-how without devoting years to acquiring it or spending a fortune on global consulting companies? The challenge illustrates one potential value of an ecosystem approach to venture creation—that of tapping global market intelligence or scaling networks.

Suppose, for example, your supporting ecosystem includes the right kind of business network or global NGO—with feet on the ground in many countries—and that group is fully motivated to help you succeed. Rotary International, for example, is a business network with branches in many countries which supports numerous social causes; gaining the support of a local branch in, say, India, could lead to introductions and help in a dozen countries. CARE is a global NGO with field operations and offices in dozens of countries, and it is increasingly interested in partnering with business to achieve the organization's social objectives. Recently, CARE played an important role in BP's efforts to scale its cookstove business in India.

Ashoka's Fellows—to cite an example I have personal experience with—comprise a network of nearly 3,000 experienced social entrepreneurs in 60 countries. More than 400 of them work in some aspect of health care, so they know an enormous amount about the health-care challenges, needs, opportunities, and political/business realities in their respective countries. Even before I joined Ashoka, I called up a former colleague who represents Ashoka in the Philippines and explained the health-care model I was developing. He said he would pull together people for me to talk with the next time I came through Manila—and he more than kept his promise. In four days of meetings, I talked to half a dozen entrepreneurs, the country's largest generic drug manufacturer, one of the country's leading industrial families, some key policymakers, and respected academics in the health area. I came away with a clear sense of the market opportunity, potential partners and investors, ways of dealing with regulatory issues, and a promise of political/regulatory backing—in short, invaluable market intelligence and access to potential partners that can make scaling globally much easier.

Those partnerships have since jelled, and we expect to launch a pilot in the Philippines shortly. Similar market investigations that leverage the Ashoka network are already underway in a number of countries; indeed, Ashoka may help pilot the Healthpoint model in multiple geographies well ahead of when the company could pursue this activity by itself. The prescription? When planning for scale, figuring out how to leverage existing global networks and include them in your supporting ecosystem is a vital building block.

Creating an ecosystem to support scale can be viewed as extending to BoP markets approaches that have worked well in traditional venture creation. Entrepreneurial partnerships, social and commercial fundraising networks, technology networks, scaling networks, advice networks, incubators—all can be viewed as part of an ecosystem that nurtures and supports entrepreneurial ventures. Such ecosystems have long been part of the U.S. venture creation process; arguably, they are at the heart of Silicon Valley's success. Yes, the process is more difficult for BoP ventures, but it is not fundamentally different. Part of the game plan for the social entrepreneur pursuing scale must be to consciously build a supportive ecosystem that is both local and global, can nurture both bottom-up and top-down elements of the venture, and can help propagate the idea across national borders.

Hybrid Models as a Novel Ecosystem Approach

One way to build ecosystems is to use hybrid models that open up partnerships and access channels outside of commercial entities. Of course, universities have long played a key role as incubators of new technology businesses, and large corporations frequently support local NGOs or community groups, but here I mean something more—explicit business partnerships between ventures and civil society groups that share a common goal, or at least have overlapping goal sets. To distinguish the hybrid organizations of interest here from corporate philanthropy or corporate social responsibility activities, we want to focus on partnerships that generate substantial value for both (or multiple) partners as well as, commonly, some clear social benefits. The relationship should be a real partnership—in other words, not just a patron/beneficiary or simple buyer/supplier relationship—and it should generate real business value. It may or may not be reflected in joint ownership of the activity.

These definitions are still emerging, so it should not be surprising that there has been very little systematic research into the characteristics of successful hybrid approaches—including whether "success" is to be measured in financial or social-impact metrics or both—or the critical factors underlying success and failure in such partnerships. Nonetheless, there is growing interest in the potential of this approach, driven by the constant experimentation of social entrepreneurs, the growing number of NGOs seeking sustainable models, and the rise of impact investing as an alternative to traditional philanthropy. This interest is driven by the fact that hybrid partnerships have a potential competitive advantage: Because they draw on the advantages, capabilities, and financing sources of both for-profit ventures and noncommercial or citizen-sector organizations, they can potentially lower the barriers to entry in BoP markets and also be more effective in creating new markets and cocreating new products and services.

Hybrid organizations operating in BoP markets can be seen as a particular instance of the BoP as a source of innovation, as described in other chapters of this book—helping pioneer new business models outside the rigid rules of the developed world. At the same time, those rules are changing. (Witness the recent introduction in the U.S.—and, soon, in other countries—of a new corporate form, the low-profit limited liability company or L3C, that is itself a hybrid, a business with an explicit social purpose that enables philanthropic as well as corporate investment.[14]) At the very least, hybrid models potentially offer the partnership the flexibility of wearing both a business hat and an NGO hat as the occasion demands—thus engaging a larger, richer ecosystem in which to pursue scale.

Enabling Value at the Operational Level

Recent preliminary research undertaken at Ashoka provides a useful typology of hybrid organizations or partnerships and a tentative characterization of success factors. The research scanned 71 hybrid partnerships in Africa, Latin America, Asia, and North America and conducted interviews with 44 of them. It identified 5 common partnership models:

- *Sourcing partnerships*, in which the NGO partner typically helps a business find or organize small-scale producers
- *Distribution or marketing partnerships*, in which either an NGO or a business helps the other partner(s) to reach or develop a market
- *Product co-development*, whereby the combined insights and resources of the partners generate a hitherto unattainable solution
- *Franchising*, whereby either an NGO or a business helps the other partner(s) to establish and sustain a network of independent small or microbusinesses that sell a product or deliver a branded service
- *Financing*, in which either an NGO or a business helps the other partner(s) by providing loans or risk guarantees

Most, but not all, of these hybrid partnerships featured a local partner in a developing country and a global partner (which might be the local branch of a global entity). As such, they also exemplify the local-global criteria suggested here as a model for scalable BoP enterprises.

The Ashoka study also yielded some preliminary insights into success criteria for hybrid partnerships. For example: To an overwhelming extent, successful hybrid activities were guided by *the primacy of profit*—that is, meeting day-to-day business needs became the mantra and the route to successful and profitable operation. When this did not happen—when, for example, the NGO partner allowed its social mission to distract it from executing well on its business tasks or became concerned or jealous of the value (profit) being created within the business partner, the partnership often failed. From this perspective, therefore, *a successful hybrid activity is one that incorporates an NGO into a business ecosystem*, rather than the reverse. Alignment of goals was often important, especially in forming the partnership or hybrid organization, but in the successful cases studied, the alignment was not always complete or perfect.

A second characteristic of successful hybrid partnerships was *strong personal relationships and trust between key leaders in the business and the NGO*. Some cases suggest that trust can be deepened by good and regular communications, retreats, and similar tactics. Accordingly, some interviewees stressed the importance of finding the right person with whom to form a partnership; others stressed the importance of the effective use of information technology to enhance communications and good management. Continuity can be important: A change of leadership in the NGO partner can lead to rapid collapse of the partnership, especially if the new leadership has different values or mistrusts the intent of the business partner. I have some direct experience of this phenomenon; there are still many people in the NGO community (and the academic public health community) who deeply mistrust for-profit activities or even believe that making a profit from serving the poor is morally wrong.

While a few of the cases studied featured a deep integration of operations at many levels between partners, the more common feature of successful hybrid activities was *a strong co-dependence*, based on clear, mutually agreed definitions of roles and responsibilities. Interestingly, this co-dependence and operational clarity, as well as an appropriate risk/reward ratio for both (all) partners, seemed more important than formal legal structures or agreements.[15]

Enabling Value at the Strategic Level

Focusing only on operational advantages of hybrid partnerships, however substantial, would omit an even wider range of strategic activities that such partnerships can potentially undertake and which may well may have significant advantages over businesses or NGOs operating alone. These include innovative public/private partnerships and a wider range of potential partnerships (a more diverse support ecosystem) than would be typical of most new ventures; hybrid financing structures that combine both grants and other forms of social capital (low-interest debt, impact equity investments) as well as commercial capital; the ability to focus policymakers' attention and stimulate action on barriers confronting the partnership through, for example, regulatory reform partnerships that might include both business groups and major foundations; and the ability to stimulate collaborative entrepreneurship or research to solve common problems or create scale.

In effect, a hybrid model allows a venture and its nonbusiness partners far greater scope to enlist a wide range of organizations in their supporting ecosystem. This includes many organizations that do not commonly partner with new business ventures—citizen's groups, local NGOs, major foundations, development agencies, and corporate executives in their personal capacity.

To give an example of the collaborative research hybrid partnership: The healthcare venture I am engaged in has a compelling need for a locking medicine-dispensing device with some additional features. It turns out that such a device, called a "medstation," was invented decades ago and is still in common use on U.S. hospital wards. The patent on the medstation (I learned from its inventor) has expired. So I have partnered with a U.S. engineering school that is setting student teams to reimagine/redesign the device in an inexpensive version suitable for developing countries—for example, adding remote (Internet-based) controls so that a nonlocal pharmacist could dispense medicines reliably and securely. Essentially, I have asked them to come up with an enabling technology for telepharmacy—one that simultaneously addresses the shortage of licensed pharmacists in rural areas and the high incidence of 1) inventory leakage and 2) fake drugs in rural dispensaries. As the design begins to emerge, we will pair the student team with an experienced Indian manufacturer of technologies for use in rural areas. In effect, the venture, the university, and the manufacturer are pooling their different knowledge sets and skills to solve a problem *collaboratively* and at minimal expense to the venture.

Another example concerns advanced point-of-care diagnostic devices now under development for use in low-income communities in developing countries. The high-tech companies behind these emerging diagnostics are good at building "labs on a chip" or similar innovative approaches, but not necessarily at knowing what will work on the ground. Many of the activities (social enterprises, rural hospitals, or clinics) that could constitute a market for these devices either don't know about them or are too focused on immediate challenges to provide good advice—including my healthcare company.

Ashoka, however, has a broader agenda and because of its partnership with Healthpoint Services, is very knowledgeable about these advanced diagnostics and their potential to bring better healthcare to all. So Ashoka is seeking to form a collaborative—of healthcare social enterprises, diagnostic companies developing advanced prototypes, and a major foundation—that can jointly field test prototypes in clinics or other social enterprise settings and give companies useful feedback on user interfaces, pricing, medical utility, and similar features. The longer-term goal, of course, is to accelerate the availability and enhance the utility of these exciting new tools. Ashoka may even seek to catalyze the formation of new distributors for BoP-focused point-of-care diagnostics. These are not tasks that Healthpoint Services, still a small company, could or should undertake. And yet, it can both participate in the activity, and ultimately perhaps benefit from it because of its partnership with Ashoka.

Again, these examples perhaps suggest the potential for hybrid models as part of an ecosystem strategy for venture creation and scaling and underscore the value of building a supporting ecosystem.

Ideas into Action

How might one apply the ideas in this chapter to the formation of a new venture, to maximize its chances of achieving scale? I offer as a concrete example one work in progress in the field of healthcare. As is well-known, the problems confronting rural healthcare are multiple and seemingly intractable. They include limited access to doctors and other medical professionals, low quality (and often fake) medicines tendered by an unreliable supply chain, an almost complete lack of affordable access to modern diagnostic tests, and in many cases, no access to important commodities, such as clean drinking water, that can help ward off disease.

We're confronting these problems in a way that captures the key prescriptions included in previous pages. Here are some of the key events in the formation of Healthpoint Services, some of the choices we have made or are making, and the rationale for those choices:

- ***Cocreating a solution.*** I was already focused on pharmacies enhanced by modern diagnostics when I met Amit Jain, then of the Naandi Foundation and the entrepreneur behind an innovative new approach to providing safe drinking water at a community scale. We spent two weeks together at the Santa Clara GSBI event in 2008, and discovered that the Naandi water model and my pharmacy model fit together perfectly. So we cocreated a better solution that led to Naandi playing an important role in launching the venture and eventually to Amit joining me in the venture.

  In the same time period, I had joined Ashoka to incubate the venture and so met Ashoka's new health-care advisor, Todd Park, the cofounder of the innovative ehealth company athenahealth. Todd and I traveled to India together and studied telemedical solutions and related technologies (such as electronic medical records and clinical decision support tools) as they were being used in India, evolving that aspect of what became the Healthpoint model. So in effect, I helped cocreate the solution with two NGOs, both of whom became incubators of the venture.[16]

- ***Going global/local from the start.*** Potential solutions to many of the problems we faced already existed. These were solutions that I had studied intensively from a global perspective for several years, most of which involved deployment of advanced technology in innovative ways. But how is a local entrepreneur to source these solutions globally in efficient and productive ways? There is enormous interest in, and hence potential funding for, viable solutions to health care and clean drinking water—which are, curiously, two separate and almost nonoverlapping funding communities—but again, these are difficult for a local entrepreneur to source effectively. Both of these were strong reasons for creating a global/local structure—a global holding company with

a skeletal global management team and a local operating subsidiary with a strong local management team—from the start.

- **Creating a hybrid partnership at the global level.** Ashoka
  offered to incubate the healthcare venture described here,
  providing a base of operations from which to build a supportive
  ecosystem for a potential venture. Thus, as just described,
  Ashoka peers offered advice and contacts. An Ashoka
  researcher helped me identify and build partnerships with a
  number of start-up companies that were developing advanced
  new diagnostic devices for "last-mile" BoP use—one of the key
  technology solutions mentioned here. An Ashoka colleague,
  Todd Park, also became the lead investor in the venture and
  tapped his contacts list to help find other investors; Bill Dray-
  ton, Ashoka's founder, provided key insights and advice and
  also opened additional doors to investors.

  It quickly became clear that Ashoka's worldwide network of
  social entrepreneur fellows would offer unique market intelli-
  gence/market access when the venture was ready to scale.
  Thus, Ashoka became a partner in the venture, as well as a critical source of introductions to and credibility with investors. As
  it turned out, a majority of the initial seed round of investment
  came from individuals with close ties to Ashoka.

- **Creating a hybrid partnership at the local level.** In addition to diagnostics and ehealth tools, the key technologies
  needed for the venture are broadband connectivity in rural
  areas (to enable telemedicine) and low-cost production of clean
  drinking water. But adding these technologies into the mix
  would raise new questions. For example, we heard strong arguments that deploying many or all of these solutions simultaneously would complicate our operational challenges and
  increase the amount of capital required, even as it lowered the
  risk, achieved synergies and efficiencies, and raised the potential social impact. We also faced some critical business hurdles—how could we be sure (or plausibly convince investors)
  that we could persuade rural customers to adopt our services
  and governments to welcome our effort?

  To lower these risks and reduce our operational and political
  challenges, we formed a partnership with a local NGO in
  India—the Naandi Foundation—that was already at scale with

one of the solutions (water treatment), had demonstrated a remarkable command of social marketing skills in the development of their water business, and had strong credibility/brand value with both local and state government. That choice was made easy because Amit Jain, a partner in conceptualizing the business—the local part of local/global, the source of the water part of the solution, and a major factor in why we chose India as the launch country—was employed at Naandi.

- **Building a diverse supporting ecosystem.** The Ashoka platform, as well as personal connections, gave us access to major foundations, several of which we expect to partner with the venture in one way or another—as investors, as regulatory reform partners in India, or as grantors for child health/nutrition activities that will extend our reach in villages. Through Ashoka, we created a collaborative effort with a number of health entrepreneurs pursuing models similar to ours in different geographies—sharing problems and solutions to our mutual benefit.

The Naandi partnership led to an explicit invitation from the Punjabi government to pilot the venture in that state, with a promise on their part to cut red tape. To a gratifying extent, they did just that: We were able to build facilities, obtain pharmacy licenses, hire staff, and start treating patients barely three months after we incorporated in India.

Other networks (and of course, lots of persistence) led to contacts with social equity funds and the growing impact investing community (and the innovative social debt funding discussed here), as well as to potential international funders such as the IFC. The local management team in India found ways to deepen and broaden our access to low-cost diagnostics, as well as to attract the attention of a major venture capital firm, which liked the global/local structure as well as the concept of the venture and the venture's mastery of the relevant technologies. Both global and local connections brought access to highly placed Indian leaders who are potential advisors and/or investors.

The ecosystem-building process will continue, as will the local process of building out the value chain. Scale is still a promise, rather than a reality. Certainly, more challenges and tough decisions lie ahead; and ultimately, the market will render its verdict. Nonetheless, with nine months' operating experience under our belt, it is clear that our customers like the service. Our waiting rooms are full, our pilot units are nearing profitability, and we think that our success in raising money globally in an extremely difficult environment, while also launching a complex venture locally, suggests that we have at least some of the right DNA for scale.

And this brings us back to the core premise of this chapter. We have seen that the purely top-down driven BoP enterprise is likely to face frustrations, brought on by its lack of on-the-ground knowledge and connections and its relative inability to collaborate and invent locally. At the same time, purely local BoP enterprises find it extremely difficult to address simultaneously all of the challenges that sit between that enterprise and the scale that will enable it to survive and prosper.

Every BoP entrepreneur who is trying to bring a successful venture into being needs to plan for scale. I hope the strategies and models discussed here provide useful guideposts along that road.

Notes

[1] Ashoka, with which this author is affiliated, is a global association of social entrepreneurs. Additional details are provided later in the chapter.

[2] See, for example, the discussion of the "green leap to the base of the pyramid" in Stuart Hart's chapter in this book.

[3] C.K. Prahalad, 2009. *The Fortune at the Bottom of the Pyramid*, 2nd edition, Wharton School Publishing, Upper Saddle River, N.J.

[4] See http://www.scu.edu/sts/gsbi/

[5] See also Erik Simanis's and Ted London's discussions of market creation in their respective chapters in this book.

[6] Pat Guerra, personal communication.

[7] See, for example, Erik Simanis's and Ted London's summaries of the PUR venture in their respective chapters in this book.

[8] Al Hammond, Jim Koch, Francisco Noguerra (summer 2009), "The need for safe water as a market opportunity," *Innovations*, 107–117.

[9] For more on co-creation, see the chapters in this book by Stuart Hart, Ted London, and Erik Simanis.

[10] For more on ventures that straddle the formal and informal economies, see Ted London's chapter in this book.

[11] See http://www.huskpowersystems.com/home.htm

[12] See http://www.thamel.com/

[13] Steve Godeke and Raul Pomares, 2009. *Solutions for Impact Investors*, Rockefeller Advisors, New York.

[14] See http://www.nptimes.com/09Sep/npt-090901-3.html

[15] See the chapter by Ted London in this book for more on hybrid approaches and the importance of developing co-mingled competitive advantage between partners from different sectors.

[16] For more on the subject of venture co-creation directly with beneficiary communities—a promising but still largely unproven approach to achieving scale—see the chapters in this book by Patrick Whitney, Madhu Viswanathan, and Erik Simanis.

Conclusion

A Continuing Journey

by Ted London, William Davidson Institute and Ross School of Business, University of Michigan; and Stuart L. Hart, Johnson School of Management, Cornell University

Co-editors Ted London and Stuart Hart look at "the journey ahead"—both in terms of the future of BoP-oriented ventures, and in terms of the research that needs to be done to help advance our understanding of the field—which ultimately will help those BoP-oriented ventures succeed. They present—and begin the debate about—five core assumptions that underpin the BoP domain, which collectively help set the BoP agenda of tomorrow.

We conceived and developed this book with the guiding idea of proposing the next generation of strategies for base of the pyramid (BoP) business. We believe that BoP venture development is here to stay. The incentives to identify new business opportunities have perhaps never been greater, and the need to seek out new approaches to poverty alleviation and sustainable development has arguably become society's greatest challenge. Without a proactive focus on change, however, old ideas and outdated mindsets can persist.

Venture development based on "finding a fortune at the BoP," for example, initially offered a new way of thinking about the role of business in serving the poor. Yet, as time passed, lessons emerging from the field indicated that this perspective was insufficient. Basing BoP venture development on estimations of the current size of the market segment seems limiting; a better framing, we contend, is to focus on co-creation—in other words, generating more wealth collaboratively *with* the BoP.

We also have no doubt that business leaders and development professionals can work together to create better ventures to serve the BoP and meet their respective performance goals. The challenge is finding the right framing—and associated strategies—to ground these collaborations. Time is too short to sit back while old approaches fail to deliver on expectations. BoP venture development, we believe, will begin to truly flourish when the key players move to the next generation of enterprise strategies. Business, nonprofit, and development leaders must collaborate by embracing this new perspective on venture development and cross-sector partnerships.

The Journey Ahead

Given the unique character of BoP ventures and their potential significance to sustainable development and the global economy, we hope that the chapters of this book help to stimulate an evolution—or even better, a revolution—in the thinking about BoP business. In that spirit, we have covered a lot of territory, articulating the need for a "fortune-creating" perspective in combination with in-depth discussions of key aspects of next-generation BoP business strategies. The coauthors identified frameworks and roadmaps for enhancing BoP business success, explored the strategic challenges of market creation and environmental sustainability, and provided specific guidance on understanding the local context, designing for BoP market success, and scaling ventures to increase their reach.

While we hope and believe this book makes a substantial contribution to the development of the BoP domain, we also know that it won't be the final word. Roughly a decade ago, Prahalad and Hart first articulated the potential for a "fortune at the base of the pyramid." This "fortune-finding" call to action catalyzed interest in the domain and helped to bring us to the current state of the art. As with all innovations, the original conceptualizations not only solved problems, but also identified new challenges. It is for this reason that we now believe that business leaders, entrepreneurs, development professionals, and forward-thinking scholars should not only transition to a "fortune-creating" perspective, but also remain open to what comes next. One thing is certain: our mindsets—and the questions we seek to answer—must continue to evolve.

With this in mind, we decided *not* to focus this concluding chapter on summarizing what has already been discussed. Rather, we thought the best use of this last chapter would be to shed some light on our perspective about the way forward: What are the major issues that we didn't consider in this book? What additional questions emerge? Where might the domain go from here?

The stakes are high—both for business leaders looking for new market opportunities and for poverty-alleviation professionals seeking a more sustainable form of development. We must therefore maintain a commitment to continue to extend our understanding of what is required for successful BoP venture development.

Additional Key Topics Worthy of Deep Discussion

We focused this book on next-generation strategies, recognizing that we could not possibly cover the entire landscape of issues, opportunities, and challenges associated with BoP business development. Through interactions with the authors as the various chapters took shape, as well as ongoing conversations with other thought leaders, we identified some key areas worthy of further consideration which the book does not directly address. Three areas, in particular, emerged as crucial to the successful development of BoP ventures. These include:

- The internal organizational challenges associated with BoP business
- The importance of a holistic understanding of the impact of BoP ventures on local communities and the natural environment
- The role of government and donor agencies in facilitating BoP ventures

These three concerns, of course, are not meant as an exhaustive list. Instead, our goal is to stimulate and encourage a continuing journey that enhances and extends our understanding of—and capability in—the BoP domain, particularly when a "fortune-creating" frame is used to formulate BoP business strategy. Each is therefore discussed in greater detail here.

The Organizational Challenges of BoP Business

For both BoP entrepreneurs and BoP ventures emerging from incumbent organizations, internal challenges are substantial. The chapters by Al Hammond and by Robert Kennedy and Jacqueline Novogratz shed light on organizational difficulties faced by start-up and social entrepreneurs; these include building management capacity with the requisite skills, raising "patient" capital, and organizing the venture for eventual scale-up.

For established companies, however, the organizational challenges can be even more substantial, given that BoP ventures must be incubated within a larger existing structure that is geared toward incremental improvement, line extension, and geographic expansion of ongoing businesses.[1] Indeed, without proper protection, corporate BoP initiatives can be burdened with unrealistic expectations for short-term growth and profitability or forced prematurely into a philanthropic mode of operation.

Each of the editors of this book has, in his prior work, considered some of these issues. For example, London, in his doctoral dissertation and later work, tracked the development of eighteen BoP-oriented initiatives in six companies over an extended time period. He found that three factors—that is, where corporate BoP initiatives were placed in the organization, whether learning-oriented metrics were included, and which boundary–spanning approaches were used to solve problems—had a determining effect on the company's ability to launch a venture focused on BoP markets.[2] He recommended framing corporate BoP initiatives as "business model R&D." By positioning BoP initiative development as a form of research and development, it is possible to avoid the expectation for rapid growth and short-term returns so often associated with new product development or geographic expansion.

In his book *Capitalism at the Crossroads*, Hart also addresses this key concern.[3] Drawing upon his extensive experience with corporate BoP experiments, he similarly concluded that the creation of a protected "white space" is crucial to corporate BoP venture success. Furthermore, such a protected space must involve a coalition of internal supporters, including a senior executive champion as well as a BoP leadership team composed of key business and functional area leaders. This coalition must possess the clout to define and defend an alternative set of metrics and milestones for the BoP initiative— thereby creating a set of norms that will buy the time necessary for co-creation and embedding prior to expectations for profits and scale-out.

While the BoP organizational challenge has received only modest attention in this book, we recognize that it plays a critical role in an incumbent's ability to develop and launch ventures. These challenges become even more daunting when organizations ground their venture development with a "fortune-creating" mindset. In this case, venture leaders may well need to find nontraditional co-investors, build their business models based on cross-sector and community-based partnerships, and convince top management that initial success should be measured against metrics that embrace learning and experimentation. Clearly, these and other aspects of the organizational challenge of BoP business deserve additional attention in the future.

Assessing and Enhancing the Impacts of BoP Ventures

For the past two centuries, business has played a critical role in creating wealth and well-being around the world. But as we also know, business development can generate substantial negative impact, including unequal distribution of economic gains as well as undesirable social and environmental outcomes. We should therefore expect BoP ventures—like any form of enterprise—to create both positive and negative outcomes.

This volume only sets the stage for an in-depth treatment of the importance of impact assessment to poverty alleviation and sustainable development. The chapters by Ted London and Madhu Viswanathan, for example, discuss the importance of mutual value creation in venture development and the need for a deep understanding of local context at the earliest stages of venture design. Hart's chapter explicitly recognizes the importance of environmental sustainability to successful BoP venture development. Obviously, though, there is room for much more on the topic.

As with the organizational challenges discussed here, each of the book's editors has, in prior work, focused on the critical importance of BoP venture impact assessment. Hart, for example, developed an approach to assessing the "triple bottom line" impact of BoP enterprises—a model for evaluating the effects of a business on social, environmental, and economic outcomes, with a special emphasis on identifying and addressing unintended consequences. He also suggested focusing on the extent to which BoP ventures remove constraints for the poor, increase their earning power, and create new potential in low-income communities.[4]

More recently, London developed a "BoP Impact Assessment Framework," which offers managers of such ventures a systematic process for understanding, measuring, and improving the effects their activities have on the ground.[5] The framework provides venture leaders with a structured approach for enhancing the positive and mitigating the negative impacts on three local constituencies: sellers, buyers, and communities. For each, the framework facilitates an assessment of potential changes in economic, capability, and relationship well-being, including how the venture affects the natural environment. The framework rests on the logic that the better the venture meets the needs of the BoP—those they seek to serve—the better the venture's overall performance. Understanding and enhancing impact is an investment worth making; indeed, no leadership team should launch a venture without the ability to tap into the voices of its key BoP constituencies.

There is a growing body of research and practice on impact assessment. Much of this assessment work emphasizes providing information to donors and other external stakeholders on the social returns from their investments. Adopting a "fortune-creating" mindset for venture development, however, requires a renewed focus on generating real-time information that *business leaders and their partners* can use to proactively improve their ability to address the unmet needs of local consumers and producers. Creating a fortune with the BoP requires an in-depth understanding of the type, amount, and allocation of value created. One area that deserves more attention, therefore, is the *integrated* assessment of impacts—one that includes how BoP ventures' financial performance is affected by their social and environmental performance.[6]

The Role of Government and Donors

While BoP strategies have tended to focus on the role of the private and nonprofit sectors in venture development, governments and the donor community also play a critical role by fostering a more favorable market environment, through both removing existing barriers and providing further incentives. As Hart notes in his chapter in this book, there is a clear bias in favor of large-scale international development solutions—infrastructure-building and industrial development, for example. Throughout the world, small-scale, enterprise-based approaches are often slighted in favor of more centralized solutions. Hammond, London, and Kennedy and Novogratz, in their chapters in this book, also discuss some of the important roles that donors can play in facilitating BoP venture development. London, for example, points to the need for a new paradigm in collaboration between business leaders and donor community professionals. In this realm, as in the others discussed previously, there is a clear opportunity for deeper analysis.

While some multilateral agencies have recently launched programs focused on BoP business development—including the Inter-American Development Bank, the United Nations Development Program, and the International Finance Corporation—much more could be done on this front to "level the playing field" when it comes to national development policy. Models already exist. For example: SNV—a nonprofit, international development organization, based in the Netherlands—worked with the government of Ecuador to create a National Policy of Economic Inclusion in 2007.[7] The policy consists of a small- and micro-producer promotion program, an economic inclusion-through-government-procurement initiative, and an inclusive business promotion effort.

Governments and donors can—and should—focus much more attention on BoP venture creation as a strategy for sustainable economic development.[8] Such support might include reducing regulatory barriers to enterprise creation; offering "smart subsidies" and below-market-rate funding to early-stage companies interested in launching BoP business experiments; and, perhaps, providing targeted financial assistance (for example, a voucher program) to enhance access to critical products and services (such as nutrition, health, clean water, and renewable energy) and to make these markets more attractive to private sector investment.

Applying a "fortune-creating" perspective to government and donor support for BoP ventures also can reframe the questions that are asked. When one adopts this perspective, the question of "should BoP ventures receive subsidized support?" seems largely irrelevant. Incumbent industries serving top of the pyramid markets have long received substantial incentives and subsidies (such as R&D support, access to government-owned land and other resources, tax incentives, and so on) based on the view that encouraging these business efforts creates value for the general public. If governments and donors want to create a fortune with the BoP, they will need to adopt similar approaches to support BoP venture development. The more relevant questions, therefore, center on determining which ventures should receive support and the type, amount, and length of any support that is given. Given their potential to accelerate poverty alleviation and sustainable development, the role of government and donors in catalyzing BoP business is thus a topic that deserves extensive future consideration.

Reflections from the Field

Another source of insight regarding priorities for future BoP work came from the conference, *Creating a Shared Roadmap: Collaboratively Advancing the Base of the Pyramid Community*, which the editors hosted at the University of Michigan in October 2009 (see the appendix for a list of the attendees). This event offered a platform for the book's authors to share initial thinking on their respective chapters. The first day and a half was designed around that premise, and we received some invaluable feedback. At the same time, we knew that not everyone would agree with our views or our areas of focus. As a result, we decided to build the last day around discussing what had *not* been covered up to that point.

In advance of that final day, we asked participants—thought leaders from the private, nonprofit, development, and academic communities—to identify topics, issues, and concerns that they believed were worthy of further consideration. We asked them to come prepared the next morning to present and discuss these ideas. We kicked off the day by listening to those ideas and placing them together in appropriate clusters. The participants then self-organized into groups that focused on the clusters they were most interested in. These groups subsequently met together in break-out rooms for deeper dialogue on their topics.

Each group was tasked with articulating a clear rationale for the importance of their topic and developing a preliminary agenda for moving their ideas forward. Each then presented its collective thinking to all the conference participants for comments and feedback, as well as suggestions for further developing lines of inquiry. Emerging from this discussion was both a clear recognition that this book could catalyze a new perspective on the BoP domain, and a reinforcement of the view that there were other issues worthy of exploration beyond the material in these chapters.

In addition to the three topics discussed earlier, our conference attendees also noted several other areas deserving of future focus and attention. For example, representatives from the development sector emphasized the importance of more proactively linking approaches to serving BoP producers with efforts targeting BoP consumers.[9] It was a perceptive observation. By integrating both elements more effectively into BoP business models, it may be possible to better address social and environmental problems in poor communities, offering another lens on venture strategy and impact assessment.

Other participants in the conference focused on the issue of scale. One group, for example, proposed the development of a "platform" approach to BoP business to enable more rapid scaling of firms entering low-income markets. (A "platform," as defined by this group, is a public/private system for distribution and sale of goods and services.) Another set of participants focused on the particular challenges associated with health care in BoP markets; they proposed an integrated approach, or "roadmap," which included the development of small-scale diagnostic technologies, mobile health care facilities, telemedicine capabilities, and microhealth insurance provision.

Finally, one of the break-out teams looked at the roles of different players in the BoP ecosystem. They proposed paying particular attention to the opportunity for smaller, "national" corporations in launching BoP ventures. While not global in scope, they noted that these domestic companies might have a greater vested interest in improving local communities, as the health of their operations would be more tightly aligned with the well-being of their countries.

Looking Forward

Taken together, the chapters of this book—as well as the additional topics outlined here—have significant implications for the trajectory of the BoP domain. We close, therefore, with some thoughts about an agenda for future action. This agenda is organized around what we believe to be the five fundamental assumptions that underpin the BoP domain:

- Raising the BoP is a worthy objective.
- BoP ventures can and will play a key role in this process.
- BoP ventures can be economically self-sustaining.
- BoP ventures will achieve their greatest success and impact when they are scalable.
- BoP ventures can help to catalyze a more environmentally sustainable form of global development.

Few, we think, would argue with the first assumption. The other four, however, are still being actively debated and will therefore require focused effort and attention to evaluate and refine. Our own modest contribution to that effort follows.

The Importance of BoP Ventures in Raising the BoP

For nearly six decades, government aid and philanthropy have served as the primary vehicles for addressing the daunting problems of poverty and inequity in the developing world. It is now clear that these approaches, as important as they have been, are insufficient: There is simply not enough aid and philanthropic money in the world to overcome the scope and scale of the challenges we face. To complement these resources, the world needs business-oriented approaches that both alleviate poverty and allow development-oriented investments to reach more people.

In recent years, the donor community has increasingly recognized the importance of enterprise-based models for poverty alleviation and development. Growing numbers of aid and philanthropic programs now provide funding for initiatives designed to enhance the capabilities of local entrepreneurs and the output of local producers, including small holder farmers and artisans. Microfinance, for example, has exploded in the past decade, and now provides an important vehicle for the poor to expand their own income-generating activities.

Yet as important as these market-based initiatives have been, much more needs to be done. Most enterprises owned by the poor remain at the micro level, most larger local businesses don't view the BoP as an attractive market, and most development agencies provide support that is location- and time-bound. As we look to the future, therefore, we must learn how to build BoP ventures—in collaboration with donors and other partners—that have both business models that straddle the formal and informal economies and financial models that can achieve self-sufficiency and scale.

The financial performance of these ventures, however, must not rely on an extractive orientation. Beyond the social and ethical implications, any venture based on cross-sector partnerships is likely to collapse quickly with this framing. Instead, BoP ventures will need to emphasize creating mutual value. They will also need to invent business models that sidestep the assumed trade-off between societal and financial performance. Furthermore, as discussed earlier, BoP ventures—like any intervention—will surely have both positive and negative impacts. Thus, we should not promote BoP venture development—or indeed, any poverty-alleviation approach—if we do not also have the ability to assess and enhance its on-the-ground impacts. By building impact assessment and community engagement into the business model from the start, BoP ventures may succeed in providing value for *all* stakeholders simultaneously, rather than elevating one over the other.

The Opportunity of Economic Self-Sufficiency

By building competitively viable strategies that demonstrate strong financial performance over an extended period of time, BoP ventures can achieve economic self-sufficiency. But as the authors of this book have argued, doing so requires embracing the next generation of BoP business strategies. These "fortune-creating" strategies will necessitate a concerted effort not only by the private sector, but also on the part of civil society and government. Indeed, developing productive cross-sector collaborations requires that all partners consider abandoning their existing—and potentially outdated—ideologies and mindsets and emphasize innovating in new and "nontraditional" directions. Companies will have to reinvent strategies, business models, and engagement processes; civil society will have to enter into a new era of collaboration and mutual value-creation with business; and government and donors will need to create new policies and incentives that enable private sector approaches to more effectively engage the four billion-plus people who have previously been excluded from the global economy.

We must therefore focus on better understanding how BoP ventures can develop the leadership potential, internal capabilities, and external relationships needed to become economically self-sufficient. Leadership teams must be able to understand the BoP context and at the same time recognize the value propositions of their partner organizations. Ventures must develop internal capabilities—most likely premised on creating and maintaining a diversity of relationships—that allow them to establish competitive advantage in the marketplace. To sustain this competitive advantage, venture teams must ensure their business models and societal impacts remain aligned while continually evolving over time. Such BoP ventures will enjoy the greatest success if their strategies help them become socially embedded and underscore their commitment to cocreating mutual value with the local communities they serve.

Concurrently, we must also explore new strategies for government and the development community. Governments, with the encouragement of donors, should evaluate the benefits from and identify policy frameworks associated with promoting BoP ventures. In addition, the development community must take on a greater role in encouraging market creation and in working with the private sector to achieve its poverty alleviation goals. These efforts will require ongoing assessments of the holistic impacts of any investment, including carefully tracking and continually enhancing the approaches employed.

Achieving Impact Through Scale

Grant-based aid and philanthropic models require a continuous stream of donor capital to address the challenges of poverty and environment. In contrast, enterprise solutions rely on the development of a self-sustaining and scalable *investment-based* model. At a minimum, BoP ventures are expected to cover their operating costs, thereby allowing their efforts to continue indefinitely. Better yet are BoP ventures that actually earn sufficient profits to extend to new contexts and enter new markets. Even better are the BoP ventures that develop a value proposition that allows them to scale faster and further by attracting additional investment capital from new sources, including not only the emerging "patient capital" sector, but also more traditional providers of financing, such as venture capitalists and investment banks.

Combining the power of enterprise with the resources of the development community and the more traditional investment realms offers the potential to create ventures with the scale necessary to turn the tide on the world's most pressing problems. To do so, though, requires a better understanding of the opportunities and challenges in connecting viable BoP business models with different sources of investment capital. Ventures must build business models that can attract investments from sectors with different success metrics, as well as create capabilities that transfer across contexts and markets. The leadership team must be skilled and flexible enough to work with partners in the business, nonprofit, development, and investment sectors, and at the same time maintain an intimate connection with a diverse set of BoP constituencies.

Catalyzing Environmental Sustainability

To introduce this final topic, we need to restate some basic premises. To date, nearly two-thirds of humanity have been bypassed or ignored by economic globalization. As a consequence, raw-material and energy consumption remains heavily concentrated at the top of the economic pyramid, where 20 percent of the population consumes in excess of 80 percent of the world's resources, and in the process creates the bulk of the world's waste. With our current models that ignore or neglect environmental limitations, we are already pushing the boundaries of the world's natural systems to support human activity. Raising the base of the pyramid will require creating unprecedented new production and consumption opportunities for the underserved 80 percent of the world's population. Clearly, the *approach* to this growth must be fundamentally different from that which fueled the industrial age in the developed world.

Governmental regulation and international conventions have been the primary mechanisms for confronting the growing environmental challenges associated with the expansion of global capitalism. As the climate-change debate demonstrates, however, relying on these tactics alone is insufficient, especially as global growth becomes more inclusive. It is crucial, therefore, that BoP enterprise be based on technologies and business models that respect the environment and resource constraints. Unconstrained extraction and unchecked waste must give way to renewable resources and closed loops.

The lack of infrastructure and the poor services currently delivered to most BoP communities are, of course, troubling. At the same time, this inadequate status quo also provides a unique context in which to realize this vision. With no legacy systems to overcome, BoP markets offer the prospect of incubating the clean technologies of tomorrow and commercializing new business models outside of the embedded constraints and mindsets that limit innovation in the developed world.

Better understanding this cycle could lead to even further benefits. Sustainable innovations developed in BoP markets might also "trickle up" and create a more sustainable way of living for the entire world. Identifying and investing in these "green" BoP ventures thus could potentially generate benefits to both the BoP and their wealthier counterparts, who (we must remind ourselves) share the same planet and its finite set of resources.

In Closing

We believe that the contours of a next generation of BoP business strategies have begun to emerge from the pages of this book. By connecting, in new and productive ways, business development investments with efforts to alleviate poverty and enhance environmental sustainability, we can *create* a fortune *with* the base of the pyramid. We hope that the opportunities, strategies, and action steps outlined in this volume provide an initial roadmap that can catalyze increased experimentation and learning—and ultimately, greater success—in the years ahead.

There is a paradoxical quality—something new, yet also something encouragingly familiar—about the next-generation BoP strategies proposed here. On the one hand, BoP markets clearly present a different context and a unique set of challenges for business. As we have discussed in this book, creating a fortune with the BoP requires new skills and capabilities, innovations in business models and technologies, changes in relationships and mindsets, and a set of metrics that effectively captures mutual value creation.

On the other hand, BoP business leaders must still address the same fundamental challenges facing *every* enterprise in the world. How can we surprise and delight those we seek to serve? How can we create a business model and set of capabilities that provides a sustained competitive advantage? How can we build and retain the right set of collaborations and partners? How can we create a value proposition that satisfies all of our stakeholders, including the communities and environments in which we operate?

We contend that the challenges facing BoP business are clearly daunting but certainly not insurmountable. The terrain is new, yet many of its features are familiar. With the right framing in place, the real opportunity space begins to unfold in front of us. We can create a fortune *with* the BoP, and perhaps, in the process, move all of us toward a more inclusive and sustainable future.

Notes

[1] For more on the differences between evolution and revolutionary routines, see Mark Milstein, Ted London, and Stuart Hart. 2007. "Revolutionary routines: Capturing the opportunity for creating a more inclusive capitalism." *Handbook of Transformative Cooperation: New Designs and Dynamics*, ed. S. K. Piderit, R. E. Fry, & D. L. Cooperrider (Stanford: Stanford University Press), 84–103.

[2] See Ted London. 2005. *How are Capabilities Created? A Process Study of New Market Entry* (Unpublished Dissertation). University of North Carolina, Chapel Hill; and Ted London, 2010. "Business model development for base-of-the-pyramid market entry." In G. T. Solomon (Ed.), *Academy of Management Best Paper Proceedings*.

[3] Stuart L. Hart. 2005. *Capitalism at the Crossroads*, Upper Saddle River, NJ: Wharton School Publishing. The third edition of this book, published in 2010, provides even more extensive coverage of the organizational challenge.

[4] Hart, op cit.

[5] Ted London. 2009. "Making better investments at the base of the pyramid," *Harvard Business Review* 85(5): 106–113.

[6] Thanks to Okano Hiroshi, URP Osaka City University, Japan, and his colleagues for proposing this idea at the BoP Conference in November 2009. Exploring the relationship between venture strategy and poverty alleviation outcomes is also a central component of Ted London's research activities at the William Davidson Institute at the University of Michigan.

[7] Thanks to Neil Ghosh, Director of SNV-USA and Adrian Hodges, Senior Advisor and Former Managing Director, International Business Leaders Forum, for this information.

[8] In addition, governments and donors in the developed world may want to adopt a "BoP strategy" to address some of the challenges faced by declining cities in the U.S. and elsewhere.

[9] For more on strategies for ventures serving BoP producers, see Ted London, Ravi Anupindi, and Sateen Sheth. 2010. "Creating mutual value: Lessons from ventures serving base of the pyramid producers," *Journal of Business Research* 63(6): 582–594.

Appendix

Attendees at the "Creating a Shared Roadmap" Conference
Ann Arbor, Michigan, 2009
Collaboratively Advancing the Base of the Pyramid Community

Last Name	First Name	Affiliation
Adams	Andrew	Monitor Group
Alvarez	Sharon	The Ohio State University
Antúnez de Mayolo	César	PAD, Escuela de Dirección, Universidad de Piura
Anupindi	Ravi	Ross School of Business, University of Michigan
Asiala	Laura	Dow Corning Corporation
Babcock	Lee	ACDI/VOCA
Balasubramaniam	Rashmir	Bill & Melinda Gates Foundation
Barhyte	Bonnie	Academy for Educational Development
Barkema	Harry	RSM Erasmus University
Barney	Jay	Ohio State University
Beale	John	VillageReach
Beckwith	Colin	Emory University

Last Name	First Name	Affiliation
Billou	Niels	European School of Management and Technology
Binder	Erin	Acara Institute
Bishop	Tim	CARE International, UK
Branzei	Oana	Richard Ivey School of Business, University of Western Ontario
Braswell	Kimberly	Ashoka
Budinich	Valeria	Ashoka
Bundick	Paul	Academy for Educational Development
Burand	Deborah	International Transactions Clinic, University of Michigan Law School
Canter	David	William Davidson Institute at the University of Michigan
Chaudhary	Asha	Jaipur Rugs
Chertok	Michael	Bill & Melinda Gates Foundation
Chervela	Kalyani	Mack Center for Entrepreneurship, Wharton Business School
Chowdhry	Pradeep	Soalni Healthcare Private Limited
Clyde	Paul	Ross School of Business, University of Michigan
Dalsace	Frédéric	HEC Paris
Duke	Duncan	Cornell University
Elaydi	Raed	Penn State University
Enk	Gordon A.	Partners for Strategic Change
Esper	Heather	William Davidson Institute at the University of Michigan
Flammer	Martina	Pfizer

Last Name	First Name	Affiliation
Fujioka	Taka	Sasin Graduate Institute of Business Administration, Chulalongkorn University
Gardetti	Miguel Angel	Center for Study of Corporate Sustainability
Ghosh	Neil	SNV Netherlands Development Organization
Grogan-Kaylor	Andy	University of Michigan School of Social Work
Hallstrup	Mikal	Designit
Hammond	Allen	Ashoka
Hansen	Ole Lund	DI International Business Development
Hart	Stuart	Cornell University
Hartmann	Jorg	GTZ GmbH
Hebbar	Harishchandra	Manipal Centre for Information Sciences
Henning	Nina	Ascension Health
Herrndorf	Martin	Institute of Management, University of St. Gallen
Hodges	Adrian	International Business Leaders Forum
Horrocks	Mike	Experian
Husted	Bryan	Schulich School of Business
Ishikawa	Eriko	International Finance Corporation
Jain	Anuj	CARE International UK
Jenkins	Beth	CSR Initiative, Kennedy School of Government, Harvard University
Jiwa	Farouk	CARE USA
Jung-Rozenfarb	Francois	CARE USA
Kandachar	Prabhu	Delft University of Technology

Last Name	First Name	Affiliation
Kassalow	Jordan	VisionSpring
Katz	Rob	Acumen Fund; NextBillion.net
Kennedy	Bob	William Davidson Institute at the University of Michigan
Kim	Hyung	Ascension Health
Kim	Namsuk	United Nations Development Programme
Kistruck	Geoffrey	The Ohio State University
Koch	James	Santa Clara University
Lewis	Gerald	World Vision International
Lindeman	Sara	Helsinki School of Economics
Liu	Guozhong	Redbud Textile Science and Technology Corp.
Liu	Hongzhi	Wuxi Municipal Government, China
London	Ted	William Davidson Institute & Ross School of Business, University of Michigan
Madsen	Sally	IDEO
Majumder	Mahbub	GE Healthcare & Grameen Partnership
Martin	Ed	Hershey
McKague	Kevin	Schulich School of Business, York University
Mejia	Francisco	Inter-American Development Bank
Menasce	David	HEC School of Management
Milstein	Mark	Johnson School, Cornell University
Mitchell	Susan	Abt Associates Inc.
Moodley Naidoo	Roshini	Oxfam America
Moreno Barcelo	Israel	CEMEX, Patrimonio Hoy

Last Name	First Name	Affiliation
Novogratz	Jacqueline	Acumen
Okano	Hiroshi	Urban Research Plaza, Graduate School of Business, Osaka City University
Owens	John	SC Johnson
Pulik	Linda	Bao Design Lab
Rashid	Shaikh Saif Al	CARE Bangladesh
Ritchie	Robin	Carleton University
Ros	Luiz	Inter-American Development Bank
Rosa	José Antonio	University of Wyoming
Rose	Fred	Acara Institute
Schneider	Robert	US Agency for International Development
Schuler	Doug	Jesse H. Jones Graduate School of Management
Shaw	Will	Academy for Educational Development
Sheats	Jayna	Terepac Corp.
Sheth	Sateen	William Davidson Institute at the University of Michigan
Simanis	Erik	Cornell University
Sridharan	Srinivas	University of Western Ontario
Subbiah	Ponni	Pfizer
Tharmaratnam	Geetha	Aureos Advisers Limited
Touesnard	Monica	Cornell University
Tseng	Albert	Harvard John F. Kennedy School of Government
Uddin Ahmed	Asif	CARE Bangladesh
Varghese	Zubin	Siemens Corporate Technology-India

Last Name	First Name	Affiliation
Viswanathan	Madhu	University of Illinois, Champaign-Urbana
Waller	Nigel	Movirtu Limited
Whitney	Patrick	Director, Institute of Design, Illinois Institute of Technology
Widmer	Rex	GE Healthcare Systems
Wille	Edgar	Ashridge Business School
Wulczyn	Kirstin	Global Alliance for Improved Nutrition
Wyatt	Jocelyn	IDEO
You	Xiaojian	William Davidson Institute at the University of Michigan
Zhang	Guangqi	Jiangsu Redbud Textile Science and Technology Co. Ltd.
Zhang	Wenhong	Nanjing University

Thank you to the following University of Michigan student volunteers for their logistical assistance during the conference:

Anita Bhat, Kathy Dasovich, Colm Fay, Ashish Gupta, Kangana Gupta, Rosemary Lapka, Parvati Patil, Aileen Payumo, Tim Polkowski, Eric Rosenthal, Saulo Rozendo, Patricia Stansbury, Amrita Vijay Kumar, and Chris White

Thank you also to the following staff at the William Davidson Institute for their assistance:

Rosemary Harvey, Heather Esper, Laurie Gendron, Cynthia Koenig, Sergei Kolomeitsev, Moses Lee, Chris Simmons, and Sinia Whatmore

INDEX

IkoToilet malls, 66
Immelt, Jeff, 90
impact, achieving through
   scale, 229
India
   economic growth, 92-93
   housing, 180
      context, 180-181
      options, 184
      reframing, 181-183
information deficiency, 107
innovation, embedded
   innovation, 117-118
innovation gap, 171-174
innovation strategies, market
   creation, 117-122
innovations, patient
   capitalism, 59
   D.light Design, 70-73
   Ecotact, 63-66
   LifeSpring Hospitals, 60-62
   WHI, 66-69
installments, customization, 141
Institute of Design (ID), 179
The Inter-American
   Development Bank, The
   Opportunities for the
   Majority, 8
interactions in BoP
   marketplace, 140-141
investment-based model, 229
iPhone, 165, 167
ITC, xxxiii, 35-36
iTunes, 165

J

Joshi, Bal, 199

K

ka-torchi, 173
Kelkar, Anjali, 180
Kennedy, Bob, 12
kerosene, 70
Kinnebrew, Alexis, 180
Kiran, D.light, 72
Kumar, Anant, 60
Kuria, David, 63

L

L3C (low-profit limited liability
   company), 206
LED techology, 70
leveraging social
   embeddedness, 34-37
literacy, developing socio-
   culturally embedded
   marketplace literacy, 144-146
LifeSpring Hospitals, 59-62
literacy, 134
   low literacy, 135
      self-esteem issues, 137
      Sumitra, 135-138
   marketplace literacy, 151, 156
   pictographic thinking, 135
local business structures,
   199-200
localization, Chotukool, 189
London, Ted, 217, 220

M

make-and-model work-
   shops, 119
managing failures, 28-31

In an increasingly competitive world, it is quality of thinking that gives an edge—an idea that opens new doors, a technique that solves a problem, or an insight that simply helps make sense of it all.

We work with leading authors in the various arenas of business and finance to bring cutting-edge thinking and best-learning practices to a global market.

It is our goal to create world-class print publications and electronic products that give readers knowledge and understanding that can then be applied, whether studying or at work.

To find out more about our business products, you can visit us at www.ftpress.com.